P9-BXZ-743

FOOD ALLERGY
COOKBOOK

FOOD ALLERGY
COOKBOOK

INCLUDES THE 5 MAJOR ALLERGY GROUPS
Gluten • Soy • Eggs
Nuts • Dairy

LUCINDA BRUCE-GARDYNE

Reader's Digest

The Reader's Digest Association, Inc.
Pleasantville, NY / Montreal / Sydney / Singapore / Mumbai

A READER'S DIGEST BOOK

This edition published by The Reader's Digest Association, Inc.,
by arrangement with Rodale Ltd. an imprint of Pan Macmillan Ltd. 2008

Pan Macmillan
20 New Wharf Road
London N1 9RR
Basingstoke and Oxford

FOR RODALE
Photography: Ian Greig Garlick
Food Styling: Lorna Brash
Editor: Jillian Stewart
Illustrator and original concept designer: Simon Daley
Designer: Emma Ashby

FOR READER'S DIGEST
U.S. Project Editor: Andrea Chesman
Copy Editor: Fiona Hunt
Canadian Project Editor: Pamela Johnson
Designer: Wayne Morrison
Associate Art Director: George McKeon
Executive Editor, Trade Publishing: Dolores York
Associate Publisher: Rosanne McManus
President and Publisher, Trade Publishing: Harold Clarke

Library of Congress Cataloging-in-Publication Data
Bruce-Gardyne, Lucinda.
    The food allergy cookbook : how to cook over 100 family-friendly recipes / by Lucinda Bruce-Gardyne.
        p. cm.
    Includes index.
    ISBN-13: 978–0–7621–0896-1
    ISBN-10: 0–7621–0896-7
    1. Food allergy—Diet therapy—Recipes. I. Title.
    RC588.D53B78 2007
    616.97'50654—dc22

                                    2007029706

We are committed to both the quality of our products and the service we provide to our customers. We value your comments, so please feel free to contact us.

The Reader's Digest Association, Inc.
Adult Trade Publishing
Reader's Digest Road
Pleasantville, NY 10570-7000

For more Reader's Digest products and information, visit our website:
www.rd.com (in the United States)
www.readersdigest.ca (in Canada)
www.readersdigest.com.au (in Australia)
www.readersdigest.com.nz (in New Zealand)
www.rdasia.com (in Asia)

NOTE TO OUR READERS
Eating eggs or egg whites that are not completely cooked poses the possibility of salmonella food poisoning. The risk is greater for pregnant women, the elderly, the very young, and persons with impaired immune systems. If you are concerned about salmonella, you can use reconstituted powdered egg whites or pasteurized eggs.

Printed at Butler and Tanner in the UK
1 3 5 7 9 10 8 6 4 2

To my mother, Margie Monbiot,
whose health would have benefited hugely
from the improved understanding and wealth
of information on food allergies that we have today.

Acknowledgments

A special thank you to my husband, Hew, for his constant support, guidance, and involvement through all stages of this book, and to my three sons, Angus, Robin, and Otto, for inspiring me to write it in the first place. I am also immensely grateful to Penny Webber, my oracle at the start of this project; to Lucie Nason for introducing me to Websters; to Millie Scott-Dempster for being a wonderful caregiver to Otto; to Dorothy Bruce-Gardyne—Granny—who has held the fort on a regular basis; and to Mary Stansfeld for her gluten-free cooking tips. Thank you also to my friends and family, without whose support this book would have been much harder to write.

I would also like to thank the team at Websters, namely Anne Lawrance, Jillian Stewart, and Emma Ashby, for the thought and sheer hard work they have put into producing this book. Thanks also to Ian Greig Garlick and Lorna Brash for taking such care over the photographs.

CONTENTS

INTRODUCTION 8

Part i LIVING WITH FOOD ALLERGIES

1 AVOIDING PROBLEM FOODS IN DAY-TO-DAY LIFE 12

2 EATING OUT AND TRAVELING 19

3 EATING A BALANCED DIET ON A RESTRICTED DIET 27

Part ii HOW TO SUBSTITUTE INGREDIENTS

4 SUBSTITUTING FOR EGGS 34

5 SUBSTITUTING FOR WHEAT AND OTHER GLUTEN-RICH GRAINS . . .40

6 SUBSTITUTING FOR DAIRY PRODUCTS 50

7 SUBSTITUTING FOR NUTS 55

8 SUBSTITUTING FOR SOY 58

Part iii THE RECIPES

9	STOCK, SOUPS, AND SAUCES	.62
10	FRYING	.86
11	BROILING	.105
12	ROASTING AND OVEN-BAKING	.109
13	POACHING AND STEWING	.124
14	POTATOES	.135
15	GRAINS, RICE, AND PASTA	.138
16	HOME BAKING	.149
17	DESSERTS AND SWEET SAUCES	.188
18	BABY FOODS	.210
	CHILDREN'S PARTY FOODS	.219
	INDEX	.220

INTRODUCTION

The diagnosis of a food allergy is at once a blessing and a source of anxiety. It is a blessing because it often comes after a long and frustrating search for the cause of the debilitating symptoms from which you have been suffering. And the anxiety? That is inevitable, as you now face changes in your lifestyle or circumstances to accommodate or overcome the problem. At first it may feel as if your "can eat" list would fill no more than a Post-it note in comparison to the tome that is your "cannot eat" list and, if you allow it to, this can quickly impact on the rest of your life. After all, many of the things we enjoy in life—celebrations, birthdays, get-togethers with friends —revolve around food, and when you see food as a problem, it dampens your enjoyment of life.

In a funny way, we were lucky. Our eldest son was a tiny baby when we discovered he was acutely allergic to both dairy and egg. Because he was so small we had time to adjust as a family, and we adapted and grew together. He has never known the taste of dairy products and so does not "miss" them and, because his reaction was so severe, there was no decision to be made: we had to go dairy- and egg-free as a family and that was that.

That was seven years ago. We now have three boys who, between them, cannot eat dairy, eggs, anything containing gluten, and, bizarrely, potato. Yet despite these restrictions we manage to have an interesting, varied diet, using the wide range of ingredients that we can eat. Our experience is that we can conquer allergies without the need to adopt the sort of approach that necessitates living on a limited range of foods. How? The answer is simple: cook your food yourself using fresh ingredients.

When you cook your own food from scratch, you'll find that there are surprisingly few restrictions as to what you can eat. Gone are the days of worrying about the traces of allergens in all those ready-made meals. In addition, you'll find that your food is fresher, purer, tastier, and will become a focus of family life. And if that conjures up images of hours spent slaving over a hot stove, think again. Contrary to what you might believe, cooking from scratch doesn't have to be time-consuming or difficult. By taking a few minutes to plan the week's menu, writing out a shopping list, cooking in advance in batches and freezing, it is possible to eat an exciting, healthy, and varied diet without spending all your time in the kitchen. There is also no reason why eating this type of diet should be more expensive. In fact, it can be cheaper to buy fresh, basic ingredients rather than processed versions or the few ready-made meals that will cater specifically to your dietary requirements.

More importantly, being able to cook for yourself will help you cope better in everyday life. If you understand the ingredients to which you are allergic and how they are used in food, you will be able to anticipate problems when eating away from home and hence avoid them before they arise. It will help you to be more confident in suggesting easy alternatives to friends and family who would like to cook for you. An understanding of how food is cooked will also help you identify "safe" foods on the menu when eating in a restaurant and the right questions to ask to check that your needs are understood by the staff. In short, it will give you far greater control over your life.

I have had to find out how to do all of this over the last seven years. Even as a professionally trained chef, I have found this challenging, and I have been surprised that I haven't been able to find a book that approaches food allergies from the perspective that food can and should be normal and enjoyable—naughty even (after all, everyone needs a treat now and then). With this book I hope to fill that void—it's full of delicious real food; it's food that we eat all the time and it's the stuff we really enjoy.

The book is divided into three parts. The first part, Living with Food Allergies, looks at the key rules that will help you cope with food allergies in daily life, such as how to avoid cross-contamination of food in the kitchen, preparing for traveling, and eating away from home. There's also plenty of help for those with children, including how to help your child's day care or school cope with their allergy and how you can ensure your child enjoys birthday parties without feeling excluded or "different." The section also covers the basics of nutrition and balancing your diet. When you have to cut things out of your diet, you may well be missing a key source of nutrients, minerals, or vitamins and chapter 3 provides a checklist of alternative sources of these nutrients. It is by no means an exhaustive guide, but it will help point you in the right direction.

In part two you will find out why ingredients are used and the general rules for using substitutes for the foods you can't have. The most common food allergens—dairy, wheat, egg, nuts, and soy—are also some of the most common and versatile ingredients and, in order to be able to adapt a recipe successfully, you must first know the purpose that the food is serving in the recipe. Armed with this knowledge you'll find that food will come alive for you. Rather than look at a recipe in a book and think "I can't have that because it contains…," your response will be "That looks delicious – I'll just use…instead."

Of course, you have to walk before you can run, so before you launch yourself into adapting your own recipes, familiarize yourself with the cooking techniques and recipes in part three. In all of the recipes I have aimed for simplicity. First, as far as possible I have used normal ingredients that you can find in your local supermarket. If you are on a gluten-free diet, you may need to visit a health food store to get some of the gluten-free flours, but even these are gradually becoming more widely available. Second, I have kept the methods as simple as possible. After the formal testing process for the recipes, I gave them to my husband, Hew, to try—to make sure that the instructions were sufficiently clear and complete for the novice cook. He was really pleased with the way they turned out and how much he learned in the process. If he can cook them, anyone can (sorry Hew!). Last, I have tried to be realistic. There are limits to what can be adapted. The more a recipe relies on an ingredient that you cannot have, the harder it will be to create a workable substitution. While it is important to recognize these limitations, don't beat yourself up over the food you can't eat: look at all the delicious things you *can* enjoy.

If you haven't cooked—seriously—before, this book will get you up to a very good level of proficiency. It's not as hard as you might imagine, and the rewards—in terms of conquering your allergies, regaining control over your life, and improving the healthfuless and taste of your diet—are definitely worth the effort.

USING THE RECIPES

Before you begin cooking any of the recipes, please note the following:
- Many of the recipes in this book are suitable for all the featured food allergies, without any adaptations. Where a recipe is not suitable for a particular allergy and cannot be adapted, this is made clear in the introduction—although in many instances I have provided an alternative, similar recipe.
- The flagging system that is used in the recipes indicates the ingredients you need to subsititute in order to make the recipe suitable for your particular allergy (or to alert you to an ingredient that potentially could be a problem). Where no quantity is given for the alternative ingredient, the quantity is the same as the standard ingredient.
- At the start of each section, you will find guidance on preparation techniques and the suitability of that particular cooking method or food for each of the food allergies —it is helpful to read this information before making any of the recipes that follow. The techniques are covered in much more depth at the beginning of each chapter, because it would be impossible to include detailed guidance in every recipe.
- Unless the recipe states otherwise, all spoon measures are level, all eggs are medium (as are vegetables), and onions, garlic, shallots, and ginger are peeled.
- All stock featured in the recipes is made using the recipes in chapter 9.
- Sunflower, corn, and olive oil are used as cooking oils throughout the book because they are free of nut and soy oils. If you have a nut allergy and are also allergic to seeds, cook with corn oil or olive oil.
- Use one set of measurements—i.e. metric or imperial—because they are not interchangeable.

Part I
LIVING WITH FOOD ALLERGIES

Chapter 1 | AVOIDING PROBLEM FOODS IN DAY-TO-DAY LIFE

When you—or your child—suffer from food allergies, you need to make some very basic changes not only with regard to what you eat but how you store, prepare, and cook food. This might sound daunting—and there's no doubt food allergies make life more challenging—but you and your family can lead a full life, by planning ahead and taking time to explain to friends and family how food allergies can be managed. As well as avoiding unsuitable foods in the diet, contamination of safe foods with unsafe foods must be prevented by storing and preparing them separately, and by using clean hands and clean utensils. Mealtimes away from home need to be planned and your condition explained to anyone who prepares food for you. You will also require the cooperation of your colleagues at work, and, if it is your child who has an allergy, the staff caring for your child at school. Food allergies have a bearing on the restaurants you choose, the vacation accommodation in which you choose to stay, and how you plan to travel.

EATING AT HOME

At home you are in control of the food you prepare, and control is the key. Allergic reactions to food are caused by eating or coming into contact with the foods you must avoid. To prevent allergic reactions occurring at home, you therefore need to:
- know what you are eating
- keep safe and unsafe foods separate
- ensure you and your food do not come into contact with contaminated surfaces, utensils, tableware, and people eating or preparing unsafe food.

Before eating or preparing food, take time to read the ingredients lists on food labels (see box opposite and the "What to Look for on Food Labels" sections in chapters 4 to 8).

KEEPING SAFE AND UNSAFE FOODS SEPARATE

- Store safe foods separately from allergy-causing foods. For example, store wheat flour and gluten-free flours on separate shelves.
- Prepare foods separately to reduce the risk of cross-contamination via hands, utensils, or work surfaces.
- Prepare safe foods before unsafe foods so that your hands, work surfaces, and utensils are free of traces of unsuitable foods.

Making life easier for yourself

If you are cooking for a family, there is no reason why you should always go to the trouble of preparing separate meals for allergenic and non-allergenic members—why not make the same safe food for everyone? This saves time and means no one will feel different or left out. This book is full of familiar recipes that are easily adapted for dairy-, gluten-, egg-, soy-, and nut-free diets—they taste great, too.

Understanding food labels

To avoid exposure to food allergens always check the list of ingredients on the label of packaged foods before buying or eating them. The latest FDA food labeling rules have made food labels much easier to understand. They require manufacturers of packaged food to state clearly in the ingredients list when food products contain ingredients that are derived from the eight major allergenic foods: milk, eggs, fish, crustaceans, tree nuts, peanuts, soybeans, and wheat.

Food products containing any of these allergenic ingredients must clearly list them next to the specific ingredient and after the list of ingredients. The label could read, for example:

"lecithin (soy), flour (wheat), and whey (milk)." Immediately after or next to the ingredients list there will be a "contains" statement, as in "Contains Wheat, Milk, and Soy." Continue to check products you buy regularly because manufacturers change their recipes and may, at any time, add ingredients to which you are allergic.

For terms used on food labels to describe ingredients derived from gluten, dairy, egg, nuts, and soy, see the information about food labels at the end of each of the "Substituting for" chapters.

AVOIDING CONTAMINATION OF SAFE FOOD

In the kitchen
- Always wash your hands and make sure the work surfaces, pots, pans, and utensils are clean before using them to prepare food.
- Use separate cloths or disposable paper towels to mop up spills containing food allergens, for general cleaning, and for wiping the hands and face of allergic children.

At mealtimes
- Make sure the table is clean before people sit down. Traces of food left on it may cause a reaction.
- Wash your hands before setting the table and serving food, to prevent contaminating cutlery and serving spoons with traces of unsafe foods.
- Keep safe foods and allergy-causing foods away from each other on the table.
- Serve safe and allergy-causing foods with separate spoons.
- If you have a small child who is allergic, put the child in a clean high chair (invest in a portable one that can be taken to other people's homes, and restaurants).
- Keep serving dishes and serving spoons used for unsuitable food out of the reach of allergic children.
- Sit allergic children out of reach of other children eating unsuitable foods.
- Before cleaning an allergic child's face and hands after a meal or snack, make sure both your hands and the face cloth are clean.

EATING AWAY FROM HOME

Visiting friends and family should be an enjoyable event and not a source of stress or anxiety. Provided you take time to discuss your dietary requirements beforehand, it is possible to maintain the level of control necessary to ensure you eat safely and enjoy your time away from home. If you explain which foods have to be avoided but also offer to bring your own food, your host can decide to cook or ask you to provide food without embarrassment. By mutually agreeing to bring your own food you may both feel relieved and more relaxed knowing that your food will not contain any allergens.

VISITING FRIENDS AND FAMILY

Whether your hosts would like to cook for you or would prefer you to bring your own food, the following points are worth discussing to make your visit "allergy free" and enjoyable.

When your hosts would like to cook for you

- Ask what they are planning to serve. The menu may be perfectly suitable or easily adapted. To be certain, ask whether the recipes contain any of the ingredients you cannot eat.
- If the menu is not suitable, help them by listing the foods you can eat and suggest safe dishes that are familiar and enjoyed by everyone.
- Alert your hosts to allergy-causing ingredients they may not be familiar with on food labels.
- If you are staying overnight or for longer, offer to bring key foods that you rely on, such as gluten-free bread, dairy-free milk, and suitable snacks and drinks. This will save your hosts time and effort when shopping for your visit. If they offer to buy these products for you, give all the details they require to buy the right product: this is particularly important if you have allergic children, who may not eat unfamiliar products. It also makes shopping easier for the hosts.
- While you are visiting, offer to help your hosts prepare the food and to serve at mealtimes. This may be a relief for your hosts and reduces the risk of contamination.

When the hosts are nervous about cooking for you

It is perfectly possible to take easy-to-prepare ingredients or ready-prepared meals and snacks for a day or so. For longer, it is best to take staples with you and shop for basic ingredients nearby. Ask the host what she plans to cook so that you can plan a similar meal or menu for yourself.

WHEN YOUR CHILD IS IN THE CARE OF OTHERS

If you have an allergic child, controlling the diet can be difficult once he or she is outside the home. Inevitably, as your child grows, and he or she visits friends and family or begins day care or school without you, you will need to trust other people to ensure your child does not come into contact with allergy-causing foods. However, in spite of having dietary restrictions, it is important that your child learns to enjoy periods of time away from you, with trusted friends and members of the family, and feel normal and included at day care or school. This section outlines ways of ensuring your child is safe when he or she is in the care of others.

Family and friends may be unused to dealing with food allergies. When they first invite your child to play, or to a party, explain that certain foods and food containing those ingredients make him or her allergic and offer to supply suitable snacks and meals. Depending on how daunting the hosts regard your child's dietary requirements, they may be happy to provide suitable food for your child or ask you to supply your child's food. Discuss the following points so that you all feel confident that your child's visit will be safe and allergy free.

When friends and family would like to cook for your child

Although the same guidelines apply here as for "When your hosts would like to cook for you" (opposite), other precautions must be in place for allergic children. Because toddlers and small children are mobile and are prone to eating anything within their reach, suggest that the snacks, meals, and drinks served are suitable for all the children present (see page 219). This way, if the children share cups, swap food, or wipe it on each other it doesn't matter.

When friends and family are nervous cooking for your child

For your allergic baby or small child, supply purees, snacks, drinks, milk, bibs, dishes, spoons, and a portable high chair with a tray and face cloth. This way, you can be assured that your child is unlikely to come into contact with unsafe foods while he or she is eating. If possible, provide a meal similar to the meal served to other children present so your child does not feel different and tempted to try unsuitable foods on the table.

Irrespective of whether the host or the parent has provided the food, the person looking after the child should be able to recognize the symptoms of an allergic reaction and treat them swiftly and correctly. In order for them to do so:

- Supply and explain how to use any medicines in the event of an allergic reaction.
- List any early signs or symptoms of an allergic reaction so that the caregiver can quickly recognize and deal with the reaction before it has time to escalate into something serious.
- Make sure the caregiver can contact you easily.
- Ask them to call for an ambulance immediately if your child suffers from anaphylactic reactions to food.

You may have taken all the precautions possible regarding your own child, but other children there may present a risk:

- Ask the caregiver to explain to any other children old enough to understand that they must not hand food to your child.
- When your child is old enough to understand, teach him or her to be responsible for what he or she eats (see page 18).

Children's parties

Invitations to parties for very small children are usually extended to one or both parents too. This arrangement means you can take your own food, keep your child away from unsuitable food, and inform other parents present of your child's allergies so they can make sure their child does not pass food to or wipe sticky hands on your child.

Parties for children aged between 4 and 7 often do not include parents and can instill dread and anxiety in parents of allergic children. You may not know the parents hosting the party very well; traditional party food including sandwiches, pre-packed snack food, cakes, and cookies are likely to contain food allergens; and sweets that may also be unsuitable for your child are often given as small prizes and included in party bags. It is also inevitable that the parents will be busy during the party and cannot watch your child's every move.

There are many ways that you and the parents hosting the party can make the party safe, inclusive, and enjoyable for your child. Accept an invitation to a children's party by speaking directly to the parents hosting the event so you can discuss your child's dietary requirements.

When food will be provided for your child

- Once the parents have decided on the menu, go through it carefully to agree which foods are safe and which are not.

- Suggest how birthday cake, other home-baked foods, and sandwiches may be adapted using alternative ingredients. Offer to give them ideas and recipes for simple, safe party foods (see page 219) or provide food that may be difficult to find in the supermarket or is difficult for the parents to make.

- Offer to provide suitable sweets for games and party bags.

When you are providing your child's food

Discuss the menu and if possible provide similar food, birthday cake, snacks, and any sweets for games and your child's party bag.

Other ways of making a party safe for your child

- When you arrive at the party, confirm that the food the hosts say is suitable is OK.

- Ask the hosts to show your child which foods he or she can and can't eat on the table.

- Suggest that safe foods are assembled on a party plate, ready to serve. The parents then need only place the plate of safe food in front of your child when he or she is seated at the table. This means the child will not stand out as different and both you and the host parents will feel confident that your child is eating safely.

- Ask that unsuitable food is kept out of reach of your child.

- Explain the symptoms of an allergic reaction so that the parents will recognize the condition if it occurs.

- Provide all necessary treatments for your child's allergies and explain how to administer them.

- Give contact phone numbers so that you can be reached immediately in an emergency.

- If you are worried that your child may eat the wrong foods, or requires an Epipen to treat allergic reactions, ask if you can stay to help.

- Ask the parents to mark foods that are safe and unsafe by placing safe foods on paper plates of a particular color so that your child can choose his food without drawing attention to himself.

CHILDCARE AND SCHOOLING	It can be a worrying time when your allergic child starts day care or school, because it involves trusting virtual strangers to keep your child safe and happy during mealtimes and throughout the day. The organization may or may not have dealt with your child's particular food allergies and a detailed discussion regarding your child's requirements is essential before he or she begins there. When you first visit the day care or school, talk to the staff who will teach, care, and feed your child to ascertain how much experience they have in dealing with food allergies and how much additional information they require to ensure your child is safe in their care. By talking to the staff, you will also gauge how adaptable, creative, and sensitive they are to your child's requirements.

Ask the teachers or staff responsible how they guard against children with food allergies feeling different and isolated during mealtimes. Children with special dietary requirements are often seated together or among older, more responsible children who are more aware of not touching and swapping food. Provided your child is out of arms reach of the other small children, sticky fingers, scattered food, and spilt drinks, your child can enjoy a sociable meal. It is also worth asking how they plan to prevent your child from feeling excluded from any classroom activities using allergy-causing foods. For example, are they prepared to adapt recipes used in cooking activities so your child can take part?

If you are confident that the day care or school will make every effort to make your child's life in their care as happy and as "normal" as possible, make another appointment to discuss the specific details of your child's diet and medication before the term begins. If you are not impressed with the general attitude, it may be advisable—in extremis—to look at another day care or school in the area.

When the day care or school is happy to provide food for your child
- Provide a clear list of the food and drinks your child cannot eat. This list must also include a list of all the terms for unsuitable ingredients used on food labels.
- Provide an extensive list of the foods that your child can eat, because this will help the kitchen staff enormously when they plan lunch menus for your child.
- Arrange to meet the head of the kitchen to go through the weekly menus. You may both be pleasantly surprised and encouraged to see how many dishes can be made suitable with simple adaptations to recipes.
- Offer suggestions for other lunch dishes that would be practical for them to cook.
- Suggest products they can order in, such as dairy-free milk, yogurt, and ice cream or gluten-free flours.
- Ask how they will provide food for your child on school outings. Would they prefer you to provide food?

If the day care or school does not have the facilities to cook for your child
- Ask to see their weekly menus and provide similar food where possible.
- Find out what other food and drink they would like you to provide—such as suitable dairy-free milk, cookies, gluten-free bread and cakes—so your child does not feel left out, for instance, when it's snack time or when birthday cakes are brought in by other children.

Teaching your child responsibility

By the time children reach school age they usually have a good understanding of the foods that make them ill and can be given more responsibility in ensuring they do not eat unsuitable food. They will be fully aware of how ill they feel when they become allergic and this should be enough to persuade them to be careful. Ensure they are aware of the following:

- Exactly which foods they need to avoid and the various terms used for those foods on labels.

- They must read food labels carefully before eating something they are offered. Teach them to ask "Does this contain...?" before accepting any food, even from an adult.

- They must not help themselves to food unless they know it is safe to eat.

- They must not swap food with other children in the playground or at mealtimes unless they are sure it is safe for them to eat.

HELPING STAFF RECOGNIZE AND TREAT ALLERGIC REACTIONS

In the event of your child having an allergic reaction, it is vital that the staff know what to do. Before your child starts:

- Confirm that all staff dealing with your child are aware of and understand your child's dietary needs.
- Provide a list of initial symptoms of your child's food allergy so that they can recognize the first stages of an allergic reaction. Although it is very obvious to you when your child is suffering an allergic reaction, the staff in a busy classroom may not notice.
- Provide all necessary medicines and clear instructions for administering them if a full allergic reaction occurs. If your child carries an Epipen, the staff may require training to use it.
- Provide contact numbers and ask that they contact you immediately if a reaction occurs.
- Confirm that medicines will be taken on school outings.

| # EATING OUT AND TRAVELING

At home you are in control of the way in which food is stored, prepared, served, and eaten. When you are eating at restaurants, traveling, or on vacation, you are less able to protect yourself or a member of your family from allergy-causing foods. The knowledge that you are no longer in control is powerful and can be debilitating to such an extent that you may feel confined to your home. Although food allergies make eating out and traveling more complicated, it is still possible to lead a normal and fulfilling life by:

- planning mealtimes
- choosing carefully where to eat
- being prepared to ask questions about the food available to buy in shops or on menus
- taking food with you.

In this chapter you will find advice on selecting restaurants and safe food from menus, traveling and flying safely, and choosing appropriate vacation accommodation.

EATING OUT

For most people, eating out is a treat, providing an opportunity to try new foods and to relax with friends, with no cleaning up afterwards. However, for those with food allergies, it can be an anxious, frustrating experience. Unless you visit a particular restaurant, café, or fast-food outlet regularly, you have no established relationship or connection with the people running it and no way of knowing how food is stored or prepared. You must either take your own food, or place your trust in waiters, managers, and chefs. You will need to be confident that they will communicate your requirements to each other, check their dishes for the ingredients that could make you ill, and take care to prepare and serve safe and unsafe foods separately. Many people have suffered serious allergic reactions as a result of traces of unsafe food present on unwashed or carelessly washed pots, pans, utensils, and hands.

CHOOSE YOUR RESTAURANT WISELY

In order to eat out safely and for the experience to be enjoyable, it is vital to choose your restaurant wisely, book well in advance, and plan your menu with the restaurant manager and/or the chef before you eat there.

If possible, choose restaurants that have experience in dealing with food allergies and are careful to prepare your food on clean work surfaces with clean utensils and hands. The safest restaurants are those that prepare food from scratch and offer roasted, broiled, or pan-fried meat, poultry, or fish cooked to order. This way, you can choose simple ingredients, cooked plainly in suitable oil, and served simply with their cooking juices. When restaurants rely on ready-made food, which will almost certainly contain the common food allergens, there is very little they can do to cater to your needs.

It also makes sense to choose restaurants serving food that does not rely heavily on the ingredients to which you are allergic. For example, Asian cooking uses very little dairy but frequently includes soy and nuts in sauces and garnishes, and nut oil for frying; in contrast, the cuisine of northern France uses dairy products, wheat flour, and eggs in many dishes.

PLANNING
AHEAD

If possible, book your table at least two to three days in advance. This gives you the opportunity to talk to the restaurant manager—and, if necessary, the chef—to establish whether the menu includes dishes you can eat. If it doesn't, ask whether the chef could prepare a suitable dish for you. If they don't understand your requirements or are not helpful, then choose another restaurant.

If the chef is happy to cater for you, help him to plan your menu by telling him what you can eat as well as the ingredients you can't. Ask him to contact you to run through the ingredients in the proposed menu to confirm the food is safe for you to eat. It is also a good idea to contact the restaurant the day before you are due to eat there, to confirm with the restaurant manager and head chef on duty that they haven't forgotten about you, and to run through the dishes they are planning to serve you, to double check they understand your requirements.

CHOOSING SAFE FOOD FROM A MENU

If the restaurant has prepared a special menu for you, run through the ingredients with the waiter, manager, or chef once more before ordering. Even after the efforts both you and the restaurant staff have gone to, food allergens in basic ingredients may slip through the net. If the dish turns out to be unsafe for you to eat, do not take the risk. Most restaurants will be very apologetic and will make every effort to provide you with a safe alternative.

When you have not had the opportunity to book ahead, if possible explain to the manager or waiter on arrival how serious your food allergy is and run through the menu with them to look for suitable dishes or simple adaptations that could be made.

If they are not confident they can provide a suitable meal for you, it is safer not to eat there. Once you are confident they can cook for you, look for a familiar, simple dish that is normally safe for you to eat and can be freshly cooked to order, such as plain broiled, pan-fried, or roasted meat or fish, cooked with a suitable fat, and served with its cooking juices. Ask for a plain salad with oil and vinegar, served separately, to make your own dressing, or plain boiled or steamed vegetables. Desserts, more often than not, are made with dairy products, wheat, eggs, and nuts, because they add richness, and flavor and help to lighten delicate foods. Avoid rich desserts and look for those made with fresh fruit, such as poached fruit, fruit salads, sorbets, water ices,

Self-service restaurants

These are generally too risky for those with a serious food allergy. While some of the foods may be suitable, it is too easy for them to become contaminated by food from other dishes falling into them or by serving spoons that are used for a number of dishes.

and fresh strawberry or raspberry coulis, because they tend to be the safest options. Your meal may not be as interesting as you would like it to be, but you will have chosen safely.

If you have a dairy allergy

- Does the sauce, gravy, soup, casserole, or braised dish contain butter, milk, cream, yogurt, or cheese? What are they garnished with? Soup is often garnished with croutons or croûtes, often made with butter, or topped with a swirl of yogurt, sour cream, cream, or crème fraîche. If the sauce is unsuitable, ask for olive oil and wedges of lemon to moisten and flavor plainly cooked food.
- Is the food roasted, baked, pan-fried, or broiled with oil, or do they use butter or ghee (a clarified butter used in Indian food)? If so, can they prepare food for you cooked with a suitable fat?
- Has the food been marinated before cooking? If so, check the ingredients in the marinade—it may contain dairy products.
- Are the vegetables served plain or are they cooked or tossed in butter? If the vegetables are buttered, could they prepare you a salad or plain boiled or steamed vegetables to order? Roasted, baked, and broiled vegetables are normally cooked with oil but always check. Pureed vegetables, such as mashed potatoes, are best avoided because they normally contain milk and butter.
- Does the salad dressing contain dairy products? If so, ask for oil and vinegar as a simple alternative.
- When ordering pizza, confirm the dough is dairy free and ask the chef to make a cheese-free pizza. Before eating your pizza, drizzle with olive oil, or an oil flavored with garlic or herbs, to moisten it.

Other tips for eating out gluten free

If you are going to an Italian pizza restaurant, call the restaurant manager in advance to ask if you can bring along a gluten-free pizza base for them to top or gluten-free pasta for them to cook; ask for a gluten-free sauce, such as fresh Italian tomato sauce.

If a dish is normally flavored with soy sauce, ask if they can use the gluten-free equivalent, tamari, instead—if necessary, take your own bottle with you.

Ground white pepper can contain flour to bulk it out. To be sure, ask for a pepper mill to grind fresh pepper on your food.

Don't forget that there are a number of drinks you must avoid, too. Many alcoholic drinks, such as beer, lager, ale, stout, and whiskey are made from malted barley, which contains gluten. Some soft drinks served in restaurants are also questionable: tomato juice may be thickened with wheat flour, while cloudy fruit blends and fizzy drinks may contain wheat starch.

If you have a gluten allergy

- Are the sauces, gravy, braised dishes, soups, and casseroles thickened with flour? If the restaurant uses stock cubes or gravy granules to make sauces, these may contain gluten.
- Is the meat, poultry, or fish in pan-fried dishes coated in flour before frying? Meat and fish seasonings can also contain wheat flour.
- Are other fried dishes floured, battered, or crumbed?
- Do the sauces contain soy sauce, barbecue sauce, or Worcestershire sauce? (All are common sources of hidden gluten.)
- Has the food been marinated before cooking? If so, check the ingredients in the marinade—some of them may contain wheat flour or wheat derivatives.

- Do sausages, stuffing, and terrines contain flour or bread crumbs? Store-bought meat products often contain "rusk," or dried bread crumbs.
- Are bulgur, couscous, semolina, barley, oats, or rye used in the dish (all of these contain gluten)?
- Is the salad dressing freshly made? (Manufactured salad dressings are often thickened with wheat flour.) If they are not sure, ask for an undressed salad with oil and vinegar served separately, to make your own dressing. Also choose plain new potatoes, baked potatoes, rice, and plain cooked vegetables.
- Which desserts contain wheat flour? Many desserts, including some manufactured ice creams, contain wheat flour. To be safe, choose plain fresh fruit or fresh fruit salad, meringues, poached fruit, cheese and fruit, or homemade sorbet.

If you have an egg allergy
- Do the salad dressings contain egg? (Restaurant salad dressings often contain a small quantity of egg to emulsify and thicken them or are made with a mayonnaise base.) If they are unsure, ask for oil and vinegar so that you can make your own salad dressing.
- Which of the sauces contain egg? Avoid egg-based sauces, such as hollandaise and béarnaise sauce.
- Are fried foods battered or crumbed? If they are, they will contain egg. Are baked foods glazed with egg?
- Do your hamburgers, meatballs, sausages, and fish cakes contain egg? Foods made with processed or minced meat or fish are often bound with egg to prevent them from crumbling when cooked.
- Does the pasta or noodles contain egg?
- Do any of the stir-fried dishes contain egg? If you ask for stir-fried food without egg, confirm they will be frying your food in a clean pan and not in an unwashed one previously used to cook a dish containing egg.
- Most baked goods and desserts contain egg. To be safe, ask for a fresh fruit salad with a fresh fruit coulis. Homemade sorbets may also be suitable, provided they do not contain egg white.
- Do any of your drinks contain egg? Egg is often added to hot drink mixes, including hot chocolate and cappuccino, to make them frothy.

If you have a nut allergy
- Are there any nut oils in the salad dressing? (They are sometimes added to give flavor.) If they are unsure, ask for vinegar and olive oil to make your own dressing.
- Are oils containing nut oil used for frying? If so, could they fry your food in a suitable oil in a clean pan?
- Are nuts and seeds used to garnish salads and other savory dishes?
- Are nuts and seeds present in the bread?
- Are there nuts present in any of the stuffings, meat terrines, sausages (mortadella is one example), and processed meats?
- Are ground nuts used to thicken and flavor sauces? Be especially aware of curry sauces, satay sauce, and pesto.

- Many desserts, including ice cream and baked goods, may contain nuts and are not safe to eat in restaurants. Also avoid marzipan and nougat.
- Be aware of nut syrups and nut liqueurs (Amaretto and Frangelico) added to coffee and hot chocolate.

Be especially careful with Japanese, Malaysian, Thai, Chinese, Indian, Middle Eastern, and vegetarian dishes (nuts are often used in vegetarian "meat").

If you have a soy allergy
- Does your chosen dish contain the soy-based flavoring ingredients soy sauce, tamari, shoyu, or miso? Also ask about salad dressings, spreads, dips, marinades, and sauces (including Worcestershire, barbecue sauce, and mayonnaise), because these often contain soy.
- Which dishes contain tofu or tempeh (which are soy-based)?
- Do they use soybean oil or vegetable oil, which contains soybean oil, for frying? Can they use an alternative cooking oil, such as corn or olive oil?
- Are soups, stews, and sauces flavored with stock cubes? Stock cubes often contain soy-based ingredients. Canned soup and dried soup can also contain soy.
- Are baked foods, such as pastry and cakes, homemade or bought? Manufactured baked foods may contain soy flour and margarine made with soybean oil.
- Is the tuna canned or fresh? Canned tuna is often stored in soybean oil.
- Which dishes contain bean sprouts? (They are likely to be soybean sprouts.)
- Are breaded foods homemade or bought? (Manufactured breaded foods often contain soy.)
- Are the desserts manufactured rather than homemade? (Homemade desserts are much less likely to contain soy.) If homemade desserts are available, ask if margarine containing soybean oil has been used to make them. Otherwise, choose a simple dessert made with fresh fruit, such as poached fruit or fresh fruit salad.

Be especially careful with Japanese, Malaysian, Thai, Chinese, Indian, and vegetarian dishes, because soy in various guises is a common ingredient.

SHOW YOUR APPRECIATION

When restaurant staff have been helpful during your visit and you have eaten well and safely, it is worth returning. Tip them well and let them know how pleased you are. They will appreciate your comments and are more likely to remember you next time you book. When you book another time, be just as careful to discuss and plan your menu as the first time. And remember, menus and staff change, and your second experience could be different.

Take your medication with you

Always take your medication with you when you go out to eat, especially if you carry an Epipen. If you become allergic despite the precautions you have taken, immediately stop eating, tell the people you are with, and take your medication. If the allergic reaction is becoming serious, ask your friends to call for an ambulance.

TRAVELING

When traveling for the day by car, boat, or train, make sure you take satisfying and nutritious meals and snacks to last the journey, because the majority of foods available for you to buy on the way may not be suitable. Although traveling by air is also perfectly possible for people with food allergies, it is made more complicated by restrictions on luggage and carrying medication, the limited range of food available on board, sitting in such close proximity to fellow passengers, and the risk of delays.

TRAVELING BY PLANE

Plan your journey carefully in order to give yourself and the airline an opportunity to plan for your food allergy, so that you can travel in safety and comfort. The following guidelines will help.

BOOKING YOUR FLIGHT

- Book your flight directly with the airline as early as you can. This gives you the opportunity to discuss your food allergy with a member of the airline staff.
- Let them know if you or a member of your family have a serious food allergy.
- If you suffer from peanut allergy, request a flight when peanuts are not served on the airplane. Morning flights are usually nut free.
- If your allergies are easily managed with medication, you may want to request a special meal if the airline is able to provide it.
- If you feel safer taking your own food, find out how much luggage you can take on board. You will want to take your maximum allowance for long journeys to ensure you have sufficient food to last until you get to your final destination.
- Ask what documentation is required from your doctor to enable you to carry your medication on board. Airlines usually request that all medicines are stored in their original containers that show dosages and clearly identify the drugs for customs officials. If you carry an Epipen, airlines also ask you to carry a letter from the doctor confirming the drug and an explanation of why it is essential you carry it.
- If possible, book your seat. A window seat means you have a passenger on one side only, and food will not be passed above you as it is served and cleared away.

PREPARING FOR YOUR FLIGHT

- Visit your doctor to discuss which medication you should take with you. Ask them to prescribe more than you would normally need and to prepare the documentation required by the airline to enable you to carry the medication on board.
- Contact the airline twenty-four hours before your flight to confirm that you have all the medical documentation you need; that they have special meals on hand if you have ordered them; the volume of luggage you can take on board. If you have arranged to travel on a nut-free flight, confirm it will be so.
- If you are away for a few days, pack staples you may not be able to find at your destination in your checked baggage.
- Store delicate foods that squash or crumble easily in airtight containers. Pack containers of satisfying, filling foods—and avoid anything that is likely to deteriorate on a long journey. Allow for delays and provide for yourself as generously as your hand luggage allowance permits.

Flying with allergic children

Taking lots of food on the plane is a great way to keep children happy. If your children are old enough, give them a small backpack to carry filled with safe snacks. This way you can take more food on board. Keep them busy with small bags of dried fruit, small boxes of raisins, apples, carrot sticks, rice cakes, bread sticks, suitable fruit and cereal bars, and cookies. These are all ideal snacks for traveling.

Keep a close eye on your child for symptoms of an allergic reaction during the flight. Treat any symptoms at the earliest opportunity to avoid complications.

- Even if you have ordered special meals, take satisfying snacks with you in case of delays or to tide you over if the special meal does not materialize.
- Pack your medication where it is easy to access.
- Take a small packet of wipes for wiping down trays and arm rests.
- Arrive at the airport in plenty of time. This will allow you to advise check-in staff you will be carrying medication on board, confirm that they have special meals for you, and reserve your seat (choose a window seat or an aisle seat so that you are not sandwiched between people who may be eating food that could cause an allergic reaction). Reconfirm the above with the cabin staff at the gate.

ON THE PLANE
- If you are allergic to nuts and they are likely to be served on the flight, request that they are not served to people sitting around you.
- Wipe the food tray and arm rests to remove any traces of food allergens.
- Explain your food allergy to your fellow passengers. Their cooperation is essential if you are to have a safe, stress-free flight.
- Inform the flight crew that you suffer from food allergies, that you have ordered special meals, and explain you have all necessary medication with you.
- If you have ordered a special meal, run through the ingredients with a member of the cabin crew before you eat it.

CHOOSING VACATION ACCOMMODATION

Accommodation that has cooking facilities is usually the best option for those with food allergies. Even if you only have a small refrigerator in which to store fresh ingredients, some basic cooking utensils, and a hot plate to cook on, it means you are in control. By cooking for yourself or your family, you may not be trying local specialties in the restaurants every night, but you will still have the chance to purchase and prepare local produce (though do exercise caution with anything you are unfamiliar with, unless you are sure it is safe to eat).

Although hotels are in theory more relaxing than rentals with cooking facilities, this does not necessarily follow when you or someone in your family suffers from food allergies because you are forced to rely on restaurants or the hotel kitchen.

If you choose to stay in a hotel
- Stay in a hotel that has experience with cooking for people with for food allergies or provides cooking facilities, too, so you are not totally reliant on the hotel kitchen.

- Help the hotel plan your stay. Send a list of foods that you can and can't eat to the kitchen manager in advance. Follow up with a call to make sure he understands your restrictions.
- When you arrive at the hotel, introduce yourself to the kitchen manager or head chef so they know for whom they are cooking.
- Choose a region where the local cooking does not rely on the ingredients to which you are allergic. For example, eating in hotels and restaurants in northern France can be very limiting for someone on a dairy-free diet, because many of the local dishes contain butter, cream, and cheese. However, in southern France, the diet is lighter and relies more on olive oil, fruit, and vegetables, offering a wider range of suitable dishes.

Useful ingredients to take on vacation

Because there is no guarantee that you will be able to find the products you rely on back home, it is advisable to take essential basic ingredients and snacks with you. You can then supplement these with suitable local ingredients.

FOR A DAIRY-FREE DIET: It is possible to live without dairy-free spread and soy yogurt for a short period of time, but milk is difficult to live without, particularly when you are traveling with children. Get in touch with the resort and find out whether your favorite brand of dairy-free milk is available—children get used to one variety and may refuse to drink other brands. Alternatively, calculate the minimum quantity of dairy-free milk you require and buy it in small cartons of UHT dairy-free milk to limit the volume of milk that is open at one time. (Milk will go bad more quickly in warm countries.) Use a water bottle for carrying milk once the carton is opened. Dairy-free cookies and other snacks are also useful to have.

FOR A GLUTEN-FREE DIET: Take gluten-free flour for thickening sauces and flouring food for frying, as well as gluten-free pasta, breakfast cereal, and cookies. If bread is an important part of your diet, take ready-mixed gluten-free flours, packets of dried yeast, and a loaf pan to make your own bread.

FOR AN EGG-FREE DIET: Take egg-free cookies and snacks you are unlikely to find while you are away, to keep you going between meals.

FOR A NUT-FREE DIET: Take nut-free snacks and breakfast cereals you are unlikely to find while you are away. You may also want to take a trusted brand of nut-free cooking oil for cooking and salad dressings.

FOR A SOY-FREE DIET: Take soy-free cookies and snacks you are unlikely to find while you are away, to keep you going between meals. You may also want to take a trusted brand of soy-free cooking oil with you for cooking and salad dressings.

| Chapter 3 | # EATING A BALANCED DIET ON A RESTRICTED DIET |

Dairy products, wheat, eggs, nuts, and soy products are more than just simple ingredients. Due to their availability, low cost, high nutritional value, and versatility in the preparation of homemade and manufactured food, most of the world's population rely upon them to provide basic nutrition. This chapter outlines the nutritional role of these core ingredients and the wealth of alternative food sources that provide the same nutrients to help ensure your diet is balanced and varied.

THE COMPONENTS OF A HEALTHY DIET

A healthy, balanced diet is achieved by eating good-quality, fresh ingredients, prepared from scratch, which are collectively rich in the essential nutrients: carbohydrate, protein, fiber, fat, vitamins, and minerals. Specific sources of these nutrients are outlined in the tables at the end of this chapter.

- **Carbohydrates** are produced by photosynthesis in plants and are stored as sugars in fruit and vegetables, or as starch in tubers, such as potatoes, and seeds. Starchy ingredients make food more satisfying and filling to eat, while sugary ingredients enhance the flavor of food that would otherwise be bland. Both starch and sugars are converted by the body into glucose, which is used to generate energy or added to our fat stores in the liver and muscles.
- **Protein** provides the building blocks for our bodies to create, maintain, and repair skin, hair, bones, organs, muscles, enzymes, hormones, and genes. Foods high in protein are richly flavored and make food more satisfying to eat.
- **Fats and oils** provide us with energy, enable the absorption of fat-soluble vitamins, and are broken down into essential fatty acids that cannot be made by the body. Fatty acids are essential for utilizing the energy contained in the fat stores of the body, for normal growth, behavior and maintenance of cell membranes, the skin, a working immune system, and balanced hormone levels. Ingredients rich in fat add flavor and richness, moisture, and succulence to a whole variety of basic ingredients including meat, fish, fruit, vegetables, and starchy foods, and are used widely to make both savory and sweet food interesting and delicious to eat. Used in moderation, fat has an important place in our diet.
- **Fiber** remains relatively unchanged as it passes through our digestive system, assisting the carriage of food through our gut and regulating the absorption of nutrients, such as glucose and cholesterol. Fiber derived from both gluten-rich and gluten-free whole grains, whole-wheat flour and bran, nuts, beans, fruit, and vegetables gives a hearty flavor and texture to the foods we eat.
- **Vitamins** are organic substances required in small amounts In the diet. They enable the body to use proteins, carbohydrates, and fat to produce energy for growth, maintenance, and repair of healthy tissue. It is essential that we consume the correct

levels of vitamins because most vitamins are either produced in limited quantities by the body or not at all. Some vitamins are only found in animals, others only in plants, so we have to eat a wide variety of foods to obtain the nutrition we need to be healthy. A number of basic foods, such as milk, bread, and flour are fortified with vitamins to improve their nutritional value because a large proportion of their nutritional content is lost during processing and refining. The principal vitamins are the water-soluble vitamins, B and C, and the fat-soluble vitamins A, D, E, and K. Vitamins B and C are not stored in the body so rich sources of both must be eaten daily. To maintain the levels of fat-soluble vitamins stored in the liver and body fat, rich sources of these vitamins must be eaten regularly.

- **Minerals**, like vitamins, are essential for regulating and building the cells that make up the body. To maintain good health, calcium, phosphorus, potassium, sodium, and magnesium are required in quantities exceeding 100 mg a day. Iron, manganese, and zinc are required in lower amounts, and trace minerals, such as selenium and copper, are required in minute quantities. Plants and products derived from plants, including fruit, vegetables, grains, beans, nuts, and seeds, are the richest sources of minerals because plants absorb minerals directly from the soil through their roots. Animal products, including dairy products, eggs, meat, poultry, and fish, contain slightly lower levels of minerals, derived from plants eaten by the animals.

All these nutrients are found in a diet that regularly includes fresh meat, poultry, dairy products, eggs, fish, fruit, vegetables, nuts, beans, and whole grains. Milk, from which all dairy products are derived, and egg (often eaten as a meal in its own right) are both complete sources of protein, fat, minerals, and vitamins, designed by nature to support new and growing life. Similarly, wheat grain, soybeans, and nut kernels are the seeds of plants in which carbohydrate, protein, fat, vitamins, and minerals are stored to provide energy for the germination and growth of new plants. Soybean products such as soy milk and tofu are as rich in protein as foods derived from animals.

When you are allergic to one or a number of these highly nutritious ingredients, it is essential to eat other foods that are collectively rich in the same nutrients, in order to provide the energy and materials that keep your body healthy (and, in the case of children, promote growth). For example, milk and dairy products are a principal source of calcium in the Western diet, hence those with a dairy allergy must turn to other calcium-rich foods, such as green leafy vegetables, nuts, and calcium-fortified dairy-free milk, in order to obtain sufficient calcium. This is especially important for growing children. The following tables show which foods contain the nutrients you may be lacking as a result of omitting dairy, gluten, eggs, nuts, or soy from your diet.

MAIN NUTRIENTS

IF YOU CUT OUT...

DAIRY	EGG	WHOLE-GRAIN WHEAT	WHITE WHEAT FLOUR	SOY	NUTS	You may be missing	What it does	Rich sources include
X	X	X	X	X	X	Carbohydrate (starch)	Provides the main energy source in the diet. Carbohydrates are split into sugars, which are then broken down to release energy	Gluten-rich and gluten-free breakfast cereals, grains, bread, pasta, beans, potatoes, and bananas
X			X			Carbohydrate (sugars)	Sugars are broken down to form the simple sugar glucose, the primary source of energy used by the body and brain	Fruit and sweet vegetables, milk, whole grains, honey, white and brown sugar, syrups
X	X	X	X	X	X	Protein	Provides the building blocks for our bodies to create, maintain, and repair skin, hair, bones, organs, muscles, enzymes, hormones, and genes	Red meat, organ meat, poultry, fish, seafood, eggs, dairy products, gluten-rich and gluten-free grains, beans, soy products, nuts, and seeds
X	X			X	X	Fat	Provides a source of concentrated energy and fatty acids and enables the body to absorb fat-soluble vitamins A, D, E, and K	Red meat, poultry skin, oily fish, eggs, dairy products, nuts, beans, seeds, vegetable oils, and margarine
		X		X	X	Dietary fiber	Aids digestion and absorption of nutrients and passage of food through the gut	Beans, fruit and vegetables with thin skin that can be eaten, nuts, seeds, whole grains, whole-wheat bread, brown rice, soy bran, green leafy vegetables, dried fruit, bananas

IF YOU CUT OUT...

DAIRY	EGG	WHOLE-GRAIN WHEAT	WHITE WHEAT FLOUR	SOY	NUTS	You may be missing	What it does	Rich sources include
X	X	X		X		Vitamin A	Keeps the skin and immune system healthy and is important for bone growth and night vision	Liver, eggs, dairy products, soy, green leafy vegetables, dried fruit, orange foods (carrots, mangoes, sweet potatoes, apricots, pumpkins), fish oils, beans
	X	X	X	X	X	B vitamins*	Break down carbohydrates, proteins, and fats into energy for growth; help repair of skin and ensure a healthy nervous system and red blood cells	Red meat, organ meats, poultry, fish, seafood, eggs, dairy products, fortified dairy-free milk, soy, fruit and vegetables, beans, fortified cereals, whole grains, whole-grain bread, brown rice, dried fruit, nuts, seeds, yeast extract
X	X	X	X	X	X	Folic acid B12	Enables the formation of red blood cells; necessary for growth and a healthy nervous system	Red meat, organ meats, poultry, eggs, dairy products, soy, green leafy vegetables, beans, cereals, bread, brown rice, citrus fruits, dried fruit, potatoes, bananas, nuts, seeds
						Vitamin C**	Maintains healthy skin, teeth, gums, tendons, bones, immune system; necessary for wound healing, energy production, and growth	Most fruit and vegetables (especially citrus fruits), green leafy vegetables, green peppers, strawberries, broccoli, cabbage, potatoes, tomatoes, melon
X	X			X		Vitamin D	Enables the absorption of calcium to maintain healthy bones	Produced by the skin when exposed to the sun. Also in white fish, oily fish, shellfish, mollusks, eggs, dairy products, soy milk
	X			X	X	Vitamin E	Maintains good muscle control	Eggs, soy, green leafy vegetables, cereals, bread, nuts, seeds, olives, corn, fish oils and vegetable oil, beans
	X			X		Vitamin K	Aids blood clotting	Red meat, organ meats, poultry, eggs, dairy products, green leafy vegetables, strawberries, beans, and lentils

*The B vitamins include B1 (thiamine), B2 (riboflavin), B3 (niacin), and B6 (pyridoxine).
**Vitamin C intake is not affected by cutting out any of the common food allergens, but it is an important part of the diet so it is vital to get an adequate daily intake.

MINERALS

IF YOU CUT OUT...

DAIRY	EGG	WHOLE-GRAIN WHEAT	WHITE WHEAT FLOUR	SOY	NUTS	You may be missing	What it does	Rich sources include
X	X	X	X	X	X	Calcium	Maintains healthy bones and teeth and muscle function	Milk and fortified dairy-free milk, dairy products, tofu, fish with fine bones that are eaten (i.e. sardines and whitebait), green leafy vegetables, beans, apricots, nuts, seeds, eggs
X	X	X	X	X	X	Phosphorus	Maintains, with calcium, strong bones, teeth, and muscle function and is a vital component of cells	Red meat, organ meats, poultry, fish, seafood, eggs, dairy products, soy, green leafy vegetables, cereals, bread, beans, dried fruit, nuts, seeds, rice
X	X	X	X	X	X	Potassium	Maintains, with sodium, the water balance of the body by controlling the composition of blood and other body fluids	All meats, fish, seafood, eggs, dairy products, fruit and vegetables, soy, cereals, bread, nuts, seeds, beans, rice
X	X			X	X	Sodium*	Maintains, with potassium, the water balance of the body by controlling the composition of blood and other body fluids	Salt, red meat, organ meats, poultry, fish, seafood, eggs, dairy products, fermented soy products, salted nuts and seeds, processed foods
	X	X	X	X	X	Magnesium	Maintains the function of nerves and muscles in artery walls and reduces the risk of diabetes	Red meat, organ meats, poultry, fish, seafood, eggs, dairy products, soy, green leafy vegetables, cereals, bread, beans, dried fruit, nuts, seeds
	X	X		X	X	Iron	Forms hemoglobin in red blood cells to transport oxygen in the blood around the body	Red meat, organ meats, poultry, fish, seafood, eggs, soy, green leafy vegetables, cereals, bread, beans, dried fruit, potatoes in their skins
	X				X	Zinc	Enables growth and development	Red meat, organ meats, poultry, fish, seafood (particularly oysters), cereals, bread, peas, beans, dried fruit
	X	X	X	X		Selenium	A potent antioxidant that strengthens the immune system to help protect the body from bacteria, viruses, and cancer	Red meat, organ meats, poultry, fish, seafood, eggs, cereals, bread, beans, cabbage, broccoli, green peppers

*Very few of us lack sodium in our diets because of the amount of salt added to processed foods. High sodium intake is more of a problem and is linked to disorders such as high blood pressure. It Is not recommended that you consume lots of salted products. Only those who eat a very pure unprocessed diet and avoid a number of food groups are likely to need extra sodium in their diet.

Part II

HOW TO SUBSTITUTE INGREDIENTS

Chapter 4 | SUBSTITUTING FOR EGGS

The properties of eggs provide versatility in cooking unmatched by any other ingredient. Whole eggs are rich in fat, protein, and color, constituents that enhance a wide range of foods, from sauces, pastry, and fresh pasta, to cakes, tarts, and puddings.

Because egg seems ubiquitous in many dishes, it may, at first glance, appear very limiting to try and cut it from your diet. However, although there are some foods, such as meringues and whisked sponge cakes, that cannot be made without egg, there are many more where egg can be replaced with other ingredients or even left out entirely. For example, egg is often used to glaze the tops of pies and breads, but the pie or dough can just as easily be brushed with milk to add shine and color.

Due to its versatility, there is no single "egg substitute." This means that in order to adapt a recipe successfully, you first need to understand why egg is being used. This chapter will help you understand what purpose the egg component of any recipe is fulfilling and how to substitute for those properties.

Egg is used in cooking to:
• Make cakes
• Bind or hold ingredients together
• Lighten, add volume, and enable mixtures to rise
• Thicken custard sauces and custard-based ice creams
• Set custard puddings and custard fillings in tarts
• Emulsify and thicken sauces
• Soften the texture of sorbets
• Glaze or add shine to baked foods

By looking at the type of food you are preparing and how egg is handled in the recipe, you should be able to recognize which of these eight roles the egg is fulfilling:

Form of egg used	Preparation/Recipe type	Role of egg
Beaten whole egg or white and yolk whisked separately	Cake	**Binding and lightening** see Making Egg-Free Cakes, page 37
Beaten whole egg	Stuffing mixture or other foods made from ground meat or fish—such as beef burgers or fish cakes; anything with a bread crumb or batter coating; batter cakes such as brownies, pastry, cookies, pancakes	**Binding** see page 37
Whisked egg whites only	Meringue or a mousse	**Lightening** see page 38
Egg yolk only	Mixed with milk or cream, and stirred over low heat Custard-based sauce or ice cream	**Thickening** see page 38
Egg yolk only	Mixed with milk or cream and baked gently Custard tart or a quiche	**Setting** see page 38
Egg yolk only, raw, beaten	Mixed with oil and vinegar Mayonnaise or a mayonnaise-based sauce	**Emulsifying** see page 39
Egg white only, used raw, not whisked	Sorbet	**Softening** see page 39
Whole egg, egg yolk or egg white, beaten	Brushed onto the surface of food before baking	**Glazing** see page 39

Egg substitute	Quantities needed to replace 1 egg in recipe	Comment
Custard	¼ cup/50 ml thick cold custard (made with 1 Tbsp. custard powder and 1¼ cups/290 ml milk or dairy-free milk + ½ tsp. baking powder added to the flour.) Add the custard to flour, fat, and sugar and beat together. Mix self-rising flour with the extra baking powder to ensure the cake rises	Gives the cake a moist consistency and delicate, sweet flavor **Useful for:** Sponge cakes, fruit cakes, and muffins
Applesauce	¼ cup/50 ml applesauce (see page 166) + ½ tsp. baking powder added to the flour. Sift the baking powder with the flour; add the applesauce to the flour, fat, and sugar and beat together	Gives cakes a delicate fruity flavor **Useful for:** Sponge cakes, fruit cakes, and muffins
Apricot puree	¼ cup/50 ml apricot puree (see page 166) + ½ tsp. baking powder added to the flour. Sift the baking powder with the flour; add the puree to the flour, fat, and sugar and beat together	Adds a pleasant yellow coloring and rich fruity flavor **Useful for:** Rich-flavored sponge cakes, fruit cakes, and muffins
Mashed banana	1 small mashed banana or ½ a large banana	Makes a moist binder for light cakes and muffins, but strongly affects the flavor **Useful for:** Banana cakes, muffins, and bread
Milk, self-rising flour and baking powder	¼ cup/50 ml milk, replace all-purpose flour with self-rising flour and add 1 tsp. baking powder for every 1 cup/110 g flour in the recipe	Best used in strongly flavored, moist cakes where the flavor of leavening agents is masked **Useful for:** Fruit loaves and batter cakes
Arrowroot powder	1 Tbsp. arrowroot, ½ tsp. baking powder + 1 Tbsp. water per 1⅛ cups/140 g flour. Sift the arrowroot powder and baking powder into the flour. Add the water to the butter, flour, and sugar before beating	Arrowroot is flavorless, but can leave a "dry" taste in the mouth **Useful for:** Sponge cakes, fruit cakes, and muffins

MAKING EGG-FREE CAKES	While sponge cakes cannot be made egg-free because they consist mainly of whisked egg foam (plus sugar and a little flour), richer, heavier cake mixtures can be successfully adapted. Quickbreads, fruit cakes, and batter cakes contain a higher proportion of butter, sugar, and flour, and egg is usually beaten in to lighten, moisten, and hold the cake ingredients together. This is a role that can be filled by egg-free binding ingredients, such as milk, cornstarch-thickened custard, and fruit purees, along with wheat flour mixed with chemical leavening agents (see opposite). In the home baking chapter you will find examples of how to use egg substitutes to make delicious cakes.
BINDING FOODS	Beaten egg is added to a wide variety of mixtures to hold ingredients together, for example stuffing, burgers, sausages, and fish cakes. It also helps stick bread crumb coatings to fish or meat for frying. By binding ingredients together, beaten egg also enriches the flavor and improves the texture of coating batters, pancakes, cookies, and pastry by making them less crumbly and dry. But there are alternatives…

EGG-FREE BINDING AGENTS

To make ...	Use substitute binder...	Recipe example
Pancake batters	Tapioca flour and arrowroot powder blended with all-purpose wheat flour	Egg-free Pancakes (page 197)
Coating batters	Cornstarch/self-rising flour + sparkling water or lager	Battered Cod (page 102)
Bread crumb coatings	Coat moist foods, such as fresh fish and meat, in fine, fresh bread crumbs only	Crispy Fish Ribbons (page 104)
Stuffing	Replace each egg with 1 Tbsp. fine white bread crumbs	Stuffings
Beef burgers and sausages	Provided meat is very fresh and cold, it will bind together well without egg	Burgers with Tomato and Corn Salsa (page 92)
Fish cakes	Mashed potato: before frying, roll fish cakes in seasoned flour or bread crumbs to prevent them from breaking up while they cook	Salmon Fish Cakes (page 89)
Rich shortcrust pastry	Extra 1 Tbsp./15g butter rubbed into flour + 1 Tbsp. cold water per egg to be replaced	Rich Shortcrust Pastry (page 152)
Cookies	Replace each egg with ¼ cup/50 ml milk and use self-rising flour in place of all-purpose flour	Chocolate Chip Cookies (page 180)

REPLACING THE LIGHTENING PROPERTIES OF EGGS

There are a number of egg-free ingredients that can be used to add volume and lightness to dense mixtures. Whipped cream is often used to add volume and lightness to rich mousses and other light-textured creamy puddings (see Rich Chocolate Mousse, page 190).

When whisked egg foam is folded into mixtures, it helps them to rise when baked, because the air bubbles in the foam expand in the heat. Once the egg foam reaches a given temperature, it sets to support the risen mixture so that it remains light and bubbly once cooked. Yeast or chemical leavening agents, present in baking powder and self-rising flour, are frequently used with or in the place of egg, to lighten and add volume to baked foods by filling the mixture with bubbles. If eggs are not included in the recipe, then other binding ingredients must be used in the mixture to trap the bubbles that lighten and enable the mixture to rise in the oven (see Yeast and Leavening Agents, page 183).

THICKENING CUSTARD SAUCES

A rich, smooth cream sauce, very similar to egg-rich crème Anglaise, can be made with heavy cream, milk, sugar, vanilla, and a small quantity of custard powder. The custard powder contains cornstarch, which helps to stabilize and thicken the cream and milk as the mixture is heated, and its yellow hue adds subtle color to the sauce to enhance its appearance (see Vanilla Cream Sauce, page 208).

SETTING TARTS AND PUDDINGS

Savory custard tarts normally contain other ingredients in the filling to add flavor and texture, and the creamy custard holds them in place. Egg is central to savory baked custards because it is the only setting agent that sets liquids in a hot oven, necessary to develop the flavor and brown the surface of the filling to an appetizing golden color. (Gelatin and agar-agar are used to set chilled liquids.)

Egg-free tarts with a creamy filling similar to savory custard tarts can be made using an equivalent quantity of Rich White Sauce (page 74) to bind the ingredients. Provided the sauce is seasoned well, it can be used as it is or flavored with herbs or grated cheese. Unlike egg custard, it does not set firm while the tart bakes but browns well and sets as the tart cools. So the tart filling is firm enough to slice, allow the tart to cool down and set, then gently warm it in a low oven just before serving.

Sweet custard tarts are baked very gently to lightly set the custard. If custard is baked for too long, it loses its sweet creamy consistency and takes on unwanted color and a stronger baked flavor. Because the eggs are used only to set the custard, they can be replaced with gelatin. To make lightly set creamy puddings without egg, substitute 1 heaped teaspoon of gelatin for every three eggs in the recipe. Eggs are liquid ingredients and the volume of egg in a recipe must be replaced with an equivalent volume of water, milk, or cream to ensure the gelatin does not set the mixture too firmly.

One beaten egg measures approximately ¼ cup/50 ml. Measure out the equivalent volume of water required to replace the volume of eggs used in the recipe and use it to soak the

Using egg replacers

Egg replacers, developed to replace the binding, rising, and setting properties of egg, are made from a blend of potato starch, tapioca flour, leavening agents, and natural gums. Although egg replacers can be whisked to a foam, they are unsuitable for lightening mousses or making meringues. Read the label carefully when buying egg replacers because some are made for people on cholesterol-free diets and contain egg derivatives.

gelatin before melting it and adding it to the cream mixture. Alternatively, if liquid ingredients, such as lemon juice or coffee are used to flavor the dessert, use it to soak the gelatin and add extra cream to replace the volume of egg (see Lemon Tart, page 162).

EMULSIFYING SAUCES

Although manufactured egg-free mayonnaise is available in good health-food stores, there are no other ingredients available that can replace egg successfully for making mayonnaise at home. Instead there are many ingredients and recipes that can be used instead. Mustard Cream Dressing, for example (page 85) provides an egg-free creamy dressing for salads. To accompany cold fish and meat, make Horseradish Cream (page 85) and make creamy dips with sour cream or plain yogurt (see Mayonnaise-Based Dips and Sauces, page 84). Sandwiches can be spiced up and made more interesting with chutneys and mustard.

SOFTENING SORBETS

Sorbets do not need egg white in them to make them smooth and soft textured. Churn the half-frozen sorbet mixture to the consistency of softly whipped cream and return to the freezer. Once it is frozen, remove it from the freezer 15 minutes before serving, and its texture will be soft and smooth (see Raspberry Sorbet, page 202).

GLAZING BAKED FOODS

Although the shine will not be as great, replace egg with milk or soy milk, mixed with a pinch of salt or sugar. Alternatively, enhance the appearance of bread and scones by sprinkling the top with flour before baking. Sweet pastries and cookies look lovely sprinkled with granulated or Demerara sugar.

WHAT TO LOOK FOR ON FOOD LABELS

Whole egg, egg white, egg yolk, and isolated proteins—obtained from egg white and egg yolk—are used to enrich, add color, bind, emulsify, coagulate, flavor, and thicken processed foods. Food manufacturers in the United States and the European Union are now required to display "contains egg" when egg or ingredients containing egg are used in a product. In addition to obvious sources of egg, these less familiar terms indicate some form of egg:

• Albumin lysozyme conalbumin
• Livetin simplesse (a fat substitute made with egg white and whey)
• Ovalbumin
• Ovoglobulin
• Ovomucin
• Ovomucoid
• Ovovitellin
• Ovotransferrin
• Lecithin vitellin

Chapter 5 | SUBSTITUTING FOR WHEAT AND OTHER GLUTEN-RICH GRAINS

This chapter deals with two different but inseparably linked issues: allergies to wheat or other similar grains and allergy to gluten. Since it is impossible to remove the gluten entirely from wheat, the task is the same: remove the wheat and other gluten-containing grains from the diet. In order to remove it, you must first know where to find it.

The most commonly used gluten-rich grains in the Western diet are wheat, barley, and rye. These three grains must be avoided by those with a gluten allergy. Oats are also off limits because they contain a protein that is similar to gluten and, because they are usually processed and stored in the same mills as wheat, they are therefore often contaminated with gluten. In order to eliminate these grains from the diet, it is important to recognize the many forms they take in foodstuffs.

Barley is used to make breakfast cereals and is added to hearty soups and casseroles. Fermented, it is used to make beer, whiskey, and malt, a flavoring found in a whole host of products. Rye and oats are less widely used. Rye is used in cereals and to make bread and crackers. Oats are mainly used to add texture to baked goods—such as cookies and flapjacks—and to make oatcakes and oatmeal.

Wheat, however, is by far the most widely used grain. It features in an astonishing array of foodstuffs because it has many useful properties and has a versatility unmatched by any other grain.

It is used in a number of forms. Whole wheat grain is rolled to form wheat flakes used in cereals or cracked to make bulgur and couscous—starchy staples in the Middle East and North Africa. It is also ground to make nutty flavored whole-wheat flour. To produce white flour, the starchy center of wheat grain is ground once the fibrous outer layers have been removed. Both whole-wheat and white flour form the basis for bread and other baked foods, pasta, and noodles. White flour is also used widely in both manufactured and homemade food to thicken sauces, soups, casseroles, and batters.

Wheat and other gluten-rich grains feature very widely in the food we eat, however they can be replaced with gluten-free substitutes in most cases or omitted from recipes altogether. In order to replace gluten-rich ingredients with gluten-free substitutes, it is essential to understand how and why they are used so you can make the right substitution. Choosing the right gluten-free substitutions becomes progressively more important as the proportion of gluten-rich ingredients used in a recipe increases. For example, almost any gluten-free flour can replace wheat for flouring food before frying, but gluten-free flours must be carefully selected and blended in the right proportions to produce a light, open-textured bread.

GENERAL RULES FOR COOKING WITH GLUTEN-FREE FLOURS

• Ready-mixed gluten-free flour is not necessarily the best substitute for wheat flour. Wheat flour has many properties and the importance of each property varies when flour is used for thickening sauces, coating food, and making batters, cakes, pastry, and cookies. By blending specific flours for a specific purpose, foods made with gluten-free flour can closely rival—and sometimes even better—foods made with wheat flour.
• Use binding ingredients to make up for the lack of gluten in the flour. Without binding ingredients, gluten-free mixtures are likely to taste dry and fall apart.
• Most gluten-free flours do not absorb liquid as readily as wheat flour and often produce baked foods that taste dry and crumble easily, so you must add extra egg or liquid to the recipe.
• Baked foods made with gluten-free flour dry out more quickly than those made with wheat, so eat them on the day they are made (alternatively, freeze sliced bread, scones, cookies, and cakes and defrost as required).

THE ROLES OF GLUTENOUS GRAINS IN COOKING

This chapter will allow you to work out what role the wheat component of any recipe is fulfilling and how to substitute for each of these properties. It provides alternative ingredients and methods and outlines their limitations.

Wheat and other grains are used in food and cooking:
• as a carbohydrate to add bulk—for example as pasta, couscous, bulgur, etc.
• to thicken sauces, casseroles, and soups
• as bread or bread crumbs, rather than flour, often to add bulk
• as a coating for food before frying
• to thicken and bind pancakes and batters
• to provide body and to bind pastry and cookie dough
• to bind and give structure and body to cakes
• as the principal ingredient in bread.

By looking at the type of food you are cooking, in what form the ingredient appears and how that ingredient is used in the recipe, you should be able to recognize which of these roles it is fulfilling:

Form of ingredient	Preparation/Recipe type	Role of grain/gluten
Whole grains, flakes, or pasta	Main constituent of recipe	See Substitutes for Whole Grains opposite
All-purpose flour	Soup, sauce, or casserole	Thickening see below
Bread crumbs or bread	Sausage or stuffing mixes; using bread directly (e.g. in croutons)	See Bread as an Ingredient (page 43)
All-purpose flour and/or bread crumbs	Dusted onto the outside of food before frying	Coating see Coating Food for Frying (pages 43–44).
All-purpose or self-rising flour	Mixing a batter for pancakes or coating food for frying	Battering see Coatings box (page 44) and Pancakes (page 44)
All-purpose or self-rising flour	Making cookies or pastry	Binding see Binding Agents (page 46)
All-purpose or self-rising flour	Cakes, muffins, or scones	See Cakes (page 47)
Bread flour	Bread	See Bread (page 48) or Gluten-free Bread recipes, (pages 184–87)

COOKING WITHOUT GLUTEN

Once you understand why wheat and other grains containing gluten are used in a recipe, the next step is to see if there is a gluten-free ingredient that will do the same job. Although there are no other grains with the same properties as wheat, one or a number of gluten-free grains, flaked grains, and gluten-free flours can be used instead to similar effect. See box opposite for substituting gluten-rich whole grains and pasta.

THICKENING SAUCES, SOUPS, AND CASSEROLES

All-purpose white wheat flour is used to thicken many savory dishes because it is rich in starch, which swells and absorbs boiling liquid, thickening the consistency of the dish. Its bland flavor also means that it can be used to thicken both delicate and robustly flavored sauces. The color is important, too, because it doesn't affect the appearance of white or pale-colored sauces. In addition, the soft and fine texture of white wheat flour gives a smooth consistency to sauces. The starch contained in wheat flour remains stable and does not break down and thin the sauce when it is cooked or kept warm for a period of time. This is a great advantage for dishes that are bound with flour-thickened sauces and then baked in the oven.

Most gluten-free flours are also rich in starch and have the ability to thicken liquids. However, some are gritty in texture, producing grainy sauces or are dark and strongly flavored and overpower the flavor and color of sauces.

Recipe	Usual grain content	Recommended substitutes
Boiled whole grain wheat for salads or with Middle Eastern food	Cracked wheat (bulgur) or couscous	Brown rice, quinoa, and millet, boiled (see page 136)
Winter soups and casseroles	Pearl barley	Brown rice, reconstituted dried haricot or borlotti beans
Oat bars	Wheat flakes or rolled oats	Buckwheat flakes or gluten-free puffed rice (see Chewy Rice Krispies Squares, page 178)
Muesli	Rolled oats, wheat flakes, and wheat bran	Buckwheat flakes, millet flakes, and brown rice flakes; rice bran (see Gluten-free Muesli, page 141)
Oatmeal	Rolled oats	Millet flakes, rice flakes, buckwheat flakes, or risotto rice (see page 141)
Pasta	Durum wheat	Gluten-free pasta (e.g. millet and rice pasta or corn pasta)

Replace all-purpose flour with an equal quantity of rice flour or half quantity of cornstarch. Cornstarch produces the smoothest gluten-free sauces. However, the starch in cornstarch is not as stable as the starch in wheat flour and tends to break down. Sauces thickened with cornstarch must be eaten soon after they are made (see box on page 74).

BREAD AS AN INGREDIENT

White wheat bread and good gluten-free white bread are largely interchangeable in recipes that use bread crumbs, croutons, and croûtes.

Bread crumbs are often added to homemade sausage and fine stuffing mixtures to bind and add bulk. Bread crumbs also absorb the juices of sausage and stuffing ingredients, which helps to keep the cooked mixture moist and full of flavor. Replace wheat-based bread crumbs with an equal quantity of gluten-free bread crumbs, which are just as suitable for the purpose.

For croutons, small cubes of bread fried in oil, and croûtes, thin slices of bread fried or baked with oil, substitute white wheat bread with gluten-free white bread (see Garlic Croutons, page 70).

COATING FOOD FOR FRYING

Food is coated with flour, bread crumbs, or batter to protect it and to add crispiness and color to the finished dish. The chart overleaf explains how best to use gluten-free alternatives to wheat-flour coatings, crumbs, and batters.

Coating	Uses	Recommended substitutes
All-purpose flour on its own	Slices of meat, small fish or fillets, food made with ground meat, e.g. burgers	Cornstarch, buckwheat flour, or soy flour (Avoid using potato flour and rice flour because they become mushy.)
Bread-crumb coating on fried food	White meats such as pork, veal, chicken, and white fish; sliced vegetables	For pan-fried crumbed food: bland gluten-free flours, such as cornstarch or rice flour, seasoned with salt and pepper (to flour fish or meat before coating in egg and gluten-free bread crumbs). For deep-fried crumbed food: gluten-free bread crumbs
Batter for deep-fried food (made with self-rising flour)	Small pieces of fish, chicken, and vegetables	To make gluten-free coating batter: 50 percent potato flour and 50 percent cornstarch plus 1 tsp. baking powder for every 1 cup/110 g of flour used (see Battered Cod, page 102)

PANCAKES Batters traditionally made with flour, egg, and milk are used to make pancakes as well as to coat food before deep-frying. As the ingredients of pancake batter are stirred together, the small amount of gluten in the flour develops, which helps, with egg, to bind the ingredients together so that the pancakes do not fall apart when cooked. Gluten-free pancakes rely on egg and fine flours with binding properties, including potato flour, tapioca flour, arrowroot powder, and buckwheat.

Use	Comment	Recommended substitutes
French pancakes/ crêpes	Require all-purpose flour that swells and binds in liquid to form the smooth tender texture of pancakes	50 percent fine rice flour, 25 percent arrowroot powder, and 25 percent tapioca flour mixed with egg and milk (see French Crêpes, page 195)
Buckwheat pancakes	Made with an equal quantity of wheat flour and buckwheat flour (which is gluten free)	Simply substitute rice flour for the wheat flour (see Buckwheat Pancakes with Caramelized Cinnamon Apples, page 196)

All-purpose wheat flour is used to make crisp cookies and pastry. When mixed with butter or margarine and a small quantity of liquid, such as water or beaten egg, it helps bind dough so that it holds together but is sufficiently "short" to crumble in the mouth.

Gluten-free all-purpose flours

Gluten-free flours with binding properties include potato flour, tapioca flour, arrowroot powder, cornstarch, and buckwheat flour. Bland-tasting, fine rice flour is used to provide bulk. Other useful flours include cornmeal, ground rice, and soy flour. Cornmeal and coarsely ground rice flour can make food gritty, and soy flour and buckwheat flour darken the color of food and add their own characteristic flavors to it.

THE MOST USEFUL GLUTEN-FREE FLOURS

Coating	Uses
Potato flour and tapioca flour	These flours readily absorb liquid, lightly bind mixtures, and retain moisture in cooked foods. They are especially helpful where binding and moistening properties are required in gluten-free batters and bread dough. Food made with them tends to be heavy unless they are mixed with cornstarch or arrowroot powder, which lighten the consistency of mixtures, and rice flour, which forms the bulk of mixtures.
Arrowroot powder	This has binding properties when mixed with liquid; it lightens the consistency of baked goods and is used to thicken clear sauces. It is best suited for use in batters because it tends to leave a dry, powdery taste in the mouth.
Rice flour and cornstarch	These are used to make light-textured baked goods such as cakes, cookies, and pastry, where binding properties of flour are less important. Because baked goods made with cornstarch and rice flour tend to be dry and powdery, they are blended with ground almonds or potato flour to provide added moisture.
Ground almonds	Rich in oil, ground almonds enrich and moisten, hence often make up 25 percent of the flour content of gluten-free cookies, cakes, sweet and savory pastry dough, and bread. Only use more than 25 percent ground almonds in foods that are meant to taste of almonds. Ground almonds used in larger quantities will strongly flavor and coarsen the texture of baked foods.
Soy flour	Due to its strong beany flavor and tan color, use in moderation. When mixed with bland white flours, soy flour retains moisture to produce soft crumbly cookies, and pastry that is tender and rich.
Buckwheat flour	Buckwheat flour also has binding properties but is dark and strongly flavored. It is therefore best combined with bland white flour and used for specific purposes, most notably in buckwheat pancakes.
Cornmeal and ground rice	Cornmeal has a pleasant delicate flavor. Both cornmeal and ground rice add a crisp, gritty texture to cookies and pastry.

Gluten-free pastry

When replacing gluten-rich flours in pastry:

- Use 50 percent rice flour, 25 percent cornstarch, and 25 percent ground almonds for simple, neutral-flavored shortcrust pastry (see Rice and Almond Pastry, page 155).
- Use 50 percent rice flour and 50 percent cornmeal for a coarser textured, neutral-flavored, nut-free shortcrust pastry (see Rice and Cornmeal Shortcrust Pastry, page 156).

Whole-wheat flour is used to make a coarser-textured, nutty flavored pastry for hearty savory and sweet pies and tarts. Used on its own it tends to produce heavy pastry so it is usually mixed with equal quantities of all-purpose white flour to lighten the end result. For gluten-free whole-wheat pastry, use 50 percent brown rice flour, 25 percent cornstarch (for lightness), and 25 percent finely ground whole almonds (with skin on—to add moisture and richness). For every 2 cups/225 g of this flour mixture, add 1 Tbsp. of rice bran to add extra fiber and color. (See Whole-Grain Rice and Almond Pastry, page 155.)

Pastry dough is bound with the fat in the mixture and a small quantity of cold water or a mixture of beaten egg and water. Mashed potato can also be used to bind pastry because it gives pastry a savory flavor and flaky texture. The quantity of binding liquid required to bind pastry dough depends on the flour. Wheat flour absorbs liquid more readily than gluten-free flours, so if you're adapting a wheat flour recipe to make it gluten free, it may require more liquid than the recipe states before the dough will hold together.

BINDING AGENTS FOR GLUTEN-FREE PASTRY

Binding agent	Usage/Quantities	Comment
Cold water	Pastry dough made with 2 cups/225 g flour requires 2–3 Tbsp. cold water	Used to make simply flavored, pale colored pastry with a crisp but crumbly texture
Beaten whole egg	Pastry dough made with 2 cups/225 g flour requires 1 egg, beaten with 1 Tbsp. cold water	Less likely to crumble when bound with whole egg mixed with water (Egg white in the whole egg binds the pastry more firmly; the yolk softens the texture of the crumb, enriches the flavor and deepens the color of the pastry)
Beaten egg yolk	Pastry dough made with 2 cups/225 g flour requires 2 yolks, beaten with 2 Tbsp. cold water	Beaten egg yolk enriches and colors gluten-free pastry but mainly relies on the water to bind the pastry
Mashed potato	½ cup/225 g mashed potato binds 1⅓ cups/170 g flour	Mashed potato produces rich-tasting, flaky pastry ideal for savory pies and tarts

CAKES Cakes are characteristically tender and spongy in texture. In order to achieve that spongy texture, they require just enough gluten, along with binding ingredients, such as eggs, to trap small bubbles of air incorporated into the mixture by whisking or by the use of chemical leavening agents. For this reason, cakes require the strong binding properties of either gluten or egg: cakes can be gluten free *or* egg free, but *not both*.

In order to adapt a cake recipe to make it gluten free you need to take the following steps:
- substitute a suitable gluten-free flour or combination of flours
- add extra egg to bind the mixture and to ensure the cake is not too dry and crumbly.

GLUTEN-FREE FLOURS FOR CAKES

Flour type	Gluten-free alternative	Comment
All-purpose	For light sponge cakes: 50 percent rice flour (for bulk), 25 percent cornstarch (for lightness), and 25 percent ground almonds (for richness and moisture); for heavier cakes, such as scones: 50 percent rice flour, 25 percent potato flour (for a soft, moist texture), and 25 percent ground almonds; for moist batter cakes, such as chocolate brownies: simply substitute potato flour for the all-purpose flour	These flours are bland, white, and fine in texture
Self-rising	Use the same flour mixtures as listed above and add 1 tsp. gluten-free baking powder for every 1 cup/110 g flour	Mix thoroughly by sifting the flours and baking powder together 2 or 3 times
Whole-wheat	Use 50 percent brown rice flour, 25 percent cornstarch, and 25 percent finely ground whole almonds	Use for gluten-free whole-wheat scones and for wholesome gluten-free cakes, such as carrot cake

Gluten-free cakes often require a mixing method different from standard cake making: see the gluten-free cake recipes in chapter 16 before you attempt to adapt your own recipes.

Gluten-free binding agents for cakes

Without the binding qualities of gluten, gluten-free cakes rely solely on the binding properties of egg to trap the bubbles of air and produce a light spongy texture. Eggs are therefore invaluable in gluten-free cake making. Egg in the mixture forms the bubbly structure of the cake by trapping and stretching around air bubbles and steam, enabling the dough to rise before it sets in the heat of the oven. Egg also moistens, colors, and enriches the flavor of cake. Cake recipes containing dried fruit, fruit purees, and mashed banana are ideal for adapting with gluten-free flours because all these ingredients add moisture to the cake mixture.

BREAD   Bread is characteristically chewy in texture with an open, bubbly structure. In gluten-rich breads, this structure is provided by bread flour, the rising agent yeast, sugar, salt, oil, and water. When bread flour is mixed with water, elastic strands of gluten develop, which bind the mixture, enabling the dough to trap and stretch around large bubbles produced by yeast, causing it to rise and develop its characteristic structure.

In order to produce a gluten-free bread with a similar texture, a gluten-free substitute with strong binding and elastic properties is required. Unfortunately, the properties of bread flour and gluten-free flours are so vastly different it is not possible to simply substitute a gluten-free flour for bread flour. Gluten-free bread is made by an entirely different method to take into account the lack of gluten in the mixture. When making gluten-free bread:

- gluten-free flours are carefully selected and blended
- a small quantity of xanthum gum is used as a gluten substitute to bind the mixture
- to distribute the yeast, gluten-free bread dough is mixed rather than kneaded
- gluten-free bread is not left to rise before it is baked. Gluten-free dough, even with added xanthum gum, is less able to trap the bubbles produced by yeast. If left to "rise" the bubbles produced by yeast would be lost and the bread will "collapse."

Since the method and ingredients are so different for making gluten-free bread, a straight substitution of wheat flour with gluten-free flours is not possible. Refer to the recipes given in the bread section of chapter 16.

WHAT TO LOOK FOR ON FOOD LABELS

Packaged foods in the United States have to show clearly on the label if they contain wheat, or if one of the ingredients contains wheat. However, it is good to familiarize yourself with the many different guises that both wheat and gluten can go under. Obviously you need to avoid all products that mention wheat or wheat flour—whether it's described as bleached, unbleached, white, whole wheat, all-purpose, enriched, farina, graham, durum, high-gluten, or high-protein flour, it contains gluten. So, too, do products containing semolina, rye, barley, triticale, kamut, and spelt.

Meat products, including sausages, often contain "rusk" (white bread crumbs used as a bulking agent). Foods containing soy sauce and the Japanese flavoring miso must also be avoided as they are both made by fermenting soy beans with wheat.

The use of starch and proteins derived from wheat, and other grains containing gluten, is also widespread in processed foods.

Here are the most common forms of starch and protein that may be derived from wheat:

Starches
- Edible starch
- Farina vegetable starch
- Food starch
- Gelatinized starch/hydrolyzed starch

- Modified food starch, modified starch
- Wheat starch
- Malt sugar or maltose
- Dextrin
- Maltodextrin

Proteins
- Vegetable protein (often derived from wheat protein)
- Wheat protein (derived from gluten)
- High-gluten flour, high-protein flour
- Flour protein
- Hydrolyzed plant protein (often derived from wheat)
- Hydrolyzed vegetable proteins (often derived from wheat)
- Hydrolyzed wheat protein
- Monosodium glutamate
- Natural flavoring (can be obtained from wheat protein)
- Cereal protein (obtained from cereal grains, including wheat, barley, and rye)
- Cereal extract (concentrated protein, extracted from malted cereals)
- Vegetable gum (often derived from wheat)

Wheat-free and gluten-free products

Wheat-free products are not the same as gluten-free products because they may contain other gluten-rich grains, such as rye and barley, or oats, and are not suitable for gluten-free diets.

Conversely gluten-free products may not suit those on a wheat-free diet because they may contain other wheat proteins, including albumins, globulins, and starch granule proteins.

Other ingredients that may contain wheat flour

Be aware that some powdered ingredients can contain wheat flour, because it is a good bulking agent. These include baking powder, mustard powder, instant coffee, confectioners' sugar, and cocoa. Also be careful with ground spice mixtures, such as garam masala and pumpkin pie spice. It is best to buy a well-known spice brand in a sealed container, rather than buy from a bulk supplier.

Chapter 6 | SUBSTITUTING FOR DAIRY PRODUCTS

Avoiding dairy products in the diet can be a daunting task because milk and the products derived from it—cheese, butter, cream, and yogurt—are integral to both home-cooked and packaged foods. Despite this, many recipes can be adapted successfully using one of the many good alternatives to dairy produce now available. These include products based on rice, almonds, and oats. However, the majority of dairy-free products are based on soy, because it is an outstanding source of protein, oil, minerals, and vitamins, and produces dairy-free milk, yogurt, cream, and margarine with a mild flavor, creamy consistency, and cooking properties similar to that of dairy products.

DAIRY-FREE MILKS There are a number of very good dairy-free milks on the market. The best are fortified with vitamins and minerals found in cows' milk, including vitamin D and calcium, and are subtly sweetened to match the natural sweetness of dairy milk. Unsweetened dairy-

Substitute	Nutritional content	Not suitable for
Soy milk	High-protein content, vitamins B and D and calcium	Adding to tea or coffee—it tends to curdle; unsuitable for soy-free diets
Rice milk	Low in fat and protein; available fortified with vitamin D and calcium	Foods needing a rich creamy flavor
Oat milk	High in fiber, protein, fat, vitamins, and minerals	Delicately flavored sauces and custards; unsuitable for gluten-free diets
Almond milk	High in fat, protein, omega fatty acids, vitamins, and minerals, including calcium and vitamin D	Savory dishes; unsuitable for nut-free diets

free milk tends to make food taste flat and uninteresting. The most common dairy-free alternatives to milk are generally available chilled or as UHT long-life milk.

Soy milk: Soy milk is most commonly recommended by doctors as the best alternative to dairy milk because it is an excellent source of high-quality proteins, vitamins, and minerals. Mild and rich in flavor, it has the consistency of whole milk and is very versatile in cooking. It is suitable for drinking, pouring on cereal, making fruit smoothies and milk shakes, and in recipes for soups, savory and sweet milky sauces, desserts, and baked goods.

Rice milk: Light and aromatic, rice milk has the subtle, slightly sweet flavor of rice and the consistency of skimmed milk. Chilled rice milk tastes very pleasant and refreshing drunk on its own, poured on cereal, pureed with frozen soft fruit in smoothies, and in desserts, sweet milky sauces, and in home baking. Due to its low fat and protein content, food made with rice milk is not as rich in flavor or consistency as food made with dairy or soy milk.

Oat milk: Oat milk is rich tasting with a consistency similar to 2 percent milk. It is mild and oaty in flavor and pleasant to drink chilled from the glass, poured on cereal, in smoothies and milkshakes, and used in baking.

Almond milk: Almond milk has a light, sweet flavor, the consistency of skimmed milk, and is high in nutritional value. Chilled almond milk tastes very pleasant and is refreshing drunk on its own, poured on cereal, and used to make smoothies, desserts, and sweet milky sauces.

Other dairy-free alternatives to milk

Fruit juice can be used to add moisture and fruity sweetness to sweet baked foods. Water can also be used instead of small quantities of milk in baked goods, such as cakes and breads. If a larger proportion of milk is required in a recipe, water is not a suitable substitute because it will dilute the flavor and affect the overall texture and appearance of the dish.

Soy cream: Soy cream is the best alternative to dairy cream. It is made of emulsified and stabilized sunflower oil, soy protein, and a small amount of wheat syrup and is available as a pouring cream or in a whipped consistency. Soy pouring cream resembles light cream in fat content, appearance, and consistency and cannot be whipped. Due to its mildly beany flavor, soy cream is not suitable for pouring over desserts but is great for giving a creamy consistency to soups, sauces, custards, and homemade ice cream, where its beany flavor will be masked.

Whipped-style soy cream has a less pronounced beany flavor and is slightly sweet. Although its consistency, appearance, and flavor do not resemble whipped cream, it is appreciated by those who cannot have standard whipped cream on desserts and in cakes and pastries.

Soy sour cream: Cultured dairy cream such as sour cream and crème fraîche are made by adding cultures of bacteria to cream. The bacteria convert lactose sugar (milk sugar), present in cream, into lactic acid, which thickens cream and gives it its characteristic sour, fresh flavor. Soy sour cream is very similar to dairy sour cream in appearance, consistency, and flavor and makes a very good dairy-free alternative. It can be used in place of crème fraîche, for example, to add a creamy, tangy flavor to sauces, or as a sour cream substitute, spread onto blinis, in dips, and in Mexican food.

Soy yogurt: Soy yogurt is the closest alternative to dairy yogurt in appearance, flavor, and consistency—it is also the most readily available. It is made in the same way as dairy yogurt, by thickening and souring the flavor of soy milk by adding bacterial cultures. Soy yogurt is fortified with calcium and vitamin D and is a good source of protein.

Plain soy yogurt has the same consistency and sourness as plain dairy yogurt and a rich, delicate beany flavor. It can be used very successfully to make Indian raita, Greek tzatziki, and sour cream–style dips and adds creaminess and body to Indian curries. Sweetened yogurts are available in a smooth style or with pieces of fruit and are great for adding creaminess to smoothies.

Soy cheeses: Soy cheese is made from an emulsion of soy milk, soy milk fat or vegetable oil, salt, colorings, and flavorings. The enriched and flavored milk is soured and curdled with bacteria to produce the semi-solid "soy curd" and liquid "soy whey." The curd is used to make two styles of cheese: cream cheese and hard cheese. (Check the labels of soy cheeses because they sometimes contain dairy-based casein and caseinates to give it a flavor and texture closer to dairy cheese.)

Soy cream cheese, available flavored with herbs or garlic from health food stores, is very similar in appearance, taste, and consistency to dairy cream cheese. It is not suitable for cooking purposes but is good for spreading on bread and crackers.

Hard soy cheese is made by pressing the curds to squeeze out the whey and comes in various styles, ranging from mozzarella and cheddar to blue cheese flavor. In my view, hard soy cheese is not a viable alternative to dairy cheese. It is very dense and putty-like in texture and bears very little resemblance to dairy cheese. It has an unrefined sharp acidic flavor and is very rich.

Margarine: Margarine is made from one or more vegetable oils such as soybean, corn, and sunflower. Many people assume that by definition margarine is dairy free, but many margarines, particularly the soft, spreadable ones in tubs, contain milk solids to soften them and give them a creamy flavor. Foods made with dairy-free margarine (or any type of margarine for that matter) do not taste as rich as those made with butter, but it provides the fat and pale yellow color essential for making light, moist, appetizing baked products.

Dairy-free soft margarines and spreads: Soft, spreadable margarine is made by partially hydrogenating oils to turn them from a liquid to the consistency of softened butter at room temperature. They are bland and mildly oily in flavor and are best used for spreading thinly on bread, as dairy-free fat for making cakes, scones, and soft icings, and as an alternative to the small quantity of butter used in flour-thickened sauces. Due to the soft consistency of dairy-free margarines and spreads, cookies and pastry dough made with it can be too soft and difficult to roll out. It is also unsuitable for frying foods, because it separates and scorches at high temperatures.

Oil as a dairy-free alternative

When to use olive oil in place of butter: Butter and olive oil are used in dishes where their flavor adds character to the finished dish. Although butter is traditionally used to flavor British and Northern French dishes and olive oil flavors dishes from the Mediterranean, North Africa, and the Middle East, they are largely interchangeable. The style of the dish may be altered by using olive oil in place of butter, but provided the ingredients are cooked and seasoned correctly, the end result will be just as delicious.

When used on its own to fry food, olive oil, like butter, will scorch at high temperatures. For frying, mix a light olive oil with an equal quantity of a neutral-flavored oil that is stable at high temperatures. Light olive oil can also be used in place of butter or neutral-flavored oils for basting meat, poultry, or fish as it roasts, bakes, or broils.

When to use neutral-flavored oil in place of butter: Due to its rich but neutral flavor, butter is normally used to make a roux, the flour and fat paste used to thicken delicately flavored sauces. Olive oil is unsuitable for this purpose because it is too strongly flavored. Instead use 2 Tbsp. of a neutral-flavored oil, such as sunflower or corn, in place of 3 Tbsp./40 g of butter.

In stews, soups, sauces, and other dishes where fat is skimmed off during cooking, use neutral-flavored oils to fry ingredients because it would be a waste to use olive oil.

When oil and margarine cannot replace butter: Delicately flavored savory and sweet sauces, and fruits caramelized in butter and sugar, rely on the rich, creamy flavor of butter and would not taste the same made with dairy-free alternatives. Oil as a substitute is wholly unsuitable and although dairy-free margarine and soy cream can be used in the place of butter, they give the food a disappointing oily flavor.

Uses of nuts	Substitute ingredient	Comment
Coating food before baking or frying	Dried bread crumbs, cornmeal, or rolled oats	Drizzle with oil before baking to make the coating crisp and to give a golden brown color
Garnishes for Asian food, esp. stir-fries and curries	Crunchy vegetables, (peppers, bean sprouts, chopped scallion, or diced cucumber)	Add a handful of prepared vegetables to the pan to heat through just before serving so they remain crisp
Adding texture to homemade muesli	Add an equal quantity of extra dried fruit, cereal flakes (e.g. rolled oats, rice flakes), or sunflower seeds	Add extra crunch by toasting cereal flakes in a dry pan. Add chopped fresh fruit just before eating
Adding crunch and texture to cake mixtures and cookie dough	Omit the nuts and use equal quantities of dried fruit. Although dried fruit does not add crunch, it adds chewiness, flavor, and moisture	Also try roughly chopped chocolate, especially for cookies
Decoration for cookies, cakes, and pastries	Omit and decorate with sugar, chopped or dried fruit. Avoid marzipan because it is made with ground nuts	Decorate baked rich fruit cakes with dried fruit and glaze with apricot jam
Adding texture and flavor to bread dough	Simply omit or replace with other ingredients (garlic cloves, softened onion, herbs, pitted olives, or dried fruit)	
Adding texture to stuffings, pies terrines, and pâtés	To add texture, replace with finely diced celery	Make the texture of stuffing coarser by adding cooked brown rice or bulgur
Ground nuts used in small quantities in cake mixtures, cookie and pastry dough to add flavor and richness	Replace ground nuts with extra flour	
Ground nuts used as the main ingredient in baked foods	Flour will not replace the rich flavor and moist texture of baked foods based on ground nuts	Choose an alternative recipe

Uses of nuts	Substitute ingredient	Comment
Garnishes in salads and other savory dishes to add texture and protein	Salted, plain, or garlic croutons for crunch; cooked chickpeas, beans or diced meat, poultry, or fish for protein. Soy nuts can also be used as an alternative	Other raw vegetables work well —diced celery, cucumber, peppers, onion, or bean sprouts
Peanut oil is used in Asian cooking for stir-frying and deep-frying due to its neutral flavor and stability at high temperatures	Other vegetable oils: soybean oil, blended vegetable oil (provided it does not contain peanut oil), canola oil, corn oil, grapeseed oil, safflower, or sunflower oil	These substitutes have a neutral flavor and are stable (do not burn) at high temperatures
Flavored nut oils used in salad dressings and to flavor hot dishes	Use sesame oil to flavor Asian food, extra virgin olive oil or light olive oil flavored with garlic, chile, or herbs	Butter and olive oil can be mixed with neutral-flavored frying oils to add flavor
Ground nuts used to thicken and add flavor to sauces in Asian cooking	No substitute	Choose an alternative recipe that does not rely on nuts for its consistency and flavor
Nuts ground and blended with oils to make nut butter	No substitute	Choose an alternative nut-free spread
As a snack food	Soy nuts	Although they are not "nuts" as such, they are the closest in texture and flavor and are a delicious alternative. Soy nuts are made with whole soybeans that have been soaked in water, then baked until crisp and golden brown; available plain or flavored with salt or paprika

Chapter 8 | SUBSTITUTING FOR SOY

Due to their outstanding nutritional content, mild flavor, and versatility, soybeans are the most widely grown and utilized bean in the world. Soy comes in many forms, including soy flour, soy protein, soy oil, and the emulsifier soy lecithin. It is used in around 60 percent of processed foods—including baked goods, ready meals, salad dressings, baby foods, and an increasing number of dairy-free products—to thicken, enrich, soften, add nutrition, emulsify, and stabilize. As a result of its widespread use, allergy to soy is increasing. Unfortunately food manufacturers have not kept up with this and the range of ready-made foods available for those allergic to soy is limited.

However, although the majority of manufactured foods contain soy, only a handful of soy-based ingredients are used in freshly prepared home cooking. These include soy sauce, vegetable oil (containing soybean oil), soy-based margarines, and chocolate (containing soy lecithin). While there is no exact substitute for soy sauce, recipes and cooking methods for dishes where soy is normally used can be altered to ensure they are richly flavored and colored. Soy-free cooking oil, margarine and chocolate are also available. Always read the label on packaged products before using them in your recipes to ensure they do not contain soy.

SOY SAUCE
Soy sauce is the collective name for thin, dark brown sauces, with a characteristic rich salt-sweet flavor, made from fermented soybeans. The three main varieties of soy sauce include all-purpose, rich and dark shoyu (or soy) sauce, thinner aromatic tamari, and sweet teriyaki sauce. They are used to season and add color to Asian soups, stews, stir-fries, marinades, dressings for grilled food, and are used in dipping sauces.

Soy-free alternative to soy sauce
Although there is no such thing as a soy-free soy sauce, a rich brown sauce with a sweet-salt flavor can be made to replace it in stir-fry dishes:
- Brown your fish, meat or seafood quickly and evenly in hot oil to add rich color and flavor to the dish.
- As the food is frying, mix together ½ teaspoon salt, 1 teaspoon dark brown sugar, and 1 tablespoon of rich chicken stock per 1 tablespoon of dark soy sauce in the recipe. Just before the ingredients are cooked, stir the mixture into the food. To make a substitute for 1 tablespoon light soy sauce, mix ½ teaspoon salt and ½ teaspoon dark brown sugar with 1 tablespoon of rich chicken stock; stir into the food just before it is cooked.

SUBSTITUTES FOR SOYBEAN OIL
Soybean oil, an amber colored oil extracted from soybeans, is mild in flavor, stable at high temperatures, and a versatile cooking oil for frying and using in salad dressings and mayonnaise. Vegetable oil, a generic term, is usually 100 percent soy oil or a blend of soy oil and other vegetable oils. Other general purpose cooking oils that

have similar properties to soybean oil include sunflower oil, grapeseed oil, canola oil, and safflower oil. Light olive oil can also be used for gentle frying.

SUBSTITUTES FOR SOY MARGARINE

Due to its mild taste, availability, and low cost, soybean oil is one of the most common oils used to make margarine. Margarine is also available made with mild-flavored vegetable oils including canola, sunflower, and corn oil or tropical oils such as palm oil—but check the label to ensure they have not been emulsified and stabilized with soy lecithin.

SOY IN CHOCOLATE

Soy lecithin, an emulsifier and stabilizer, is often added to conventional chocolate to reduce the quantity of expensive cocoa butter required to produce smooth, even-textured chocolate. More expensive, high-cocoa-content chocolate is usually made without soy lecithin and is widely available in good supermarkets and health food stores.

FOOD PRODUCTS MADE FROM SOY

Whole soybeans are liquidized to make soy milk; dried and ground to make soy flour; fermented to make soy sauce, miso, and Tamari sauce; and cultured with bacteria to make yogurt, cheese, tofu, and tempeh. Soy flour is used to make noodles; to improve the texture and add protein to baked products; to thicken milk drinks, sauces, dressings, and ice cream. It also adds bulk to meat products, cereals, baby food products, and diet foods. The list on page 60 outlines the most common soy products and ingredients that can be used to replace them.

WHAT TO LOOK FOR ON FOOD LABELS

When packaged food sold in the United States and the European Union is made with soy, or uses ingredients containing soy, the food label must clearly state "contains soy." However, refined soy oil, the main component of vegetable oil, is regarded by the medical profession as safe for people with soy allergies (though not everyone agrees) because the proteins that cause the soy allergy are removed during the refining process. For this reason, soybean oil is not labeled individually when used in blended vegetable oil. Remember that recipes sometimes change so always check the label for soy each time you buy a packaged food. In addition to the obvious ingredients that indicate the presence of soy—such as soy protein, soy lecithin, soybean oil, and so on—you may find the following terms on food labels:

- Hydrolyzed vegetable or plant protein (may be made from soy)
- Natural and artificial flavoring (can mean soy)
- Textured vegetable protein, or TVP (made from soy granules)
- Vegetable starch (a purified starch often obtained from soybeans)
- Vegetable gum (a soluble vegetable fiber, sometimes based on soy)

Canned and frozen vegetables

Surprising as it may seem soy can be found in some canned and frozen vegetables. Soy-based hydrolyzed vegetable protein is added to enhance the flavor of some canned and frozen vegetables, so check the label and use brands free of soy or use fresh vegetables instead.

Soy product	Soy-free substitute
Soy flour	Wheat flour and gluten-free flours
Soy nuts	Nuts
Soy milk	Dairy milk or rice, almond, or oat milk
Soy cheese	Dairy cheese
Natto (fermented soy cheese used in Japanese cooking)	No soy-free substitute
Okara (soybean pulp remaining after soy milk is squeezed from the beans). Used in Japanese cooking	No soy-free substitute
Yuba (made from the skin that forms on heated soy milk). Used in Japanese and Chinese cooking	No soy-free substitute
Soy yogurt	Dairy yogurt
Soy desserts	Creamy desserts made with milk, rice, or almond milk
Soy cream	Dairy cream
Soy custard	Custard made with dairy, rice, or almond milk
Soy sprouts (bean sprouts)	Mungbean sprouts and alfafa sprouts
Edamame (young soybeans)	Peas or other beans
Soybean granules or curds	Ground meat
Tofu (made from soy milk curds)	Cheese or meat
Miso (paste made from fermented soybeans and grain). Used to flavor Japanese food	No soy-free substitute
Tempeh (made from fermented whole soybeans)	Meat, poultry
Soy sauce, tamari	Brown food well, use richly flavored stock, and season food with salt and dark brown sugar
Teriyaki sauce	As above and add a small quantity of vinegar
Soybean oil (neutral-flavored oil used in vegetable oil blends)	Grapeseed, canola, safflower, corn, and sunflower oil

Part III
THE RECIPES

| # STOCKS, SOUPS AND SAUCES

STOCKS

Homemade stock, when prepared properly, adds depth and a freshness of flavor to risottos, soups, casseroles, poached dishes, and flour-thickened sauces that is simply not possible even with the best-quality stock cubes. Unlike stock cubes, homemade stock is also dairy-, egg-, gluten-, nut-, and soy-free. It is made by poaching fresh or browned meat, poultry, or fish bones with herbs and aromatic vegetables—such as celery, onion and carrot—in water.

There are two main varieties of stock: white stock and brown. White stock provides a delicately flavored, pale-colored liquid that can be used in both richly flavored and subtle dishes. It is made by poaching fresh carcasses of white-meat poultry (usually chicken), veal bones, or the fresh bones and heads of white fish in water flavored with vegetables and herbs. The bones left over from roast chicken or turkey also can be used; however, this produces a stock with a thinner flavor, because much of the flavor in the bones is lost in the cooking juices during roasting.

Brown stock is a richly flavored, dark caramel-colored liquid that enhances full-flavored dishes. Brown stock derives its color from first browning chicken carcasses or chopped beef bones and vegetables in a hot oven, or in a frying pan with some oil, before poaching in water.

GENERAL RULES
FOR MAKING
STOCK

- Use a pot large enough to cover the ingredients with water. Exposed ingredients will not flavor the stock.
- Do not season stock with salt. The natural salts derived from the bones and vegetables provide all the flavor stock needs. Salted stock tastes overpowering.
- Use very fresh vegetables and bones for the purest and freshest flavored stock. Choose meaty bones to make richly flavored stock.
- Before making fish stock, remove the gills from fish heads because they contain a large quantity of blood, which will make the stock cloudy and bitter.
- Avoid using vegetables that fall apart, such as potatoes and tomatoes, or green vegetables, such as broccoli, cabbage, and green beans, which become strongly flavored when cooked for a prolonged period.
- Dice vegetables so that their flavors are readily extracted. To prevent vegetables

NOTES
FOR FOOD
ALLERGY
SUFFERERS

The pure flavor of homemade stock is achieved by using the simplest ingredients. Stock made with bones, vegetables, herbs, and water makes an ideal liquid base for dairy-, gluten-, egg-, nut-, and soy-free sauces and dishes. For nut- and soy-free diets, use a suitable soy- and nut-free neutral-flavored oil to brown vegetables and bones.

from falling apart during cooking, dice them according to the length of time the stock is cooked for: ⅓ in./1 cm for stock that takes 30 minutes or less to cook; 1 in./2.5 cm for stock requiring 3–4 hours; 2 in./5 cm for stock that requires 6 hours to cook.

- Avoid using burned bones or vegetables in brown stock because they will spoil the flavor of the stock.

Stock should be perfectly clear. To keep stock from becoming fatty and cloudy:

- Trim the excess fat from bones.
- Submerge stock ingredients in cold water and slowly bring to a gentle simmer. This way fat on the bones gradually melts and blood gradually congeals and floats to the surface, where it can be skimmed off. If this scum is not removed, the stock becomes cloudy and tastes fatty.
- While the stock is cooking, use cold water to top up the water level so that the ingredients remain submerged. Adding cold water encourages fat and scum to rise to the surface, where it can be skimmed off.
- Maintain stock at a gentle simmer to ensure scum and fat gently rise to the surface and are not bubbled through the liquid, because this makes it cloudy and greasy.
- Once the stock is made, strain through a fine-mesh sieve to obtain a clear, fragment-free liquid.

USING STOCK

Stock can be used as it is in soups, delicately flavored sauces, casseroles, and so on, or it can be reduced to half its original volume (by boiling in a wide pan) to strengthen its flavor and color, making it suitable for adding depth to richly flavored and colored sauces. As stock is reduced, it should be skimmed regularly to remove any remaining fat and scum.

STORING STOCK

Stock must be stored in the refrigerator because it is highly nutritious and provides an ideal breeding ground for bacteria. To store stock in the refrigerator or freezer, it is more space efficient to reduce stock by at least three-quarters of its original volume. The stock becomes thick and syrupy and sets to a firm jelly when chilled, which keeps for up to 3 days in the refrigerator and up to 1 year in the freezer.

RECONSTITUTING
JELLIED STOCK

Jellied stock is very strong in flavor and is reconstituted with water before it is used in recipes. To make a light stock from jellied stock, add 1 heaped Tbsp. of jellied stock to 1¼ cups/290 ml water. To make a richer stock, add 2–3 heaped Tbsp. of jellied stock to 1¼ cups/290 ml water.

WHITE CHICKEN STOCK

White chicken stock can be used to enhance the flavor of almost any savory dish because it is light in color and delicate in flavor. **Makes 1 qt./1 l**

INGREDIENTS

1 chicken carcass

1 onion, cut into wedges

1 large carrot, cut into 1-in./2.5-cm dice

1 celery stick, cut into 1-in./2.5-cm dice

1 handful button mushrooms

1 sprig thyme

4 parsley stems

a grind of black pepper

1 bay leaf

1 Combine all the ingredients in a large stock pan, cover with cold water, and bring slowly to a gentle simmer. Simmer for 3–4 hours, uncovered. Do not allow the stock to boil.

2 Keep the water level topped up with cold water and lift off any melted fat and scum that rises to the surface.

3 Once the stock is cooked, pass it through a large sieve and use as required (see Using Stock, page 63).

VARIATION

BROWN CHICKEN STOCK
Roast a chicken carcass at 400°F/200°C/gas mark 6 for an hour, or until golden brown. Meanwhile, brown the stock vegetables, listed above, in 2 Tbsp. oil in the stock pan, making sure they do not burn. Add the browned bones, herbs, and ground pepper to the vegetables, cover with water, and continue as above.

FISH STOCK

White fish stock is colorless and delicate in flavor, and is used in sauces served with fish, in fish soups, and fish casseroles. **Makes 1 qt./1 l**

INGREDIENTS

1 lb./450 g white fish bones, skin, tails and heads (gills removed)

1 small onion, thinly sliced

1 small carrot, cut into ⅓-in./1-cm dice

1 handful button mushrooms, thinly sliced

1 celery stick, cut into ⅓-in./1-cm dice

1 sprig thyme

4 parsley stems

4 black peppercorns

1 bay leaf

1 Combine all the ingredients in a large stock pan, cover with cold water, and bring slowly to a gentle simmer. Simmer for 20 minutes. It is essential that fish stock does not boil or cook for longer or it will become cloudy and bitter in flavor. Lift off any scum that rises to the surface with a large metal spoon.

2 Once the stock is cooked, pass it through a fine-mesh sieve. Ensure all fish bones have been removed and use as required (see Using Stock, page 63).

BROWN BEEF STOCK

Ask the butcher to cut beef bones into small pieces for you. Brown beef stock has a stronger flavor than brown chicken stock and is used mainly in dishes containing beef, venison, or lamb, and in richly flavored and colored sauces served with red meat. **Makes 1 qt./1 l**

INGREDIENTS

2¼ lb./1 kg chopped beef bones

2 onions, cut into wedges

2 large carrots, cut into 3 chunks

2 celery sticks, cut into 3 pieces

2 Tbsp. sunflower or corn oil

2 handfuls button mushrooms

1 sprig thyme

4 parsley stalks

a grind of black pepper

1 bay leaf

1 Preheat the oven to 400°F/200°C/ gas mark 6. Place the chopped bones in a roasting pan and bake for 1 hour, or until evenly browned.

2 Meanwhile, in a large stock pan, brown the onions, carrots, and celery in the oil, stirring frequently to prevent the vegetables from burning.

3 When the bones are caramel brown, add them to the pan, along with the remaining ingredients, cover in cold water, and bring to a simmer.

4 Gently simmer the stock for 6 hours, to extract all the flavor from the bones. Spoon off the fat and scum from the surface and top the pan up with cold water every hour. Once the stock is cooked, strain it through a fine-mesh sieve, and use as required (see Using Stock, page 63).

VEGETABLE STOCK

Vegetable stock is used mainly in soups and vegetarian dishes. It is also a nutritious cooking liquid for baby food (see chapter 18). **Makes 1 qt./1 l**

INGREDIENTS

2 onions, finely sliced

2 carrots, cut into ⅓-in./1-cm dice

1 leek, cut into ⅓-in./1-cm dice

1 celery stick, cut into ⅓-in./1-cm dice

4 button mushrooms, finely sliced

4 parsley stems

1 sprig fresh thyme

a grind of black pepper

1 bay leaf

1 Combine all the ingredients in a large stock pan, cover with cold water, and bring to a simmer.

2 Simmer gently for 30 minutes, skimming regularly, then strain through a sieve and use as required (see Using Stock, page 63).

VARIATION
BROWN VEGETABLE STOCK
This stock is suitable for richly flavored and colored soups, pureed vegetable sauces, and vegetarian dishes. Using the ingredient list above, first fry the prepared onions, carrots, leek, celery, and mushrooms in 2 Tbsp. sunflower or corn oil until golden brown, stirring regularly to prevent the vegetables from burning. Add 1 tsp. tomato puree to add color and cover the ingredients with cold water. Bring to a simmer and poach for 30 minutes, regularly removing oil and scum from the surface. Strain the stock and use as required.

SOUPS

Soup is justifiably popular across the world. It is made with an endless variety of ingredients and can be thin or thick, smooth or chunky. In general, most recipes are suitable—or are easily adapted—for dairy-, egg-, gluten-, soy-, and nut-free diets (see box, page 68).

GENERAL RULES FOR MAKING SOUP

- Cut ingredients to the same size so they cook evenly and look uniform in chunky soups. Make sure the ingredients are no smaller than ¼ in./5 mm so they can be recognized and do not overcook and fall apart during cooking.
- When softening vegetables by gently frying them in butter or oil, stir frequently to prevent them from sticking and burning. Remove any burned vegetables before adding liquid to the pan or they will taint the flavor of the soup.
- Simmer, do not boil, soups. If soup is allowed to boil the ingredients are likely to overcook and lose their fresh flavor; thin, clear soups may become cloudy.
- Regularly skim the surface of the soup to remove any fat and scum—this will improve the appearance and flavor of the soup.
- Add green vegetables to soup towards the end of the cooking period so they do not overcook and lose their vivid color and fresh flavor.
- Blend potatoes until just smooth. If potatoes are overblended, the soup will become thick and gluey.
- To control the thickness of smooth pureed soup, strain the cooked ingredients and most of the liquid into a clean container. Puree the ingredients with one-third of the liquid until smooth, then gradually add the strained liquid to the puree until it reaches the required consistency.

SMOOTH SOUPS

Smooth soups that are served as a starter to a meal tend to be perfectly smooth, with the thickness of heavy cream. When smooth soups are eaten as a warming, hearty meal, they should be thicker so they are more substantial and satisfying to eat.

Smooth soups are thickened by two main methods:

1 By pureeing the cooked ingredients in a blender or using a hand-held blender until smooth (food processors tend to produce a coarse puree). This method is ideal for soups made with vegetables that naturally thicken soup when softened and pureed, such as root vegetables, potatoes, squashes, and beans. This method does not require flour to thicken the soup and is ideal for gluten-free diets (see Peppery Watercress and Spinach Soup, page 70).

2 By thickening the soup with wheat flour (or for gluten-free diets, with cornstarch). This method is used when the flavoring ingredients are unsuitable for pureeing or do not puree to a smooth, creamy consistency. Flour is mixed with fat to form a paste called a roux (see Flour-Thickened Sauces, page 72). The liquid base of the soup is then gradually stirred into the roux and brought to a simmer. As the soup simmers, it thickens to a fine, smooth consistency.

CHUNKY SOUPS

Chunky soups tend to be heartier and more satisfying than smooth soups because they usually contain ingredients rich in starch and protein, as well as vegetables that add flavor, color, and texture.

Thin clear soups, eaten all over the world, are made by gently simmering the soup ingredients in stock or broth. They are delicately flavored, low in fat, and are made more substantial with ingredients rich in carbohydrate, including pasta, noodles, rice, pearl barley, and potatoes.

Chunky soups made with a thicker base are made by simmering evenly diced or sliced ingredients together in stock until tender. The soup base is thickened by pureeing a proportion of the ingredients in the cooking liquid, or by thickening the strained cooking liquid with flour. The remaining cooked ingredients are then returned to the pan to add texture and enhance the appearance of the soup.

NOTES FOR FOOD ALLERGY SUFFERERS

DAIRY-FREE DIET: Soup ingredients are often gently fried in butter. Use olive oil, a neutral-flavored oil, or dairy-free margarine instead.

Soup is sometimes thickened with a roux, a mixture of flour and butter. In place of butter, use an equal quantity of dairy-free margarine or 1 Tbsp. oil per 2 Tbsp./30 g butter used in the recipe.

Milk and cream are often added to smooth soup towards the end of cooking to enrich its flavor. Use soy milk, oat milk, or rice milk instead. When soup is garnished with a swirl of cream, use a small quantity of pouring soy cream in strongly flavored soups, where its mild beany taste will not be evident. Alternatively, drizzle soup with a small quantity of extra virgin olive oil to add richness.

GLUTEN-FREE DIET: Smooth soups thickened with pureed ingredients are ideal for gluten-free diets. Many soups are traditionally thickened with a roux made with wheat flour and butter. Replace the wheat flour with a half quantity of cornstarch to make the roux. For soups that contain wheat noodles, pasta, or bread, replace these with gluten-free rice or buckwheat noodles, rice and millet pasta, and gluten-free bread. You can also make croutons for garnishing soup with gluten-free bread (see page 70).

EGG-FREE DIET: Egg is often included in Asian soups because it provides protein and texture. Simply omit the egg and use more protein-rich ingredients, such as fish, meat, poultry, or beans.

NUT-FREE DIET: Some Asian and Middle Eastern soups use ground almonds and other nut varieties to enrich and thicken soup. Because nuts are integral to the consistency and flavor of these soups, it is best to choose an alternative recipe that does not use nuts. When frying or browning ingredients in oil, make sure the oil is free of nut oils.

SOY-FREE DIET: Soy beancurd, more commonly known as tofu, and soy sauce are often used in Asian soups. Replace tofu with another protein-rich food, such as meat, fish, poultry, or egg. Replace soy sauce by adding ½ tsp. salt and 1 tsp. dark brown sugar per 1 Tbsp. soy sauce and a little richly flavored stock.

CHUNKY WINTER VEGETABLE SOUP

This hearty soup is ideal for lunch on cold winter days. Half of the ingredients in the soup are pureed to form a thick, creamy base for the remaining vegetables. **Serves 4**

INGREDIENTS

2 Tbsp./30 g butter or sunflower or corn oil

● DAIRY   dairy-free margarine or oil

1 onion, sliced thinly

1 leek, sliced thinly

3 large carrots, cut into ¾-in./2-cm dice

2 celery sticks, sliced thinly

Salt and freshly ground black pepper

2 potatoes, peeled and cut into ¾-in./2-cm dice

1 bay leaf

1 sprig thyme

2½ cups/570 ml white chicken or vegetable stock

1¼ cups/290 ml milk

● DAIRY   soy milk

TO GARNISH

extra virgin olive oil for drizzling

1 Tbsp. finely chopped chives

1 Heat the butter or oil in a medium-sized heavy saucepan. Add the onion, leek, carrots, celery, and a little seasoning, cover with a lid, and fry gently until very soft. This will take at least 20 minutes. Stir occasionally to prevent the vegetables from sticking to the pan. Do not allow the vegetables to brown.

2 Add the potatoes, bay leaf, thyme, and stock to the pan. Season the soup with a pinch of salt and grind of pepper and simmer for 20 minutes, or until the potatoes are tender. Do not allow the potatoes to overcook or they will break up, affecting the appearance and consistency of the soup.

3 Using a slotted spoon, lift out one-third of the cooked vegetables and reserve. Discard the bay leaf and thyme and puree the remaining soup until smooth. To remove any remaining lumps, pass the soup through a fine-meshed sieve, into a clean pan, gently pressing it through with a wooden spoon.

4 Reheat the soup, taste, and season as necessary.

5 Add the reserved vegetables and the milk and bring the soup back to a simmer to warm the vegetables through. To serve, ladle the soup into warmed soup bowls, lightly drizzle the soup with olive oil, and sprinkle with the finely chopped chives.

PEPPERY WATERCRESS AND SPINACH SOUP WITH GARLIC CROUTONS

This is a vibrant soup in both taste and color. To retain the wonderful bright green color and zingy flavor of the leaves, the watercress and spinach is wilted in the hot soup for the briefest moment before it is pureed. **Serves 4**

FOR THE SOUP

● DAIRY

2 Tbsp./30 g butter

1 Tbsp. sunflower or corn oil

salt and freshly ground black pepper

1 onion, finely sliced

1 large potato, peeled and diced

3¾ cups/860 ml White Chicken or Vegetable Stock (see pages 64 and 66)

4 oz./110 g watercress

4 oz./110 g baby spinach leaves, washed and drained

FOR THE GARLIC CROUTONS

4 slices white bread, crusts removed and cut into ¼-in./5-mm dice

● GLUTEN

gluten-free white bread

4 Tbsp. vegetable or olive oil

2 garlic cloves, cut in half lengthwise

salt

TO GARNISH

4 sprigs watercress

1 Place the butter for the soup in a medium-sized heavy pan, add the onion, season with the salt and pepper, cover with a lid, and fry gently until very soft and sweet.

2 Meanwhile, start the croutons by preheating the oven to 350°F/180°C/gas mark 4.

3 Spread the cubes of bread on a baking sheet in one layer. Set aside. In a small pan, gently warm the oil and garlic cloves for the croutons until the garlic begins to sizzle. Remove from the heat and allow the oil to cool, then remove the garlic. Drizzle the oil over the bread cubes, turning the cubes over until evenly coated. Lightly sprinkle with salt and bake for 5-10 minutes, until the croutons are golden brown. Cool on a wire rack, covered in paper towels to absorb excess oil.

4 Add the potato and stock to the softened onions. Bring the stock to a simmering point and simmer for about 10 minutes, or until the potato is soft.

5 Add the watercress and spinach leaves to the pan and simmer for 30 seconds, or until wilted.

8 Puree the soup until smooth. Bring the soup back to a simmer, taste, and season as necessary. Serve immediately in warmed soup bowls, garnished with a sprig of watercress and a sprinkling of croutons.

NOTES FOR FOOD ALLERGY SUFFERERS

DAIRY-FREE DIET: The roux in flour-thickened sauces is made with butter, but oil is used for browning and frying. Using oil or fat that collects in the base of a roasting pan from a roast is suitable for a dairy-free diet. Or sauces thickened with a flour and butter roux can be made with an equal quantity of dairy-free margarine or 1 Tbsp. oil per 2 Tbsp./30 g butter.

Flour-thickened sauces made with stock or cooking liquids used to poach or stew ingredients are safe for dairy-free diets, provided butter is not used to fry the ingredients beforehand. White sauce is traditionally made with cows' milk but can be made just as well with sweetened soy milk. For a very rich white dairy-free sauce, substitute half the soy milk with soy cream.

GLUTEN-FREE DIET: Flour-thickened sauces are traditionally thickened with a plain wheat flour and fat roux. Use a half quantity of cornstarch in place of wheat flour. It produces perfectly smooth-textured, glossy sauces.

EGG-FREE DIET: Egg is not used in flour-thickened sauces.

NUT-FREE DIET: Provided the flour is milled in a nut-free factory and the fat used does not contain nut oils, flour-thickened sauces are suitable for nut-free diets.

SOY-FREE DIET: Provided soy milk is not used as the liquid base for the sauce and the roux is made with soy-free fat, then flour-thickened sauces are suitable for soy-free diets.

SAUCES

Sauces are integral to the food we eat. They add endless variety, flavor, color, and moisture and improve the consistency and appearance of food. Sauces are extremely versatile, and ingredients unsuitable for your dietary requirements can be avoided easily or replaced to dramatically increase the repertoire of dishes available to you.

Sauces can be classified by the way they are thickened to coat or bind food: flour-thickened sauces are based on a wheat flour and fat paste, or roux (see White Sauce, opposite); reduction sauces are thickened by boiling down to a syrupy consistency (see Red Wine Sauce, page 78); pureed sauces are based on softened vegetables (see Rich Italian Tomato Sauce, page 80); emulsified sauces are thickened by whisking melted butter, oil, cream, or yogurt into water-based ingredients (see Mayonnaise, page 83).

FLOUR-THICKENED SAUCES

Flour-thickened sauces have a number of roles in cooking. Lightly thickened sauces are used to thinly coat the ingredients they accompany or to add moisture and thickness to baked dishes; thicker sauces, made with a higher proportion of roux, are generally used to bind ingredients together, for example in a pie or tart.

WHITE SAUCE

This very simple flour-thickened sauce has a smooth, creamy consistency that is perfect for lightly coating or binding delicately flavored ingredients. Due to its bland flavor, white sauce is usually flavored with herbs and vegetables or cheese (see next page).
Makes 2½ cups/570 ml

INGREDIENTS

3 Tbsp./40 g butter

● DAIRY dairy-free margarine or 2 Tbsp. vegetable oil

5 Tbsp./40 g all-purpose flour

● GLUTEN 2½ Tbsp./20 g cornstarch

2½ cups/570 ml milk

● DAIRY sweetened soy milk or rice milk

salt and freshly ground black pepper

1 Melt the butter in a medium-sized heavy pan over medium heat.

2 Stir in the flour, using a wooden spoon, to form a thick, smooth roux.

3 Cook for 30 seconds, stirring continuously. Remove from the heat.

4 Add a splash of the milk and stir vigorously until the roux has absorbed all the liquid evenly. Add another splash of milk and stir vigorously until the roux has again absorbed all the liquid and is an even texture. As more liquid is incorporated, you can add it in progressively greater "splashes."

5 Repeat this process until all the milk has been incorporated and the roux becomes a smooth sauce. Do not add the liquid too quickly or the sauce will become lumpy.

6 Place the pan back on a medium heat. Stirring continuously, bring the sauce to a boil.

7 Reduce the heat and simmer gently for 1 minute to cook the flour. The white sauce should be smooth, glossy, and the consistency of heavy cream. Add seasoning to taste.

VARIATIONS ON WHITE SAUCE

BÉCHAMEL SAUCE

White sauce is used to add creaminess to dishes such as lasagna and vegetable gratins. A slightly more upscale version of white sauce can be made by infusing the milk with herbs by bringing 2½ cups/570 ml milk to a simmer with 4 onion slices, 2 bay leaves, 6 whole black peppercorns, and 3 parsley stems. Then remove from the heat and set aside until cold to extract the flavor of the added ingredients. Strain the flavored milk through a sieve and then use as normal in the main recipe for white sauce.

CHEESE SAUCE

As well as its common use in dishes such as macaroni and cheese, this sauce is good with baked, poached, or steamed fish. Simply add 4 oz./110 g grated aged Cheddar or Parmesan to the finished sauce and stir well. Don't reheat the sauce after adding the cheese or it will lose its flavor and become greasy.

PARSLEY SAUCE

Add 2 Tbsp. finely chopped parsley to white sauce in the last few minutes of cooking. Parsley sauce is a good accompaniment to white fish and poached chicken.

SAGE AND ONION SAUCE

Gently fry 1 finely sliced onion and 1 Tbsp. of finely chopped fresh sage in 1 Tbsp. of butter or oil until soft but not colored. Stir into the cooked white sauce and gently simmer for 2 minutes. This sauce is particularly good with roast pork.

RICH WHITE SAUCE

This egg-free sauce is a good alternative to egg custard fillings in savory tarts. To make it, simply use half milk, half heavy cream in the basic white sauce recipe.

THICKENING SAUCES WITH CORNSTARCH

Do not simmer sauces thickened with cornstarch for more than a minute or keep them warm for more than 15 minutes or the cornstarch will break down and the sauce will become thin.

STOCK-BASED FLOUR-THICKENED SAUCES

Stock and poaching or stewing liquid flavored with meat, chicken, fish, and vegetables are also thickened with a roux to produce mild-flavored sauces. Due to their delicate flavor, these sauces benefit from the addition of herbs, aromatic vegetables, including onions, celery, and mushrooms, a little wine, or a squeeze of lemon juice.

VELOUTÉ SAUCE

This delicate, velvety sauce is ideal for binding chicken or game pie fillings or, with added flavoring ingredients, such as herbs, wine, and lemon, for serving with pan-fried poultry, game, and pork. **Serves 4**

INGREDIENTS

3 Tbsp./40 g butter or 2 Tbsp. sunflower or corn oil

● **DAIRY**

dairy-free margarine or oil

5 Tbsp./40 g all-purpose flour

● **GLUTEN**

2½ Tbsp./20 g cornstarch

2½ cups/570 ml White Chicken Stock (page 64) or liquid from poaching a chicken

1 bay leaf

salt and freshly ground black pepper

1 Melt the butter in a heavy saucepan over a medium heat.

2 Stir in the flour, using a wooden spoon, to form a thick, smooth roux. Cook for 30 seconds, stirring continuously. Remove from the heat.

3 Add a splash of the stock and stir vigorously until the roux is smooth. Add another splash of stock and stir vigorously until the roux is smooth again. Repeat this process until all the stock has been incorporated. Do not add the liquid too quickly or the sauce will become lumpy.

4 Place the pan back over medium heat and add the bay leaf. Stirring continuously, to prevent the sauce sticking to the bottom of the pan, bring the sauce to a boil.

5 Reduce the heat and simmer the sauce for 1 minute to cook the flour. It should be smooth and lightly coat the back of a spoon. Add seasoning to taste.

VARIATIONS

These variations can also be made with vegetable stock or white fish stock (see page 64), in place of chicken stock, to serve with pan-fried fish or shellfish.

WHITE WINE VELOUTÉ SAUCE

Off the heat, add ¼ cup white wine to the roux (before the stock) and stir continuously until it is incorporated. Gradually add the stock to the mixture. When all the liquid is incorporated and the sauce is smooth, add a bay leaf and bring to a boil. Simmer for 1 minute, stirring continuously, to cook the flour and to boil off the alcohol in the wine. Serve with pan-fried or poached chicken, game birds, pork or veal.

HERB VELOUTÉ SAUCE

Add a handful of chopped tarragon and parsley to the white wine sauce (above), just before serving. Serve with pan-fried or poached chicken, game birds, pork, or veal.

MUSHROOM VELOUTÉ SAUCE

Slice half an onion and a handful of button mushrooms and fry gently in 1 Tbsp. oil or butter until very soft, then add to the white wine sauce (above). Serve with pan-fried or poached chicken, game birds, pork or veal.

LEMON VELOUTÉ SAUCE

Make as for basic velouté sauce and add 2 Tbsp. lemon juice just before serving. Season as necessary. Serve with pan-fried or poached chicken, game birds, pork, or veal.

REDUCTION SAUCES

These sauces, characterized by their richly colored, glossy appearance and syrupy consistency, are generally made in a wide, uncovered pan used to pan-fry or roast meat, poultry, or fish. Also referred to as pan sauces, they are served with pan-fried, roasted, baked, and stewed dishes.

Much of the color and flavor of these sauces derives from the browned juices of pan-fried and roasted food on the bottom of the pan. The browned juices are loosened by adding water, wine, stock, or liquid used for poaching or stewing, to the pan. The liquid, colored and flavored by the juices, is then reduced in volume by boiling to concentrate it to a syrupy liquid that boils with large, slow-moving bubbles. As the sauce boils, fat and other impurities rise to the surface, where they can be skimmed off, clarifying and purifying the flavor of the sauce. Boiling is also an effective method for removing raw-tasting alcohol in wine and spirits used to flavor pan sauces. Cream, added to pan sauces to enrich and soften their flavor, also thickens pan sauces when boiled and concentrated.

This reducing method, an ideal thickening method for dairy- and gluten-free diets, is used to improve the flavor, consistency, and appearance of simple sauces such as Rich Italian Tomato Sauce (page 80), sauces that accompany stews, and rich, pure concentrated pan sauces served with pan-fried meat, fish, or poultry (see Red Wine Sauce with Shallots and Mushrooms, page 78).

GENERAL RULES
FOR REDUCING
SAUCES

- Use a wide shallow pan placed over medium heat.
- Seasoning a liquid before reducing its volume is likely to result in oversalted, peppery sauces. Boiling off water to thicken sauces concentrates the remaining ingredients and any seasoning present.
- Always boil acidic and alcoholic ingredients to remove their sharp, raw flavor because this will affect the flavor of the sauce.
- Recipes may call for the sauce to be reduced by half. This means that the sauce must be boiled until only half of the original volume of liquid remains, to thicken and concentrate its flavor and color.
- A recipe may specify a sauce be reduced to a syrupy consistency. This means the liquid is sufficiently viscous to cling to the back of a spoon without immediately running off. As the sauce boils and thickens, the bubbles become larger and move more slowly.
- If a pan sauce becomes too thick or too strongly flavored, add a tablespoon or two of water or stock.
- Once the sauce has reached the required consistency, season it with a small quantity of salt and freshly ground black pepper.

NOTES FOR FOOD ALLERGY SUFFERERS

DAIRY-FREE DIET: Provided meat, fish, poultry, and vegetables are browned, fried, or roasted in oil only, and cream is not added to the sauce, pan sauces are perfectly suitable for dairy-free diets.

GLUTEN-FREE DIET: Pan sauces are ideal for gluten-free diets because they are generally flour free. Flour is sometimes added to thicken pan sauces that are already richly flavored and colored, and when a large volume of sauce is required to cover the ingredients in stews. When a pan sauce calls for flour, use half the amount of cornstarch instead. Because cornstarch loses its thickening properties with prolonged boiling, mix 2 tsp. cornstarch with 1 Tbsp. water, per 1¼ cups/290 ml of sauce, and add to the sauce once its flavor is concentrated and rounded and the dish is ready to be served. Bring the liquid back to a boil for 1 minute, to cook the flour, and serve immediately.

Adding a small quantity of heavy or whipping cream to a pan sauce and boiling it until the sauce reaches thin coating consistency provides an alternative method for enriching the flavor and thickening the consistency of pan sauces.

EGG-FREE DIET: Pan sauces rarely contain egg.

NUT-FREE DIET: Pan sauces are safe for nut-free diets provided the oil used to cook the ingredients to make the sauce is nut-free.

SOY-FREE DIET: Pan sauces are safe for soy-free diets provided the oil used to cook the ingredients is soy-free.

Making cream sauces

- Use whipping cream, heavy cream, or full-fat crème fraîche for thickening pan sauces. Half-and-half and light cream curdle when boiled because they do not contain enough fat to emulsify with the sauce.
- Add cream to a sauce once it has reached the required concentration of flavor.
- Cream is likely to curdle when added to sauces that contain raw alcohol, vinegar, or lemon juice. Always boil them well before adding cream.
- Once cream is added to a sauce and boiled, it will thicken very quickly. If the sauce becomes too thick and oily around the edge of the pan, stir in 2–3 Tbsp. water.
- Once the sauce has reached the required consistency, season with a small quantity of salt and freshly ground black pepper. Taste and season again as necessary.

RED WINE SAUCE WITH SHALLOTS AND MUSHROOMS

This deliciously rich sauce is suitable for gluten-, dairy-, egg-, nut-, and soy-free diets. It improves in both flavor and color when it is added to the browned cooking juices in a pan used for frying meat. **Serves 4**

INGREDIENTS

2 Tbsp. sunflower or corn oil

1 tsp. butter

● DAIRY omit for dairy-free diet

2 shallots, thinly sliced

4 oz./110 g button mushrooms, finely sliced

salt and freshly ground black pepper

1 cup/200 ml red wine

1¼ cups/290 ml chicken or beef stock

1 sprig fresh thyme

1 Heat the oil and butter in a heavy saucepan, add the shallots and mushrooms, season with a pinch of salt and a grind of pepper, cover with a lid, and fry gently until the shallots are soft and lightly browned.

2 Add the red wine to the pan and boil for 1 minute to remove the alcohol. Then add the stock and thyme.

3 Boil the sauce over medium heat until it is thick and syrupy and boils with large, slow-moving bubbles. Carefully spoon off any fat and scum that collects on the surface.

4 Once the sauce has reached a syrupy consistency and lightly coats the back of a spoon, taste, and season the sauce with more salt and pepper as necessary. Remove the sprig of thyme and serve as required.

VARIATIONS

PEPPERCORN SAUCE
Add 1 tsp. black peppercorns to the sauce with the stock and thyme at step 2. Pass the finished sauce through a sieve into a clean pan. Bring back to a boil and serve with grilled or broiled steak.

RED CURRANT AND MINT SAUCE
Add 1 Tbsp. red currant jelly, 1 Tbsp. balsamic vinegar, and 1 sprig of mint with the stock and thyme at step 2. Pass the finished sauce through a sieve into a clean pan. Bring back to a boil and serve with broiled or roast lamb.

WHITE WINE SAUCE

Serve this light-colored, delicately flavored sauce with poultry, fish, veal, and pork. White wine sauce to accompany fish should be made with 1¼ cups/290 ml fish stock instead of the 2 Tbsp. of jellied stock stated in the recipe. Cream thickens and enriches the flavor of this sauce. **Serves 4**

INGREDIENTS

2 large or 4 small shallots, finely sliced

1 handful button mushrooms, finely sliced

2 Tbsp. sunflower or corn oil

1 tsp. butter
● DAIRY
omit for dairy-free diet

⅔ cup/150 ml dry white wine

1¼ cups/290 ml water

2 Tbsp. jellied White Chicken Stock
(page 63)

1 sprig thyme

2 Tbsp. whipping cream
● DAIRY
omit for dairy-free diet

a squeeze of lemon juice

salt and freshly ground black pepper

1 In a small pan, covered with a lid, gently fry the shallots and mushrooms in the oil and butter (if using) until very soft. Do not allow them to brown.

2 Transfer the vegetables to a frying pan, stir in the wine and half the water and boil for 2 minutes.

3 Add the jellied stock, the remaining water, and thyme. Reduce the sauce over medium heat until it thickens to a syrupy consistency. Carefully spoon off any fat that collects on the surface.

4 Add the cream (if using), boil for 1 minute, and add the lemon juice. Taste and season as necessary. Remove the sprig of thyme and serve as required.

VARIATIONS

WHITE WINE AND TARRAGON SAUCE
Add 1 Tbsp. finely chopped tarragon to the finished sauce. Heat the tarragon through and serve before it loses its fresh color.

LEMON SAUCE
For a rich, creamy lemon sauce to serve with fish, whisk 3 Tbsp. whipping cream into the sauce made with 1¼ cups/290 ml fish stock. Boil the sauce for 1 minute to return it to a syrupy consistency and add another squeeze of lemon juice. Taste and season as necessary and serve immediately.

LEEK AND MUSTARD SAUCE
Gently fry 2 finely sliced leeks instead of the shallots and mushrooms and continue as for the recipe above. For a sauce enriched with cream, whisk 1 heaped tsp. Dijon mustard into the finished sauce, taste, and season as necessary. For a sauce made without cream, use 1 level tsp. Dijon mustard so the sauce is not too sharp. Serve with poultry, pork, and firm white fish.

PUREED VEGETABLE SAUCES

Pureed sauces are made by cooking vegetables until soft and pureeing them until smooth. Such sauces are often richly flavored and colored and are served with pasta, meat, fish, and vegetables.

RICH ITALIAN TOMATO SAUCE

This rich tomato sauce is great on pasta and pizza or served with fish, poultry, and vegetables. **Serves 4**

INGREDIENTS

1 large onion, finely diced

3 Tbsp. olive oil

salt and freshly ground black pepper

1 garlic clove, finely chopped

2 (14-oz./400-g) cans chopped tomatoes

1 bay leaf

1 sprig thyme

2–3 parsley stems

1 large pinch sugar

1 Combine the onion in a heavy saucepan with the olive oil. Season with salt and pepper, cover with the lid, and fry gently, over low heat, until the onion is very soft but not colored.

2 Add the garlic and stir over medium heat for 1 minute.

3 Add the tomatoes, herbs, and sugar and bring to a simmer. Simmer the sauce with the lid off for 20 minutes.

4 Remove the herbs and puree the sauce until smooth. Pass the sauce through a sieve back into the pan and bring back to a simmer. Taste and add more seasoning as necessary. Use as required.

VARIATIONS

TOMATO AND HERB SAUCE
Add 1 Tbsp. chopped fresh herbs, such as basil, oregano, or parsley to the sauce just before serving to conserve their fresh flavor and color. Serve with pasta, poultry, fish, and vegetables such as pan-fried zucchini and eggplant.

TOMATO SAUCE WITH CAPERS AND BLACK OLIVES
Add 2 tsp. rinsed and drained capers (preferably capers preserved in salt) and 1 Tbsp. pitted, roughly chopped black olives in the last 5 minutes of cooking. Serve with grilled fish and pasta.

TOMATO SAUCE WITH BACON
Gently fry 4 oz./110 g finely chopped smoked bacon with the onion. When the onion is soft, remove the lid and stir over medium heat until the onions and bacon are lightly browned. Continue as from step 2 of Rich Italian Tomato Sauce. Serve with pasta.

<table>
<tr><td rowspan="3">

NOTES FOR FOOD ALLERGY SUFFERERS

</td><td>

DAIRY-FREE DIET: Pureed vegetable sauces are suitable for dairy-free diets provided olive oil or a neutral-flavored oil, and not butter, is used to soften onions, carrots, and any other aromatic vegetables flavoring the sauce.

GLUTEN-FREE DIET: Pureed sauces are made with vegetables that soften when cooked and have the ability to thicken liquids when pureed. As a result, flour is not required in pureed sauces.

</td><td>

EGG-FREE DIET: Egg is not used in pureed vegetables sauces.

SOY-FREE DIET: Use butter, olive oil, or a neutral-flavored oil that does not contain soybean oil to soften the vegetables.

NUT-FREE DIET: Use butter, olive oil, or a neutral-flavored oil that does not contain nut oils to soften the vegetables.

</td></tr>
</table>

EMULSION SAUCES

Emulsion sauces include vinaigrettes and rich creamy mayonnaise. Both sauces are thickened by forming an emulsion between oil and vinegar or lemon juice. Vinaigrettes quickly separate back into vinegar and oil when left to stand. Mayonnaise contains egg yolk, which acts as an emulsifier, holding the oil droplets and water-based ingredients in a stable emulsion that remains thick and creamy.

BASIC VINAIGRETTE

This is the perfect light dressing for prepared salads. **Serves 4**

INGREDIENTS

1 Tbsp. white or red wine vinegar

salt and freshly ground black pepper

2 Tbsp. neutral-flavored oil, such as sunflower, corn, or grapeseed oil

2 Tbsp. extra virgin olive oil

1 Spoon the vinegar into a bowl and add 1 tsp. salt and 4 grinds pepper.

2 Whisk the vinegar until the salt has dissolved. Whisk in the vegetable and olive oil a tablespoon at a time to emulsify and thicken the dressing.

3 Taste and add more seasoning as necessary. Serve immediately.

VARIATION
MUSTARD DRESSING
Add 1 tsp. Dijon mustard to the vinegar at step 1 and continue making the dressing as above. This dressing is thicker than Basic Vinaigrette because the mustard is a good emulsifier.

NOTES FOR FOOD ALLERGY SUFFERERS

DAIRY-FREE DIET: Basic Vinaigrette (page 81) and Mayonnaise (opposite) are dairy free. Avoid salad dressings that are enriched and thickened with cream. Mayonnaise provides a good rich, creamy dairy-free base for cold sauces and dips (see page 84).

GLUTEN-FREE DIET: Although store-bought salad dressings and mayonnaise often contain wheat flour to thicken and stabilize them, their homemade equivalents are suitable for gluten-free diets.

EGG-FREE DIET: Although Basic Vinaigrette (page 81) is suitable for egg-free diets, mayonnaise is not, because egg yolk is a core ingredient. Egg-free alternatives to mayonnaise include rich and creamy Horseradish Cream and Mustard Cream Dressing (see page 85) or ready-made egg-free mayonnaise, available from health food stores.

NUT-FREE DIET: Avoid salad dressings made with nut oils and use olive oil or nut-free neutral-flavored oils to make homemade vinaigrettes. Mayonnaise is made with neutral-flavored oil or a half and half mixture of neutral oil and olive oil.

SOY-FREE DIET: Avoid using neutral-flavored oils that contain soybean oil when making salad dressings and mayonnaise.

MAKING MAYONNAISE

Homemade mayonnaise is thick, yellow, glossy, and bears little resemblance to manufactured mayonnaise. It is greatly superior in flavor and is not hard to make, provided a few basic rules are followed.

Homemade mayonnaise is free of gluten, dairy products, and nut oils but cannot be made without egg yolk, which forms a stable emulsion between the oil, vinegar, and lemon juice. The egg yolk also contributes to the creamy consistency and rich flavor. However, mayonnaise can be replaced successfully with egg-free thick natural yogurt, sour cream, or dairy-free natural soy yogurt in dips and sauces.

GENERAL RULES FOR MAKING MAYONNAISE

- Mayonnaise is made with raw egg yolks that could contain salmonella bacteria. To reduce the risk of food poisoning, use very fresh eggs and store homemade mayonnaise in the refrigerator for no more than 2 days. It is also best to avoid serving homemade mayonnaise to pregnant women, small children, or the very old, because they are the most at risk of contracting salmonella poisoning.
- Make mayonnaise with ingredients that are at room temperature.
- Because mayonnaise is delicately flavored, it is easy to overflavor with lemon juice, vinegar, and seasoning. As the mayonnaise is being made, taste it before adding the full quantity of these ingredients. If the mayonnaise tastes too acidic, use water instead of more vinegar and lemon juice. Add half a pinch of salt and a grind of pepper at a time to avoid overseasoning.

MAYONNAISE

The delicate flavor of mayonnaise is delicious as it is, or flavored with other ingredients (see Mayonnaise-Based Dips and Sauces, page 84). Serve with French fries, cold seafood or chicken, or poached salmon, with salads, and spread in sandwiches. Mayonnaise is not suitable for egg-free diets. **Makes 1¼ cups/290 ml, to serve 4–6**

INGREDIENTS

2 large egg yolks, at room temperature

½ tsp. salt and freshly ground black pepper

½ tsp. Dijon mustard

1 Tbsp. white wine vinegar

1¼ cups/290 ml sunflower or corn oil or half olive oil, half vegetable oil

a squeeze of lemon juice (optional)

1 Combine the egg yolks, a pinch of salt, 2 grinds of pepper, the mustard, and half the vinegar in a bowl and beat with a wooden spoon.

2 To incorporate oil into the egg mixture without it curdling, add the oil very slowly at first, drop by drop, from the prongs of a fork. Stir vigorously after each addition of oil until it can no longer be seen on the surface or around the sides of the bowl. Continue in this way until the mayonnaise mixture begins to thicken. This stage should take about 5 minutes. (Do not add the oil too quickly or the mayonnaise will curdle.)

3 As the mayonnaise begins to thicken, start to add the oil a teaspoon at a time, beating the mixture continuously.

4 When half of the oil is incorporated, add 1 tsp. of the remaining vinegar to prevent the mayonnaise from curdling or becoming too oily.

5 Continue adding the oil a tablespoon at a time, beating well in between. If the mayonnaise starts to look greasy, taste it. Depending on its flavor, add the remaining vinegar or 1 tsp. water.

6 Once all the oil is incorporated, the mayonnaise should be glossy and thick enough to hold Its own shape. Taste. If the mayonnaise is bland, stir in a squeeze of lemon and a little more seasoning. Use as required or cover and store in the refrigerator for up to 2 days.

MAYONNAISE-BASED DIPS AND SAUCES

The recipe for mayonnaise provides a gluten-, dairy-, nut-, and soy-free rich and creamy base for a wide variety of sauces and dips. For egg-free diets, substitute mayonnaise with sour cream, plain Greek yogurt, or soy yogurt. Because the following sauces and dips contain mayonnaise, they must be eaten fresh or kept for no longer than 2 days in the refrigerator to reduce the risk of salmonella poisoning.

GARLIC MAYONNAISE
Follow the main recipe for mayonnaise, stirring 2 finely crushed garlic cloves into the finished recipe. Serve as a dipping sauce with crudités, cold cooked shrimp, deep-fried battered or breaded vegetables, chicken, or fish.

TARTAR SAUCE
Stir 1 tsp. Dijon mustard, 2 tsp. finely chopped onion, 2 finely chopped pickled gherkins, 2 tsp. rinsed and drained capers, and 1 tsp. each finely chopped parsley and finely chopped tarragon into 1¼ cups/290 ml mayonnaise. Taste and season as necessary with salt and black pepper. Serve with fish.

ANCHOVY MAYONNAISE
Stir 2 finely crushed garlic cloves, 6 anchovy fillets, mashed with a fork, and 1 Tbsp. lemon juice into 1¼ cups/290 ml mayonnaise. Serve with steamed asparagus spears, warm or cold poached or grilled fish, shellfish, and chicken.

CURRIED MAYONNAISE
Stir 1 finely crushed garlic clove, 1 tsp. Madras curry powder (for gluten-free diets check for wheat flour in the curry powder), 1 Tbsp. lemon juice, 2 teaspoons mango chutney (check label for nuts), salt, and pepper into 1¼ cups/290 ml mayonnaise. Serve with cold chicken, sliced raw vegetables, new potatoes, French fries, or bread sticks.

AVOCADO AND WATERCRESS DIP

This light green, creamy and slightly peppery sauce is wonderful served with cold poached salmon and new potatoes or as a dip for sliced raw vegetables, slices of toasted pitta bread, or tortilla chips. **Serves 4 as a sauce and 6 as a dip**

INGREDIENTS

1 large handful watercress

1 avocado, peeled and pitted

1 Tbsp. lemon juice, plus more as needed

1 garlic clove, crushed

salt and freshly ground black pepper

⅔ cup/150 ml mayonnaise

● EGG   sour cream

1 Boil some water in a small pan, add the watercress, and boil for 30 seconds; Place immediately under cold running water until cold. Drain well.

2 Blend the watercress, avocado, lemon juice, garlic, and seasoning together until smooth.

3 Stir in the mayonnaise and taste. If necessary, season with a little more salt, pepper, and lemon juice.

4 Serve or store covered in the refrigerator for up to 4 hours. If kept for longer, the avocado in the sauce will discolor.

HORSERADISH CREAM

This is not suitable for dairy-free diets. Sweet but sharp horseradish cream is an interesting and delicious egg-free alternative to mayonnaise to accompany cold fish and meat. **Serves 4**

INGREDIENTS

⅔ cup/150 ml fresh whipping cream

2 tsp. prepared or freshly grated horseradish

2 tsp. white wine vinegar

1 tsp. Dijon mustard

1 tsp. sugar

salt and freshly ground black pepper

1 Combine all the ingredients in a bowl and whisk together until the cream just holds its shape. Do not overwhip or the sauce will curdle.

2 To thin the sauce down to heavy-cream consistency for salad dressing, add 2 Tbsp. cold water and whisk.

MUSTARD CREAM DRESSING

This is not suitable for dairy-free diets. This sauce can be served thick, as an egg-free alternative to mayonnaise, or thinned with water to the consistency of heavy cream and used as a creamy salad dressing. **Serves 4 as a sauce and 6 as dressing**

INGREDIENTS

1¼ cups/290 ml whipping cream

4 tsp. Dijon mustard

2 tsp. superfine sugar

salt and freshly ground black pepper

Combine all the ingredients in a bowl and whisk together until the cream just holds its shape. Do not overwhip or the sauce will curdle. If the sauce becomes too thick, stir in a tablespoon of water at a time, to thin it to the required consistency.

Chapter 10 | FRYING

Frying—cooking food in hot oil—is a method mainly used to cook delicate or tender foods quickly before they become tough and dry. There are three main methods of frying: pan-frying, stir-frying, and deep-frying.

PAN-FRYING

Pan-frying is a method used to cook thin portions, slices, strips, and diced tender meat, poultry, fish, vegetables, and fruit in a small quantity of hot oil. Pan-frying is also used to cook, brown, and crisp the surface of ground and shaped foods such as sausages, burgers, and fish cakes. Larger or tougher cuts of meat, whole fish, and whole or jointed birds are also pan-fried over a high heat to brown them before stewing, braising, poaching, roasting, or baking, to add color and a rich flavor to the finished dish.

OILS AND FATS USED FOR PAN-FRYING

Both neutral-flavored oils, which tend to be stable at high temperatures, and more flavorful but less heat-stable fats and oils, are used for pan-frying. Neutral-flavored oils are used where the flavor of oil is unwanted. The best neutral-flavored oils for frying are sunflower oil, safflower oil, canola oil, corn oil, and vegetable oil (Note: this may contain soybean oil or peanut oil).

Fats and oils with flavor are used to add depth and complexity to a dish. Flavorful fats and oils used for pan-frying include butter, beef drippings, bacon fat, olive oil, sesame oil, and nut oils. Because flavorful oils and fats tend to burn at temperatures too low to fry effectively, they are usually mixed with an equal quantity of a neutral-flavored oil to increase their stability at high temperatures. Pure beef drippings is an exception—it can be used alone for frying and is ideal for browning beef for stewing. Butter and olive oil can be used on their own, but only to fry delicate foods that require very gentle frying or very little browning.

GENERAL RULES FOR PAN-FRYING AND BROWNING

- Use a wide, shallow, heavy-bottomed pan.
- The oil should be hot enough to make the food sizzle as it is added to the pan. If the oil is too cool, the food is liable to boil in its own juices and overcook before it is browned properly.
- When butter is added to oil, the oil is hot enough for frying and browning when the butter starts to foam.
- Season food with salt and pepper just before frying. Salting food too early will draw the juices out of it, making the surface wet and difficult to brown.
- Do not overcrowd the pan because the oil will cool down causing the food to boil in its own juices and not brown.
- Meat, poultry, and fish tend to stick to the bottom of the pan in the initial stages of pan-frying. Providing the oil is sufficiently hot, the food will release itself when it is fully browned after 2–5 minutes. Do not attempt to pry the meat, fish, or poultry off

the bottom of the pan because you will break the surface of the food. Turn the food once it has released itself.

- Do not cover frying food with a lid or the resulting steam will cause it to boil, toughen, and fail to brown.
- Once the food is evenly browned on all sides and cooked to your requirements, remove it from the pan to prevent it from cooking further. Keep it warm in a low oven while any remaining food is fried or a pan sauce is prepared.
- When you are frying a large volume of food, fry the food in batches. Loosen the browned cooking juices after frying each batch to prevent a build-up of juices on the bottom of the pan, because they are likely to burn with prolonged cooking and affect the flavor of your food.
- Tender strips or dice of meat, poultry, or fish should be no less than 1 in./2.5 cm thick and uniform in size so that they brown and cook at the same rate and remain moist in the center. Smaller pieces will overcook and toughen.

NOTES FOR FOOD ALLERGY SUFFERERS

DAIRY-FREE DIET: Butter used in fried savory dishes can be replaced with olive oil or neutral-flavored oil. However, when butter is used to flavor sweet dishes, it is not so easily substituted, because the dish tastes oily made with oil or dairy-free margarine.

Be aware that ghee is often used to fry food in Indian dishes. Ghee, or clarified butter, is made by removing the milk proteins in melted butter to leave pure butterfat, which has a rich, buttery flavor and is stable at high temperatures. Although the flavor of the dish will not be so rich, replace ghee with an equal quantity of a suitable frying oil, such as vegetable or sunflower oil.

GLUTEN-FREE DIET: Although all oils and fats are suitable for gluten-free diets, meat, fish, poultry, and vegetables are sometimes coated in seasoned flour or egg and bread crumbs before pan-frying. Often meat and poultry are also coated in flour and browned before stewing, to add color and flavor and to thicken the stew. In place of wheat flour, use cornstarch.

NUT-FREE DIET: Peanut oil is often used in Asian cooking for frying at high temperatures. Replace with a suitable neutral oil, such as sunflower or corn oil. Read the label before using vegetable oil because it sometimes contains peanut oil. Also be aware that seed oils, such as sunflower, safflower, and sesame oil, sometimes do not suit people with nut allergies.

Nut oils, such as walnut and hazelnut, are sometimes added to neutral oils to add their characteristic flavor to pan-fried dishes. Instead, use a neutral-flavored oil only or flavor the oil with butter or olive oil instead. The shortfall in flavor can be made up using more strongly flavored ingredients, such as garlic, ginger, and cilantro.

SOY-FREE DIET: Vegetable oil usually consists of a blend of soybean oil and other vegetable oils. Current regulations do not require manufacturers to list soybean oil on the ingredients list because it is believed to be totally safe for people with soy allergies. This is because the protein that causes soy allergy is filtered out of the oil during processing. You may still choose to use alternative neutral-flavored oils instead such as sunflower oil, canola oil, or corn oil.

CRISPY FILLET OF SEA BASS

A simple and delicious way to cook sea bass, this method is also suitable for other firm-fleshed white fish, such as cod, haddock, turbot, and halibut, and oily fish, such as salmon and mackerel. Serve with boiled new potatoes tossed in olive oil and sea salt or Oven-Baked Fries (page 136) and steamed green beans. **Serves 4**

INGREDIENTS

2 Tbsp. olive oil

4 sea bass fillets, with skin intact and scaled

salt and freshly ground black pepper

4 lemon wedges

1 Heat the olive oil in a heavy frying pan over medium heat. Season the skin of each fillet and place skin side down in the pan. The oil should sizzle when the fish is added to the pan. If it is not hot enough, wait for a few moments before trying again.

2 As the fish starts to fry, the skin will stick to the bottom of the pan. Do not attempt to loosen it because this will damage the skin or break up the fillet. As the skin becomes crisp and brown, it will free itself from the bottom of the pan.

3 Turn the fish and fry for 1 minute on the flesh side. The fish is cooked when the flesh feels firm, but remains slightly translucent in the thickest part of the fillet.

4 Serve the fish immediately, skin side up, and garnished with a lemon wedge.

SALMON FISH CAKES WITH TARTAR SAUCE AND LEMON

Fish cakes are great for a starter or an informal meal. They are also easily adapted to suit egg-free, gluten-free, and dairy-free diets. If eggs are off limits, serve these fish cakes with Parsley Sauce (page 74). **Serves 4**

INGREDIENTS

14 oz./400 g peeled potatoes, diced

1 lb./450 g salmon fillet with the skin left on

2½ cups/570 ml milk, plus more as needed

● DAIRY ▸ soy milk

1 bay leaf

2 slices onion

salt and freshly ground black pepper

2 Tbsp./30 g butter

● DAIRY ▸ 2 Tbsp. olive oil

1 egg, beaten

● EGG ▸ 1 Tbsp. poaching milk and 1 Tbsp. bread crumbs

2 scallions, finely sliced

1½ tsp. each chopped dill, parsley, and tarragon

1½ cups/140 g dried white bread crumbs

● GLUTEN ▸ gluten-free bread crumbs

¼ cup sunflower or corn oil for frying

TO SERVE

4 lemon wedges

Tartar Sauce (page 84)

1 Simmer the potatoes in boiling salted water for 20 minutes, or until tender.

2 Place the salmon, skin side down, in a frying pan. Pour the milk over the fillets. If the fillets are exposed, add extra milk or water to cover. Add the bay leaf, onion, and seasoning. Bring the milk slowly to a simmer and gently poach the fish for about 10 minutes, or until it is just cooked. Reserve the poaching liquid, and allow the fish to cool.

3 Meanwhile, mash the potatoes with ½ cup/100 ml of the poaching milk and the butter.

4 Separate the flakes of salmon and mix with the mashed potatoes, the egg (or the milk and bread crumbs), scallions, and herbs. The consistency should be soft but firm enough to hold its shape. Add 1–2 Tbsp. poaching milk if the mixture is too stiff. Taste and add more seasoning, if necessary.

5 Wet your hands to prevent the mixture from sticking to them and shape the mixture into eight round, flat cakes no more than 1 in./2.5 cm thick.

6 Press the fish cakes into the bread crumbs and brush off any loose crumbs.

7 Heat the oil in the frying pan over medium heat. When the oil is hot, place four fish cakes at a time into the pan and fry until golden brown on both sides. Remove from the pan and keep warm in a low oven while the remaining fish cakes are cooked.

8 Place two fish cakes in the center of each plate with a lemon wedge. Serve the tartar sauce separately in a bowl.

DUCK BREASTS WITH BRAISED LENTILS

These richly flavored braised lentils are an interesting hearty accompaniment to duck, other game, chicken, pork, and pan-fried white fish. Duck breasts have a thick layer of fat below the skin and do not require any additional cooking oil or fat for pan-frying. This dish is delicious served with Mashed Potatoes (page 136) and steamed green vegetables. **Serves 4**

INGREDIENTS

4 duck breasts, skin on

FOR THE SAUCE

● GLUTEN

1 Tbsp. all-purpose flour

1½ tsp. cornstarch

½ cup/100 ml red wine

1¼ cups/290 ml chicken stock

1 sprig thyme

salt and freshly ground black pepper

FOR THE LENTILS

1 Tbsp. sunflower or corn oil

4 slices smoked bacon, thinly sliced

1 onion, cut into small dice

1 carrot, finely diced

1 celery rib, finely diced

2 sprigs thyme

salt and freshly ground black pepper

1 large garlic clove, finely chopped

8 oz./200 g Puy lentils

2 bay leaves

½ cup/100 ml red wine

2½ cups/570 ml rich stock, made with 1¼ cups/290 ml jellied White Chicken Stock (page 64) and 1¼ cups/290 ml water, or more as needed

1 First make the lentils. Heat the oil in a medium-sized saucepan, and add the bacon, onion, carrot, celery, thyme, and a little seasoning. Cover with a lid and fry gently until very soft and sweet, 20–30 minutes.

2 Add the garlic and cook for 30 seconds, stirring continuously. Add the lentils, bay leaves, red wine, and stock. The lentils should be covered by an inch of liquid, so top up with a little water, if necessary. Bring to a simmer over medium heat and simmer, uncovered, for 30–45 minutes, until tender. Spoon off any fat or scum that collects on the surface and, if necessary, top up with water so the lentils remain covered.

3 Meanwhile, prepare the duck breasts. With a small sharp knife, score through the fatty skin, with diagonal cuts ½ in./1.25 cm apart and then again in the opposite direction to form a diamond pattern. Take care not to cut into the meat below.

4 Sprinkle the skin with salt and rub into the scored fat. This helps to draw the water out of the duck fat and encourages the skin to become crisp and golden brown.

5 Place a dry heavy frying pan over medium heat. When the pan is hot enough to make the duck breasts sizzle, place them well apart, skin side down, in the pan. Fry the breasts gently until the fat under the skin has melted into the pan and the skin is brown and crisp.

6 After approximately 10 minutes, the duck skin should be crisp and golden brown. Lightly season the skin with salt and pepper before turning the duck breasts over.

7 Gently brown the lean side for 8 minutes, by which time the duck breasts should be cooked medium-rare (moist and rosy pink in the center). If the duck breasts are well browned, but still very rare in the center, fry very gently for another minute or so on both sides. Place the duck breasts in a low oven while you repeat the process with the remaining two.

8 Once all the duck breasts are cooked, make the sauce. Pour out the fat and place the pan over medium heat. Stir in the flour and slowly add the wine to form a smooth sauce. Pour in the chicken stock, add the thyme, and loosen the browned cooking juices on the bottom of the pan with a wooden spoon. Boil the sauce until it is reduced by half, or evenly coats the back of a spoon. Remove the sprig of thyme, taste, and season as necessary. Keep warm over low heat.

9 Once the lentils are cooked, taste and season as necessary.

10 To serve, place a spoonful of lentils in the center of the plate, cut the duck breast in thick slices, on the diagonal, and arrange on top. Spoon over the sauce and serve immediately.

BEEF BURGERS WITH TOMATO AND CORN SALSA

Homemade beef burgers make a delicious, nutritious, and popular lunch for children and the whole family. Place the cooked burgers in soft, warmed buns (see gluten-free rolls, page 186) with the salsa, store-bought or homemade mayonnaise (page 83), and lettuce. **Serves 4 to 8**

FOR THE BURGERS

1 ½ lb./675 g good-quality lean, ground beef

½ onion, finely diced

2 tsp. dried Italian seasoning herbs

1 Tbsp. Worcestershire sauce

● GLUTEN — omit because it contains gluten

1 tsp. salt and freshly ground black pepper

sunflower or corn oil for frying

FOR THE TOMATO AND CORN SALSA

2 Tbsp. frozen or canned corn

4 ripe tomatoes, seeded and diced

½ small red onion, finely diced

1 Tbsp. freshly chopped cilantro leaves

1 Tbsp. freshly squeezed lime juice

½ tsp. salt and 3 grinds black pepper

First make the salsa. Stir all the salsa ingredients together in a bowl until thoroughly mixed. Cover with plastic wrap and store in the refrigerator. The salsa has a better flavor if made a few hours or a day before serving. Remove from the refrigerator 30 minutes before serving.

2 Preheat the oven to 250°F/120°C/gas mark ½.

3 To make the burgers, combine all the burger ingredients, except the oil, together in a bowl until well mixed. To test the burgers for flavor, fry a spoonful of the mixture in a little oil until cooked through, then taste. Add more seasoning and Worcestershire sauce as necessary.

4 With wet hands, shape the mixture into eight flat rounds ¾ in./2 cm thick, with a circumference roughly the same as the buns.

5 Heat 3 Tbsp. oil in a large frying pan over medium heat. When the oil is hot enough to make a spoonful of the mixture sizzle, place the burgers in the pan. Do not overcrowd the pan—cook in two batches if necessary.

6 Brown for 2–2½ minutes each side for rare to medium-rare burgers and 3–4 minutes on each side for medium to well done.

7 As the burgers are cooking, warm the buns in the preheated oven on a baking sheet.

8 To serve, split the warmed rolls in half, spread generously with mayonnaise (if using), arrange some lettuce on top, place the burgers on the lettuce, spoon some corn and tomato salsa over each burger, and cover with the top half of the buns.

FILLET STEAK WITH RED WINE SAUCE

This recipe uses fillet steak but sirloin or rump are just as suitable. Ask the butcher to cut fillet steak into 1½-inch-thick/4-cm portions so that they can be cooked to a deep brown on the outside and remain pink, moist and tender in the center. **Serves 4**

FOR THE STEAK

4 (1½-inch-thick/4-cm) fillet (tenderloin) steaks, at room temperature

salt and freshly ground black pepper

2 Tbsp. sunflower or corn oil

2 Tbsp./30 g butter or 1 Tbsp. oil

FOR THE SAUCE

Red Wine Sauce with Shallots and Mushrooms (page 78)

Lightly season the steaks on both sides.

2 Heat the oil and butter in a heavy frying pan over high heat. When the butter starts to foam, add the steak to the pan. (For rare steak use oil only because it can be heated to a higher temperature for rapid browning.) Do not overcrowd the pan.

3 As the steak starts to fry, it sticks to the bottom of the pan. Do not attempt to loosen the steak because this will prevent it browning. As the steak browns, it will gradually free itself. When it does, turn it and brown the other side. Fillet steak ideally should be served rare to medium-rare, to take full advantage of its meltingly tender qualities. If you prefer it medium or well done, see box below. Keep the steaks warm in an oven set at its lowest temperature, while the sauce is finished.

4 Pour any remaining oil out of the pan, pour in the sauce and bring to a boil, scraping the bottom of the pan to loosen the browned steak juices. Spoon the sauce over the steaks and serve immediately.

COOKING FILLET STEAK

RARE
• Fry for 2–3 minutes per side. Rare steak feels soft and gives easily when pressed.

MEDIUM
• Fry for 3–3½ minutes per side. Medium steak feels firmer but gives a little under the fingers when pressed.

WELL DONE
• Fry for 4–5 minutes per side. Well-done steak is firm and does not give when pressed.

Sirloin and rump steak
These steaks are slightly tougher than fillet steak so are usually cooked in thinner slices; reduce the cooking times given above by 30 seconds on each side.

HOMEMADE PORK AND APPLE SAUSAGES WITH RICH ONION GRAVY

Unlike many store-bought varieties, these sausages are egg-, dairy-, nut-, and soy-free. They can also be adaped easily for gluten-free diets. **Makes 8 sausages**

FOR THE SAUSAGES

1 lb./450 g ground pork

½ onion, very finely diced

½ Granny Smith apple, peeled, quartered, cored, and coarsely grated

2 Tbsp. fine white bread crumbs

● GLUTEN gluten-free bread crumbs

1 Tbsp. finely chopped leaves of fresh thyme, sage, and curly parsley

½ garlic clove, crushed

1 tsp. salt and 5 grinds freshly ground black pepper

sunflower or corn oil for frying

FOR THE ONION GRAVY

½ onion, finely sliced

salt and freshly ground black pepper

2 tsp. all-purpose flour

● GLUTEN 1 tsp. cornstarch

1¼ cups/290 ml Brown Chicken Stock (page 64)

1 Tbsp. red wine

1 sprig fresh thyme

1 Preheat the oven to its lowest setting.

2 Place all the sausage ingredients, except for the oil, in a bowl and mix together thoroughly with your hands.

3 Divide the sausage mixture into four and, with wet hands, shape the

quartered mixture into eight even-sized sausages no thicker than 1 in./2.5 cm. (If the sausages are thicker, they may start to dry out and crumble before the center is properly cooked.)

4 Gently fry the sausages in hot oil, turning them frequently until they are cooked through and golden brown all over, about 15 minutes. Do not crowd the pan because the sausages will be hard to turn and may fall apart. If the sausages stick to the pan, allow them to release themselves or they may break as you try to loosen them.

5 Transfer the cooked sausages to a baking sheet and keep warm in the oven while you make the sauce.

6 Pour out all except 1 tablespoon of hot fat from the frying pan, add the sliced onion and some seasoning, cover, and fry gently, until very soft. Remove the lid and continue to fry the onion, stirring continuously, until golden brown.

7 Stir the flour into the onion and gently cook for another 30 seconds.

8 Remove the pan from the heat and gradually stir in the stock and wine, to make a smooth sauce. Add the thyme and simmer over medium heat until the sauce is thick enough to thinly coat the back of a spoon. Taste and season as necessary.

9 To serve, place the sausages on warm plates and spoon over the onion gravy.

STIR-FRYING

This frying method is commonly used in Asian cooking. Shellfish, crisp vegetables, firm fish, tender poultry and meat, noodles, or rice are quickly fried in a few tablespoons of oil over very high heat until just cooked through. To prevent food from sticking or cooking unevenly, it is stirred continuously with a wooden spoon. Although a large frying pan is perfectly suitable for stir-frying, a wok is traditionally used because its narrow base and high, rounded sides allow the flames to hug the sides of the pan. This allows the food to cook on the sides and bottom as it is stirred. The high sides also help to prevent food from escaping as it is stirred.

Stir-frying is not suitable for food that easily falls apart when cooked, such as potatoes and many varieties of fish. Shrimp are ideal for stir-frying and the most suitable fish include firm-fleshed fish, such as tuna and monkfish. The best poultry and meats for stir-frying include chicken or turkey breast, and pork or beef tenderloin.

GENERAL RULES FOR STIR-FRYING

- Use a wok or large frying pan so that the frying food can be stirred and tossed around.
- Make sure the oil is almost smoking before adding your ingredients. The ingredients should sizzle noisily when they are added to the pan.
- Ingredients must be added to the wok in a particular order so they are just cooked through when served. First add the ingredients that require longer or thorough cooking, such as hard vegetables and meat, poultry, and fish. Once the first batch of ingredients is heated through, add more delicate ingredients, such as garlic, ginger, and vegetables that are more likely to wilt or burn in the hot oil if cooked for too long. Cooked noodles and rice are added last to briefly warm them through, because they break up when overcooked.
- When the ingredients are almost cooked, water, stock, soy sauce, and other flavoring ingredients are added to the pan to make a sauce. Cornstarch is often added to a stir-fry sauce to thicken it to a syrupy consistency just before serving.

NOTES FOR FOOD ALLERGY SUFFERERS

DAIRY-FREE DIET: Stir-fries rarely contain dairy products.

GLUTEN-FREE DIET: Soy sauce and wheat noodles contain gluten. Replace soy sauce with tamari sauce, which is wheat free, and wheat noodles with rice noodles.

EGG-FREE DIET: Egg is sometimes added to stir-fried dishes but can be omitted easily from a recipe.

NUT-FREE DIET: Peanut oil is often used for stir-frying. Vegetable oil may also contain peanut oil so always read the label. Seed oils, including sunflower, safflower, and sesame oil, are also sometimes not suitable for people with nut allergies. Replace these oils with another suitable neutral oil, such as canola or corn oil.

SOY-FREE DIET: Vegetable oil either contains 100 percent soybean oil or a blend of vegetable oils. Other suitable oils include sunflower oil or canola oil.

Soy sauce or tamari sauce, often used to add a salty sweet flavor to stir-fries, can be replaced to a certain degree with salt, dark brown sugar, stock, and thorough browning (see page 58).

SINGAPORE STIR-FRIED NOODLES

Once the ingredients are prepared this dish does not take long to cook. It is delicious served on its own or with stir-fried greens. **Serves 4**

INGREDIENTS

● EGG
● GLUTEN

12 oz./320 g fine egg and wheat noodles
rice noodles
rice noodles

¼ cup sunflower or corn oil

4 oz./110 g smoked bacon, cut across into thin strips

4 oz./110 g shiitake mushrooms, finely sliced

1 cup/110 g cooked chicken or pork, sliced into thin strips

4 oz./110 g peeled shrimp

2 large garlic cloves, finely chopped

1 Tbsp. finely chopped ginger

1 Tbsp. Madras curry powder
● GLUTEN check label for wheat

1 Tbsp. sugar

1–2 fresh red chiles, seeded and finely sliced lengthwise into strips

1 celery rib, finely chopped

4 oz./110 g bean sprouts (soy sprouts)
● SOY mung bean sprouts or omit and use 1 more celery rib for crunch

2 Tbsp. soy sauce
● GLUTEN tamari sauce
● SOY 1 tsp. salt, 2 tsp. dark brown sugar, and 2 Tbsp. Brown Chicken Stock (page 58)

2 Tbsp. sherry

1 cup/250 ml Chicken Stock (page 58)

salt and black pepper

6 scallions, finely sliced on the diagonal

2 Tbsp. roughly chopped cilantro leaves

1 Cook the noodles as directed on the package. Cool under running water and toss in 2 tablespoons of the oil.

2 Heat a large frying pan or wok over high heat and pour in the remaining 2 Tbsp. oil. When the oil is hot, add the bacon to the pan and fry until lightly browned. Add the mushrooms and chicken and fry, stirring continuously, until lightly browned.

3 Add the shrimp, garlic, ginger, curry powder, sugar, and chiles and stir-fry for 1 minute.

4 Turn the heat down to medium and add the celery, bean sprouts, soy sauce (tamari or salt, dark brown sugar, and stock), sherry, and stock. Bring the liquid ingredients to a simmer and warm the celery and bean sprouts through for 30 seconds, stirring continuously.

5 Add the drained noodles and toss all the ingredients until thoroughly mixed and the noodles are heated through. Do not overcook the noodles or they will break up.

6 Taste a little of the sauce and add salt and pepper as necessary.

7 Heap the noodles onto four plates, sprinkle with the scallions and cilantro leaves, and serve immediately.

STIR-FRIED SHRIMP WITH GARLIC, BLACK PEPPER, AND LIME

It is essential to use shell-on shrimp for this wonderful recipe, because the shells provide much of the flavor. As you peel the cooked shrimp the juices come off on your fingers, and it is almost a sin not to lick them. However, you may want to accompany each plate of shrimp with a finger bowl filled with warm water and a slice of lemon. Serves 4

INGREDIENTS

2 Tbsp. sunflower or corn oil

1 lb./400 g fresh, uncooked, shell-on large shrimp (approximately 8 per person)

salt and finely ground black pepper

3 garlic cloves, finely chopped

juice of 2 limes

1 tsp. sugar

4 lime wedges

1 Heat the oil in a wok or large frying pan over high heat.

2 When the oil is hot, add the shrimp and season with salt and 4 grinds of black pepper. Fry the shrimp in batches, stirring continuously until they are pink all over. Cook the shrimp in batches and keep warm in a low oven as you cook the rest. Do not overcrowd the pan because the shrimp will boil in their own juices rather than fry.

3 When all the shrimp are cooked, return them to the pan and turn the heat down to medium. Add the garlic, lime juice, and sugar. Continue to fry gently, stirring continuously, for another minute.

4 Taste the cooking juices to check the seasoning and add more as necessary.

5 To serve, pile the shrimp and a wedge of lime on the plates, spoon over any juices, and serve immediately.

STIR-FRIED LEAFY GREENS

Stir-fried leafy greens are delicious eaten with Thai curries and other stir-fried dishes. They are also a great source of calcium, particularly for those on a dairy-free diet. Because this dish is cooked extremely quickly, and it needs to be served immediately from the wok to the table, it is ideal for cooking in front of your guests. **Serves 4**

INGREDIENTS

2 Tbsp. sunflower or corn oil

1 garlic clove, finely sliced

1-in./2.5-cm piece ginger, sliced into matchsticks

4 oz./110 g spinach leaves, washed and drained thoroughly

8 oz./200 g bok choy, washed and drained thoroughly

4 oz./110 g watercress, washed and drained thoroughly

4 Chinese cabbage leaves, sliced across into finger-sized strips

4 small scallions, finely sliced on the diagonal

2 Tbsp. light soy sauce

● GLUTEN

● SOY

tamari sauce

½ tsp. salt, 1 tsp. dark brown sugar, and 2 Tbsp. Brown Chicken Stock (page 58)

1 Gather and prepare all the ingredients for this recipe before you start cooking. Once you start, it is cooked in less than 2 minutes.

2 Heat the oil in the wok or frying pan over medium heat.

3 Gently fry the garlic and ginger for about 1 minute, or until lightly browned. Garlic tastes bitter if it is allowed to brown too deeply.

4 Add the prepared leaves and toss in the pan until they are just beginning to wilt.

5 Add the scallions and soy sauce (or tamari, or salt, sugar, and stock). Warm the scallions through for 30 seconds. Taste and season as necessary. Serve immediately.

VARIATION

STIR-FRIED VEGETABLES

Substitute 4 oz./110 g of one or a mixture of thinly sliced shiitake mushrooms or green pepper, trimmed green beans, purple sprouting broccoli, baby corn, or bean sprouts for the spinach.

DEEP-FRYING

Deep-frying in hot oil is a speedy method for cooking small pieces or portions of tender meat, poultry, delicate white fish, and vegetables. The food is cooked in neutral-flavored oil that can be heated to the high temperatures required for frying food quickly.

Deep-frying is an ideal method for delicate foods that become dry and tough with prolonged cooking, because the food is usually first coated in batter or egg and bread crumbs, which protects it from the intense heat of the oil. The batter or bread crumb coating forms a barrier between the hot oil and the delicate food and seals in the cooking juices, keeping the food moist and tender. The coating also becomes crisp and golden brown, providing contrast in flavor, texture, and color to the moist, uncolored food inside.

BATTERS

Batters are made from seasoned flour mixed with liquids such as water, milk, lager, or beaten egg. The lightest batters are made with self-rising flour mixed with sparkling water or lager. The water or beer lightly binds the flour grains together and activates the rising agents in the flour to produce bubbles. The bubbles produced by the rising agents and present in the liquid aerate and lighten the mixture. As the batter cooks in the hot oil, the liquid boils away, leaving a crisp golden shell around the food.

BREAD CRUMB COATINGS

Bread crumbs are used to form a crisp, deep golden crust around delicate foods, such as poultry and white fish. The food is first dipped in seasoned flour, then into beaten egg, and then into fresh or dried bread crumbs. The flour prevents the egg from running off the food. Egg binds the bread crumbs to the food and sets as the food is cooked to seal in the cooking juices. The bread crumbs become crisp and golden in the hot oil, adding texture, flavor, and color to the food.

GENERAL RULES FOR DEEP-FRYING

- Use vegetable, sunflower, or corn oil for deep-frying because they can be heated to 350°F/180°C without smoking, the ideal temperature for deep-frying.
- Oil expands when it is heated so do not overfill the pan. The pan should be no more than a third full when cold.
- Heat the oil over medium heat to 350°F/180°C. If you do not have a thermometer, carefully lower a small piece of bread into the oil and time how long it takes to turn crisp and golden brown. If the oil has reached 350°F/180°C, the bread will turn golden brown in 40 seconds. If the bread takes longer to color, then the oil is not hot enough; if it takes less time the oil is becoming dangerously hot. To reduce the temperature of hot oil, turn off the heat source and carefully add a handful of torn bread. Remove when browned. Then, after a few minutes, test the temperature of the oil with another piece of bread.
- Food for deep-frying should be dry. Wet food will cause the oil to spit, which could cause burns.
- Coat food in batter or bread crumbs just before frying or the coating will be soggy and greasy.
- Deep-fry food in small batches to prevent it from sticking together and reducing the temperature of the oil. If the oil is not hot enough, the food will be greasy and pale.

Safety note

Never leave a pan of hot oil unattended. If the oil becomes too hot, it will start to smoke before bursting into flames. If this happens, turn off the heat and smother the flames with a fire blanket or a close-fitting pan lid. Do not pour water onto the oil because this is likely to spread the fire.

- Deep-fried food is cooked when it is crisp, golden, and floats on the surface. Uncooked food contains a high proportion of water and sinks to the bottom of the pan. As it cooks, the food loses moisture and rises to the surface.
- Once the food is cooked, lift it out of the pan with a slotted metal spoon. Place on absorbent paper towels to remove excess oil. Lightly sprinkle the food with fine salt to improve its flavor and to draw out the oil.
- To keep fried food warm while other batches are cooking, arrange in a single layer on a baking sheet, and place in a warm oven with the door ajar to allow air to circulate.

NOTES FOR FOOD ALLERGY SUFFERERS

DAIRY-FREE DIET: Cows' milk is sometimes used to make soft, tender batters. Use soy milk or use water or beer instead, for a lighter, crisper batter. Bread crumb coatings are ideal for dairy-free diets provided the bread crumbs do not contain traces of milk. Always read the label on bread before using.

GLUTEN-FREE DIET: Wheat flour in a batter can be replaced with a specific blend of rice flour, cornstarch, tapioca flour, and baking powder given in the recipes in this section. Rice flour provides body, cornstarch provides lightness, and tapioca flour—mixed with liquid—provides the binding power to adhere the batter to the food. Avoid using beer or lager in batter because both are made with barley malt, which contains gluten. Japanese tempura batter, which provides a delicate, crisp shell, is ideal for gluten-free diets because it is made with cornstarch and sparkling water. For a bread crumb coating, use gluten-free rice flour and gluten-free bread crumbs in place of wheat flour and bread crumbs.

EGG-FREE DIET: Egg is often used in batter because it binds and sets the batter around the food. Opt for a light batter made from flour and water or beer. Foods are often dipped in egg before being crumbed, but this is unnecessary if you use very fresh fish and poultry. Simply dip it directly into very fine fresh bread crumbs. The crumb coating will not be as even or as dense but will stick sufficiently to the food to form a light, crisp coating.

NUT-FREE DIET: Peanut oil is commonly used for deep-frying in Asian cooking but can be replaced with other neutral-flavored oils, including sunflower, canola, and corn oil. Avoid Arachis oil because this is also made from peanuts. Homemade batter is suitable provided it is made with nut-free flour. Bread crumb coatings are ideal for nut-free diets, provided the bread crumbs do not contain traces of nuts. Always read the label on bread before using.

SOY-FREE DIET: Vegetable oil is ideal for deep-frying but is usually 100 percent soybean oil or a blend of oils including soybean oil and sometimes peanut oil. Replace it with other neutral-flavored oils, such as sunflower or corn oil. Homemade batter is suitable for soy-free diets, provided it is made with soy-free flour. Bread crumb coatings are ideal, provided the bread crumbs do not contain traces of soy. Always read the label on bread before using.

BATTERED COD

White fish, such as cod or haddock, taste their best in crisp, golden batter and make a great treat for a family supper. Serve with Oven-Baked Fries (page 136), Tartar Sauce (page 84), and a wedge of lemon. **Serves 4**

INGREDIENTS

sunflower or corn oil for deep-frying

4 (6 oz./170 g) boned and skinned cod or haddock fillets

4 lemon wedges

FOR THE BATTER

⅔ cup/150 ml sparkling water or lager (for a robust beery flavor)

● **GLUTEN**

1 egg white, made up to ⅔ cup/150 ml with sparkling water and whisked

1 cup/110 g self-rising flour, seasoned with salt and pepper

● **GLUTEN**

½ cup/55 g potato flour, ½ cup/55 g cornstarch, 1 tsp. gluten-free baking powder, salt, and pepper, sifted together

1 Fill a deep-fat fryer or large, heavy pan no more than one-third full of oil. Gently heat the oil over medium heat until it reaches 350°F/180°C (at which point, a cube of bread will fry to golden brown in 40 seconds). Maintain the oil at this temperature over low heat.

2 While the oil is heating, make the batter. Pour the water (or egg white and water) into a wide, shallow dish. Sift the seasoned flour onto the liquid, whisking continuously with a fork. The batter

should have the consistency of thick heavy cream. If it is too thin, add a little more flour; if it is too thick, add a little more water.

3 Turn the fish over in the batter until completely coated. Lift the battered fish above the bowl to allow excess batter to run off.

4 Lower the fish into the hot oil and fry until it floats to the surface and the batter is golden brown, for 6–8 minutes. Fry only one or two pieces of fish at a time. Do not overcrowd the pan.

5 Lift the fish out of the oil with a slotted spoon and place on a baking sheet covered with two layers of absorbent paper towels. Sprinkle lightly with salt. While you fry the remaining fish, keep the cooked fish warm in a low oven with the door ajar, to allow air to circulate around it so that it remains crisp. Don't cover deep-fried food or it becomes soggy.

6 To serve, place the battered fish on warm plates with a lemon wedge.

FRITTO MISTO DI MARE

Fried mixed seafood (shown above) is great as finger food for a party—with garlic mayonnaise, hot pepper dipping sauce, or soy sauce—or as a starter or informal lunch piled on plates with lemon wedges and lightly dressed green salad.

To serve 4, dip 4 oz./110 g each of large shrimp, thickly sliced calamari rings, whitebait, and finger-sized strips of sole and monkfish fillets into the batter (see opposite) and deep-fry until the fish floats to the surface. Drain on absorbent paper towels, lightly sprinkle with salt, and serve immediately.

VEGETABLE FRITTO MISTO

To make a delicious vegetable fritto misto, use a selection of the following: zucchini, sliced on the diagonal; small florets of broccoli and cauliflower; wide strips of red and green pepper; trimmed green beans; thin slices of eggplant, cut in half; trimmed spears of asparagus; onion wedges; and whole, small or thickly sliced large mushrooms. Serve with lemon wedges and Garlic Mayonnaise (page 84).

CRISPY FISH RIBBONS

Crunchy on the outside and tender and moist on the inside, Crispy Fish Ribbons make a delicious starter or finger food served with lemon wedges, Tartar Sauce (page 84), or Garlic Mayonnaise (page 84). In this recipe the fish is coated in flour, egg, and bread crumbs. For an egg-free version, simply omit the flour and egg and roll the fish in fine fresh bread crumbs only. A thin layer of bread crumbs will stick to the moist surface of the fish to form a light, crisp coating when deep-fried. Served with ketchup, they're also a great homemade alternative to fish fingers for children's parties. **Serves 4**

INGREDIENTS

sunflower or corn oil for deep-frying

1 lb./450 g skinned sole or plaice fillets, sliced across into finger-sized strips

2 Tbsp. all-purpose flour, seasoned with salt and pepper

● **GLUTEN** rice flour, seasoned with salt and pepper

EGG omit

2 eggs, beaten

● **EGG** omit

5 cups/225 g fine fresh or dried bread crumbs

● **GLUTEN** gluten-free bread crumbs

TO SERVE

4 lemon wedges

1 Fill a deep-fat fryer or large heavy pan no more than one-third full of oil. Heat the oil over low to medium heat until it reaches 350°F/180°C (at which point, a cube of bread will fry to golden brown in 40 seconds). Maintain the oil at this temperature over low heat.

2 Place the flour and bread crumbs on large plates and pour the eggs into a wide, shallow dish. Roll the pieces of fish in the seasoned flour. This will help the egg to stick to the fish.

3 Dip the floured fish into the beaten egg and then roll in the bread crumbs until evenly coated. Gently shake the breaded fish to remove any loose crumbs. For egg-free Crispy Fish Ribbons, roll the fish in bread crumbs only.

4 Gently slip a handful of crumbed fish into the hot oil and fry until the coating is crisp and golden brown, gently turning the pieces of fish over in the oil so they cook evenly. The fish ribbons are cooked when they float to the surface and are crisp and golden brown. Do not allow the ribbons to become too dark or the fish will overcook and become dry and tough.

5 Lift out of the oil with a slotted spoon onto a baking sheet covered with absorbent paper towels. Sprinkle with salt. Keep warm in a low oven with the door ajar so air can circulate around the fish.

6 Fry the remaining fish in the same way. Serve immediately, piled high on the plate with lemon wedges.

VARIATION

CRISPY CHICKEN RIBBONS
Slice boneless, skinless chicken breasts into strips, coat in bread crumbs and fry as above. Serve with lemon wedges and Garlic Mayonnaise (page 84).

Chapter 11

BROILING

Although broiling takes a little longer than frying—because the food is not in direct contact with the heat—it provides a simple, tasty cooking method for a wide variety of foods. Food is first brushed with oil, melted butter, or a marinade before being placed under the intense, dry heat of the broiler. Although neutral-flavored oils are suitable for broiling, butter and olive oil are more commonly used to moisten, baste, and enrich the flavor of broiled food.

Ideally, food for broiling should be no thicker than 1½ in./4 cm; any thicker and the surface of the food will be overbrowned before the center is cooked. Steak, pork and lamb chops, and sausages are delicious broiled. Flattened small birds, bone-in poultry parts, and breast fillets also broil beautifully, as do fish steaks, fish fillets, small whole fish, and shellfish. Whole fish are often slashed to allow the heat to reach the center of the fish before the skin blackens. Firm oily fish, such as tuna and salmon, are especially good for broiling, because they are slow to dry out under the hot broiler. White fish is more delicate and benefits from regular basting during cooking, to prevent it from becoming dry. Some vegetables, particularly eggplant, zucchini and tomato, broil very well when brushed with oil or butter.

Recipes using the broiling method are also perfect for broiling and barbecuing.

MARINADES

Delicate white fish, lean poultry, and tender cuts of meat that tend to dry out and toughen quickly when cooked are often marinated overnight in an oil-based marinade before broiling. Marinades made with olive oil or neutral-flavored oils help to retain moisture in the food, and are often used to baste the food while it broils.

GENERAL RULES FOR BROILING

- Preheat the broiler to its highest setting 10 minutes before broiling.
- Broiling time depends on the temperature of the heated broiler, the distance of the food from the broiler, the thickness of the food, and its temperature before it is cooked. To reduce the broiling time, remove chilled food from the refrigerator 30 minutes before broiling. The colder the food, the longer it takes for the heat to reach its center, and the greater the likelihood of it overbrowning before it is cooked through.

NOTES FOR FOOD ALLERGY SUFFERERS

Broiled food is prepared with very few added ingredients—butter or oil, or a marinade made from oil, wine, herbs, spices, or seasoning—and served simply in its cooking juices. Provided olive oil is used instead of butter for dairy-free diets and oils containing nuts or soy are avoided for nut-free and soya-free diets, broiled food is largely safe for the allergies covered in this book.

- To moisten the food while it cooks and to help it brown, brush with oil or melted butter before and halfway through broiling.
- Unless the skin on a chicken breast or fish is intact, season with salt after it is broiled, because salt draws out the juices and prevents food from becoming crisp and well browned.
- Depending on the power of the broiler, position the food 1–2 in./2.5–5 cm away from it to allow the food time to cook through before it overbrowns.
- If the food is browning too fast, move it farther away from the heat. Conversely move the food closer to the broiler if it is broiling too slowly.
- A 1-inch/2.5-cm-thick fish steak should take between 5 and 8 minutes to cook through. A steak twice as thick will take around 10 minutes. If the surfaces are beginning to burn and the center is not cooked sufficiently, place in a hot oven until cooked.
- Meat is denser than fish and should be cut no thicker than 1½ in./4 cm for broiling. A 1-inch/2.5-cm-thick portion of meat, brought to room temperature before cooking, will take will take 2–2½ minutes on each side to broil to medium rare: a 1½-inch/4-cm-thick portion will take 3–4 minutes on each side.
- Halfway through the cooking time, the broiled surface of the food should be lightly browned and crisp around the edges. To ensure the food is cooked evenly on both sides, turn it over, brush with oil or butter, and broil the other side for the same length of time, or until it is evenly browned, crisp, and cooked to the required doneness. See the Pressure Test (page 112) and Knowing When Fish is Cooked (page 119).

LEBANESE CHICKEN KEBABS

Start this recipe a day in advance, to allow the marinade to flavor and moisten the meat. Children and adults alike love these delicious kebabs. Serve them with Tabbouleh (page 140) or Rice Salad with Pistachio Nuts (page 144). **Serves 4**

FOR THE MARINADE

1½ tsp. paprika

1 tsp. ground cumin

freshly ground black pepper

3 garlic cloves, crushed

3 Tbsp. lemon juice

¼ cup extra virgin olive oil

FOR THE KEBABS

1½ lb./600 g boneless, skinless chicken breasts, cut into 2-in./5-cm cubes

1 large onion, cut into eighths from root to shoot

2 large green bell peppers, cored, seeded, and cut into 2-in./5-cm squares

salt and freshly ground black pepper

4 lemon wedges

5 Place the kebabs on a rack in a roasting pan or on a clean broiler pan to catch the cooking juices. Brush the kebabs with the reserved marinade.

6 Place the kebabs about 1 in./2.5 cm away from the heat and broil for 10–12 minutes, basting them with the reserved marinade and turning them every 2–3 minutes to brown and lightly char (for extra flavor) evenly on all sides. If the kebabs are browning too quickly, move the kebabs another inch or so from the heat.

7 To check the chicken is cooked through, gently press with the thumb and index finger. The chicken should feel firm.

8 To serve, place a kebab on a plate, spoon over some of the cooking juices and garnish with a wedge of lemon.

1 A day in advance, make the marinade. Combine the paprika, cumin, 3 grinds of black pepper, garlic, and lemon juice in a bowl. Whisk together well. Drizzle in the olive oil, whisking continuously until the marinade is emulsified and thick. Set aside 2 Tbsp. to use as a baste.

2 Place the cubes of chicken, onion, and green pepper in a storage container, pour in the marinade, and turn the pieces of chicken over to ensure they are evenly coated. Cover and refrigerate for at least 4 hours or, ideally, overnight.

3 To cook, preheat the broiler for 10 minutes until it is really hot.

4 Assemble the chicken kebabs. Thread the pepper, onion, and chicken onto the skewers, alternating the ingredients. Lightly sprinkle with salt and season with black pepper.

VARIATIONS
LAMB KEBABS
Slice meat cut from the leg or tenderloin into 1-in./2.5-cm cubes, thread onto skewers, and marinate in the same way as above. Broil for 10–12 minutes so that they are lightly charred on the outside (see picture above) and still slightly pink and moist in the center.

SEAFOOD KEBABS
Marinate 8 oz./225 g shrimp; 1 lb./450 g firm white fish, cut into 1½-in./3-cm dice; and 8 oz./225 g scallops, in place of the chicken. Broil for approximately 2 minutes each side, occasionally basting the seafood with reserved marinade, to keep it moist under the broiler.

MARINATED BROILED LAMB STEAKS

This recipe makes the most of lamb's perfect match with rosemary and garlic. The marinade gives the meat a lovely rich flavor and helps to keep it moist as it cooks. Make sure the broiler is really hot so that the surface of the lamb becomes brown and crisp while the meat is still pink and rosy inside. Serve with Crushed New Potatoes (page 137) or couscous, and steamed green beans or a lightly dressed green salad. **Serves 4**

INGREDIENTS

FOR THE MARINADE

2 Tbsp. red wine

2 garlic cloves, crushed

6 grinds black pepper

¼ cup olive oil

4 (1-in./2-cm thick) lamb steaks, cut from the upper leg (or use lamb chops)

4 sprigs rosemary

salt and freshly ground black pepper

4 lemon wedges

1 To make the marinade, mix the wine, garlic, and black pepper together. Drizzle in the olive oil, whisking continuously until the marinade is emulsified and thick. Set aside 2 Tbsp. to use as a baste.

2 Arrange the lamb steaks in a single layer in a shallow dish. Pour the marinade over the lamb. Turn the lamb steaks over to cover them evenly in the marinade and place the rosemary on the lamb.

3 Cover the dish with plastic wrap and refrigerate for at least 8 hours, but ideally 24 hours, for the flavors to develop. Occasionally turn the steaks to ensure they are marinating evenly.

4 Remove from the refrigerator 30 minutes before cooking to bring them up to room temperature.

5 Preheat the broiler to the hottest setting for 10 minutes.

6 Place the steaks on a rack standing in a roasting pan to catch the juices. Sprinkle the lamb with salt and place under the broiler so the lamb is 1¾ in./4 cm away from the heat source.

7 Broil the lamb for 4 minutes and turn over, baste with some of the reserved marinade, sprinkle with salt, season with freshly ground black pepper, and broil the second side for another 3 minutes. Take the steaks from under the broiler and press the meat with the tips of your fingers to check its progress (see the Pressure Test, page 112). If the lamb is still too rare, cook for another minute on the same side, or until the lamb is brown and crisp on the outside and pink in the center.

8 To serve, place the lamb on the plates, spoon over some of the cooking juices, and garnish with a wedge of lemon.

Chapter 12

ROASTING AND OVEN-BAKING

ROASTING

Roasting involves cooking large cuts of meat and whole birds at high temperatures, in the dry heat of the oven. A small quantity of fat or oil is spooned over the food as it cooks to prevent it from drying out and to help it brown and crisp up. Using fat in this way is known as basting. Once meat or poultry is cooked, richly flavored gravy is made by loosening the browned juices on the bottom of the roasting pan with stock, wine, and the water that has been used to boil accompanying vegetables.

Vegetables are also roasted, often in the same roasting pan as the meat.

OILS AND FATS USED FOR ROASTING

Neutral-flavored oils, such as sunflower, vegetable, or corn oil, are the most suitable basting fats for meat roasted at high temperatures, because they will not burn in the bottom of the roasting pan. Burned fat affects the flavor of the meat and the cooking juices used to make gravy. Because poultry and fish are roasted at slightly lower temperatures, olive oil and butter (both of which burn at very high temperatures) are often used to enrich their flavor and the cooking juices that form the basis for an accompanying sauce.

ROASTING MEAT

Lean and tender cuts of beef, lamb, and pork are initially cooked in a very hot oven (400°F/200°C/gas mark 6 plus) to brown the meat and to melt the fat on the surface of the meat. If there is no fat around the meat, it is either rubbed with oil or covered with bacon to moisten the surface as it roasts. Once the meat begins to brown, the temperature is reduced to prevent the meat from cooking too quickly.

HOW TO ROAST MEAT

- Preheat the oven while the meat is being prepared for roasting.
- Trim any excess fat so that the top surface is evenly covered with a thin layer of fat.
- If fat is lacking, cover the top surface of the meat with bacon or rub butter, beef drippings or oil over the meat. Alternatively, the meat can be browned beforehand

NOTES FOR FOOD ALLERGY SUFFERERS

DAIRY-FREE DIET: Butter is only used for roasting because it enriches the flavor of poultry, fish, and their cooking juices. Olive oil is a great dairy-free alternative because it also adds flavor.

GLUTEN-FREE DIET: Gravy made with the cooking juices is often thickened with wheat flour. An equal quantity of cornstarch can be used instead. Alternatively, boil the cooking juices, some stock, and any water used for boiling accompanying vegetables in the roasting pan until the liquid is reduced to a delicious, syrupy gravy.

NUT- AND SOY-FREE DIETS: Avoid using peanut oil for nut-free diets and soybean oil or vegetable oil (made with soybean oil) for soy-free diets.

in hot oil, on the top of the stove, then roasted at a temperature below 400°F/200°C/gas mark 6.

- Season with salt and pepper (out of the roasting pan or your gravy will be salty).
- Weigh the prepared roast to calculate how long it will take to cook using the roasting times given in the recipe. A solid piece of boneless meat will take longer to cook than a bone-in roast of the same weight (bones carry heat to the center of the meat). The shape of the roast is also important. A long, thin roast will take less time to cook than a shorter, thicker piece of meat of the same weight.
- Every 20 to 30 minutes remove the meat from the oven, shut the oven door, and spoon the hot fat over the meat. Return the meat immediately to the oven.
- Check the meat halfway through the cooking time. It may be cooking faster than calculated (see Knowing When Meat Is Cooked, page 112).
- When the meat is cooked, remove from the oven, cover in aluminum foil, and rest for at least 10 minutes. This allows the free-flowing juices inside the meat to be reabsorbed, making the meat more succulent and easier to carve.

ROASTING POULTRY

Poultry is ideal for roasting because its flesh is tender and partially protected from drying out by the skin and the layer of fat beneath it. To add extra protection from the dry heat of the oven and to brown and crisp the skin, lean birds, such as chicken, guinea fowl, and game birds, are smeared with softened butter or drizzled with oil or covered with bacon, particularly over the breasts and legs. Because turkeys are also lean and require a lengthy time in the oven, they should be wrapped in parchment paper and aluminum foil, in addition to oil or butter and bacon, to ensure the meat remains moist. An hour before the turkey is done, remove the paper, foil, and bacon to allow the skin to brown evenly.

Duck and goose do not require butter or oil while they roast due to the thick layer of fat below the skin, which slowly renders down, moistening the meat, until only the browned, crisp skin remains.

HOW TO ROAST POULTRY

- Preheat the oven to the required roasting temperature.
- Place the bird on a board and remove any excess fat from inside the bird.
- If required, stuff the bird (see opposite).
- Weigh the bird to calculate its cooking time once it is prepared or stuffed. As a general rule, poultry requires 20 minutes per lb. (40 minutes per kg).
- Spread softened butter or drizzle and rub oil over the bird, particularly the breasts, legs, and wings, because they are most prone to drying out.
- Lightly season the bird with salt and pepper before placing it in the roasting pan.
- Place lean birds in the roasting pan. Place fatty birds, such as duck and goose, on a wire rack (to hold it above the fat that will melt off) inside a rasting pan.
- Once the bird starts to brown, baste it in the hot fat every 20–30 minutes.
- Once the bird is cooked, remove it from the oven, cover in aluminum foil, and leave to rest for 10 minutes to make the bird more succulent and easier to carve.

STUFFING FOR ROASTED BIRDS

Turkey, roast chicken, and other birds, such as pheasant, guinea fowl, and poussin, are made infinitely more special if stuffed with a fruity or herb-flavored stuffing. Stuffing absorbs the rich-flavored cooking juices produced by the roasting bird and helps to keep the bird moist as it cooks.

Birds may be stuffed with:
- Oranges, lemons, apples, onions, garlic, and herbs, placed into the body cavity of medium-sized birds to keep the bird moist and flavor the meat and gravy (see Mediterranean Roast Chicken, page 114).
- A stuffing based on ground meat or starchy ingredients, such as bread crumbs or rice, which will soak up the cooking juices.

HOW TO STUFF BIRDS

Medium-sized and small birds: Because of their small size, chickens and guinea fowl are often stuffed in the neck and body cavity (to provide enough stuffing). Spoon the stuffing into the bird until the cavity is loosely filled, because stuffing swells as it cooks. Tightly packed stuffing is liable to burst out of the bird or not cook through. Once the neck end of the bird is stuffed, secure the flap of neck skin over the stuffing with skewers.
Large birds: Because turkeys are so large, stuff the neck cavity only. If the body cavity is stuffed, the turkey must be cooked for a longer period to ensure the stuffing is cooked properly, resulting in overcooked, dry meat. Do not overstuff the neck cavity because the stuffing swells as it cooks and will push its way out of the bird. Secure the neck skin firmly over the stuffing with skewers. Any extra stuffing can be shaped into balls and placed into an ovenproof dish to bake separately.

ROASTING A STUFFED BIRD

Stuffed birds require 20 minutes per lb. (40 minutes per kg) to cook. To prevent the bird from overcooking, roast at 350°F/180°C/gas mark 4 for the first half of the cooking time, to brown the skin, and then at 325°F/160°C/gas mark 3 for the second half to cook it through.

NOTES FOR FOOD ALLERGY SUFFERERS

DAIRY-FREE DIET: Butter is often used to soften diced vegetables for stuffing mixtures. Replace it with olive oil or a neutral-flavored oil.

EGG-FREE DIET: Beaten egg is often used to bind stuffing. Stuffing made without egg will be more crumbly but just as delicious. Alternatively, in place of each egg used, add 1 Tbsp. bread crumbs and, if the stuffing mixture is dry, 1 Tbsp. water.

GLUTEN-FREE DIET: Bread crumbs are used as the base of meat-free stuffings and to bind and add bulk to meat-based stuffing. Sausage meat used as the base of meat-based stuffing may also contain toasted bread crumbs, but you can use the sausage meat recipe on page 94. Gluten-free bread crumbs or cooked brown rice are just as suitable for stuffing.

NUT-FREE DIET: Nuts are often added to stuffing to add texture and flavor. Although the flavor will not be the same, nuts can be replaced with lightly cooked celery for crunch and chopped dried fruit for added texture and flavor.

SOY-FREE DIET: Check the label of store-bought sausage meat for added soy products. To be sure, make your own sausage meat (see page 94).

KNOWING WHEN MEAT IS COOKED

THE PRESSURE TEST

Generally used to measure how well small cuts of roasted meat and individual portions of meat are cooked, the pressure test is also very useful used in conjunction with the skewer test for larger pieces of roasted meat and whole birds. To test how well meat is cooked, press it firmly with an index and middle finger: raw meat feels soft and flabby; rare meat is not flabby but feels soft and gives easily under the fingers when pressed; medium-rare meat is firmer but still soft enough to give under the fingers when pressed, but springs back as the fingers are removed; well-done meat feels firm and does not give when pressed.

USING AN INSTANT-READ THERMOMETER

Insert the thermometer into the center of the deepest part of the meat. Leave it in place for at least 30 seconds before taking your reading: 140°F/60°C is rare and still deep red; 160°F/70°C is medium-rare and pink; 175°F/80°C is well done and brown. Before testing the temperature of poaching meat, remove it from the poaching liquid.

THE SKEWER TEST

If you do not have a meat thermometer, insert a skewer into the middle of the deepest part of the meat, leave for a few seconds, then remove. If there are no juices, the meat is raw; if the juices are dark pink and trickling from the hole, the meat is rare; if light pink juices are flowing freely from the hole, the meat is medium-rare; if the juices are colorless and flow freely, the meat is well done.

KNOWING WHEN WHOLE BIRDS ARE COOKED

Twenty minutes before the end of the estimated roasting time, remove the bird from the oven to check its progress. The skin of the bird may be crisp and golden brown but use one of the following tests to confirm whether the bird is ready to eat or requires more cooking. White-fleshed birds, including turkey, chicken, and guinea fowl, must be well cooked to kill any salmonella bacteria present in the meat. Duck and goose meat present a far lower risk of salmonella poisoning and are traditionally eaten pink (despite the fatty skin, duck and goose meat is very lean and eating it when pink ensures the meat is moist and tender).

CHECKING THE COOKING JUICES

Insert a sharp, pointed knife into the deepest part of the breast and thigh: very little juice means that the meat is still raw in the center; deep pink, bloody juices trickling from the cut mean the meat is rare; slow-flowing, light pink juices mean that the meat is almost cooked or medium-rare, ideal for dark-fleshed birds such as duck, goose, and game birds such as pigeon; free-flowing, colorless juices signify that the flesh is cooked through, ideal for white-fleshed poultry, such as turkey, chicken, and guinea fowl.

USING AN INSTANT-READ THERMOMETER

White-fleshed poultry and meat-based stuffing must reach 175°F/80°C (well done) before they are safe to eat. Dark-fleshed birds, such as goose and duck, are best eaten pink at 165°F/70°C (medium-rare). For this reason, use meat-free stuffing for dark-fleshed birds because it is safe to eat cooked to 165°F/70°C.

THE PRESSURE TEST

The breast meat of birds is often pan-fried in hot oil until well browned and finished off in a roasting oven. To avoid cutting into the breast meat to check the progress of the cooking meat, use the pressure test (above).

TRADITIONAL ROAST RIB OF BEEF

There is nothing to beat the taste of rare beef with rich gravy. Serve with Roast Potatoes (page 135), steamed or boiled green vegetables, and mustard or horseradish sauce. The beef is delicious cold so even if there are only two of you, it's worth cooking a large roast and enjoying the leftovers. **Serves 6**

INGREDIENTS

FOR THE BEEF

4½–5½ lb./2–2.5 kg rib of beef

2 tsp. dry mustard powder

● **GLUTEN** ▶ check label for wheat

salt and freshly ground black pepper

FOR THE GRAVY

1 Tbsp. flour

● **GLUTEN** ▶ cornstarch

⅔ cup/150 ml red wine

1¼ cups/290 ml White or Brown Chicken Stock (page 64)

salt and freshly ground black pepper

1 Preheat the oven to 425°F/220°C/gas mark 7.

2 Place the meat on a board and rub salt, pepper, and mustard powder over the fat. Place the beef in a roasting pan and roast on the middle rack of the oven to brown for 20 minutes. Reduce the heat to 350°F/180°C/gas mark 4 and roast the beef for another 15 minutes per 1 lb.(450 g) for medium-rare meat; 20 minutes per 1 lb.(450 g) for well-done meat. To ensure the beef is cooked perfectly and does not overcook, test the meat (see opposite) 30 minutes before you estimate it will be ready. If the meat requires more cooking, return it to the oven for 15 minutes and test again.

3 When the meat is ready, transfer it to a carving board, cover with aluminum foil, and leave to rest for 20–30 minutes.

4 To make the gravy, pour the juices in the roasting pan into a transparent pitcher and leave for 1 minute to allow the fat and cooking juices to separate. Spoon 2 Tbsp. of the fat back into the roasting pan and carefully remove the remaining fat from the surface of the cooking juices.

5 Add the flour to the fat in the pan, stir to a smooth paste, and cook over medium heat for 1 minute, stirring continuously with a wooden spoon. Gradually stir in the wine and stock, loosening the browned cooking juices on the bottom of the pan, to form a lump-free sauce. Add any cooking juices collecting around the resting beef to the gravy and bring to a boil, stirring constantly. Simmer for 2 minutes to cook the flour, taste, season with salt and pepper, and keep warm over low heat. As the beef is carved, more juices will collect under the meat and these should be poured into the gravy, because they add lots of flavor.

6 Thinly slice the beef and arrange on warmed plates with the gravy served separately.

MEDITERRANEAN ROAST CHICKEN WITH VEGETABLES

This recipe is truly delicious, simple to prepare, and gives you time to do other things while it cooks. It is free from dairy, egg, gluten, nuts and soy and is a fantastic dish to serve to family and guests for Sunday lunch or an informal dinner. **Serves 4–6**

FOR THE CHICKEN AND VEGETABLES

4½-lb/2-kg roasting chicken

½ onion, cut in half

2 garlic cloves

½ lemon, cut in half

2 sprigs thyme

5 Tbsp. olive oil

2¾ lb./1.2 kg large baking potatoes, each cut into 6 long wedges

2 red bell peppers, each cut into 8 strips

2 onions, each cut into 6 wedges from shoot to root (ensure a little of the root is left to hold the pieces together as they cook)

4 ripe tomatoes, quartered

6 garlic cloves, in their skin

sea salt and freshly ground black pepper

4 sprigs rosemary or thyme

FOR THE GRAVY

1¼ cups/290 ml White Chicken Stock (page 64)

1 Preheat the oven to 350°F/180°C/ gas mark 4.

2 Remove any excess fat from the body cavity of the bird. Place the onion, garlic, lemon, and thyme in the body cavity.

3 Place the chicken in the center of a roasting pan large enough to hold the vegetables not more than two vegetables deep (so they cook and brown evenly).

4 Spread the vegetables and garlic around the chicken. Drizzle 4 tablespoons of olive oil over the chicken (taking care to include the legs, to help prevent them drying out) and the vegetables. Sprinkle with sea salt and season well with pepper.

5 Toss the vegetables, then spread out around the chicken to cover them evenly in oil and seasoning. Tuck the herb sprigs under the potatoes to prevent them from scorching. Also make sure the red peppers, onion wedges, and garlic cloves are well down in the pan to prevent burning.

6 Place the pan in the middle rack of the oven and roast for 30 minutes.

7 Remove the pan from the oven and baste the chicken with the remaining 1 Tbsp. oil and juices collecting in the bottom of the pan. Turn the potatoes and vegetables over carefully. Return the pan to the oven and roast for another 20 minutes.

8 Baste the chicken and turn the vegetables over once more. If the potatoes are golden brown on the outside and soft inside, transfer the vegetables to a serving dish and keep warm. The chicken will require at least another 15 minutes in the oven.

9 After this time, test to see if the chicken is done by inserting a small knife into the deepest part of the leg and breast. If the juices run clear, then it is cooked. Also, the cooking juices collected in the body cavity should be caramel in color. If the juices are dark red, the chicken requires at least another 15 minutes in the oven.

10 Once the chicken is cooked, place a wooden spoon in the body cavity and with the help of a slotted spoon, tip the chicken to allow the cooking juices in the body cavity to run into the roasting pan. Spoon off most of the fat.

11 Add the chicken stock to the roasting pan and boil the gravy until it thinly coats the back of a spoon. Taste and season as necessary.

12 To serve, carve the chicken and arrange on plates. Spoon over some of the gravy in the roasting pan. Pass the roast vegetables separately making sure everyone has a roasted garlic clove on their plates to squeeze and spread over their chicken.

VARIATION

Carrots, parsnips, butternut squash, new potatoes, zucchini, shallots and fennel also roast extremely well around a chicken.

BROWN RICE, MUSHROOM, PARSLEY, AND LEMON STUFFING

The brown rice, flavored with mushrooms, herbs, garlic, and lemon, absorbs the cooking juices to make a wonderfully rich, crumbly stuffing suitable for white- and dark-fleshed birds. This stuffing is also delicious made with cooked bulgur in place of rice. **Makes enough stuffing for a 4½-lb./2-kg roasting chicken**

INGREDIENTS

6 Tbsp./140 g brown rice

salt and freshly ground black pepper

2 Tbsp./30 g butter or olive oil

1 onion, finely diced

4 oz./110 g fresh mushrooms (button, flat, or wild), thinly sliced

2 garlic cloves, finely chopped

2 Tbsp. finely chopped fresh parsley

finely grated zest of 1 lemon

juice of ½ lemon, plus more as needed

1 Combine the rice and 1 teaspoon of salt in a saucepan. Cover with twice the volume of cold water and cover with a lid. Bring to a boil then gently simmer for 20–30 minutes, or until the rice is tender.

2 Meanwhile, heat the butter in a frying pan and add the onion, mushrooms, a pinch of salt, and two grinds of pepper. Cover and fry, stirring occasionally, until the onions are very soft and sweet. Add the garlic and continue to fry for another 30 seconds. Remove the pan from the heat.

3 Mix together the cooked rice, onions and mushrooms, parsley, and lemon zest and juice. Mix thoroughly, taste, and add seasoning or more lemon juice as necessary. The stuffing should taste delicately lemony. Use as required (see How to Stuff Birds, page 111).

VARIATION

BROWN RICE, MUSHROOM, OREGANO, AND ORANGE STUFFING
Replace the lemon with the zest of 1 orange and the juice of ½ orange and replace 1 tablespoon of the parsley with finely chopped oregano.

APPLE AND CHORIZO STUFFING

A really punchy, colorful stuffing that complements chicken, guinea fowl, and poussin beautifully. Serve the stuffed bird with brown rice or Crushed New Potatoes (page 137). **Makes enough for a 4½-lb./2-kg roasting chicken**

INGREDIENTS

1 small onion, finely diced

1 celery rib, finely diced

olive oil for frying

3 garlic cloves, finely chopped

1 tsp. ground paprika

½ recipe sausage mixture for Homemade Pork and Apple Sausages (page 94)

8 oz./200 g peeled, cored and coarsely grated Granny Smith apples

4 oz./110 g Spanish chorizo sausage, cut into thin slices and then across into thin strips

● GLUTEN — check label for wheat

● DAIRY — check label for dairy

● SOY — check label for soy

1 Tbsp. fresh oregano or thyme leaves, roughly chopped

1 Tbsp. finely chopped flat-leaf parsley

juice of ½ lemon

salt and freshly ground black pepper

1 Gently fry the onion and celery in 2 tablespoons of olive oil, in a covered frying pan, until the onion is soft and sweet. Add the garlic and paprika and continue to fry, stirring continuously, for another 30 seconds. Transfer to a large bowl.

2 Add the sausage meat, apples, chorizo, oregano, parsley, and lemon juice. Season with ½ teaspoon salt and black pepper and thoroughly mix everything together with your hands.

3 To check the seasoning, fry a flattened spoonful of the stuffing in a little oil until cooked through. Taste and add more seasoning if necessary. Use as required.

VARIATION

APPLE, APRICOT, AND SMOKED HAM STUFFING
For a milder-flavored stuffing, replace chorizo sausage with 4 oz./110 g smoked ham, thily sliced and cut into short strips, and replace half the grated apple with roughly chopped, ready-to-eat apricots; omit the ground paprika.

OVEN-BAKING

The term oven-baking refers to baking at high temperatures, usually to cook small pieces or individual portions of meat and poultry, small to medium-sized whole fish, or thickly sliced vegetables arranged in a roasting pan, and drizzled with oil. Assembled dishes of food, such as lasagna, are also baked in the oven until browned.

BAKING POULTRY AND MEAT

Oven-baking is a good method for cooking small portions of meat and jointed poultry. These can either be baked alone or with other ingredients—see Sticky Finger Chicken Drumsticks (page 123) or Baked Moroccan Chicken (page 121).

KNOWING WHEN THE MEAT IS COOKED

To check if small portions of meat or poultry are cooked, use the pressure test (page 112) and look at the color of the juices when the meat is pricked with a skewer. Beef, lamb, and duck are best served pink with light pink juices. Pork and poultry should feel firm when pressed. Make a small cut down to the bone on the underside of bone-in chicken portions to check the meat is no longer pink and the juices run clear.

BAKING FISH

Baking is mainly used to cook small fish, such as sardines, medium-sized whole fish, including sea bass and trout, or portions of fish that are too thick to cook through by pan-frying. Because oven-baked fish cooks quickly and has little time to brown and crisp up in the oven, whole fish and portions of fish are often browned in the frying pan first. Although the skin of fish offers some protection from the heat of the oven, both oily and white-fleshed fish are drizzled with oil or sealed in a package of aluminum foil or parchment paper with butter or olive oil, herbs, and lemon and effectively steamed.

To reduce the length of time thick fish take to bake in a hot oven, they are sometimes slashed through the skin at 2-inch/5-cm intervals, halfway to the bone, so that heat can quickly penetrate to the center. Marinating the fish in an oil-based marinade beforehand adds flavor and helps to keep the slashed fish moist as it cooks.

BAKING TIMES FOR FISH

In an oven preheated to 400°F/200°C/gas mark 6, fish will take the following amount of time to cook:

Portions of fish

- A 1-inch/2.5-cm-thick portion will take 10–12 minutes (less if it has been browned in a pan first).
- A 2-inch/5-cm-thick portion will take 20–30 minutes, depending on the density of the flesh (less if it has been browned in a pan first).

NOTES FOR FOOD ALLERGY SUFFERERS

Meat, poultry, fish, and vegetables, simply baked with a small quantity of fat or with other flavoring ingredients and served with their cooking juices are usually safe for dairy-, gluten-, egg-, soy-, and nut-free diets. However, recipes where food is baked in a richly flavored sauce are often not so suitable, though they can usually be adapted to suit your particular dietary requirements.

Many oven-baked dishes, for instance lasagna, traditionally contain dairy products, wheat, or eggs. Nuts are included in some baked dishes, but soy products are rarely used.

Whole fish

The time it takes for whole fish to cook partly depends on their shape. Long, narrow fish will take less time to cook than rounder fish. In an oven preheated to 400°F/200°C/gas mark 6:
- A small fish will take 15–20 minutes.
- A medium-sized fish will take 25–30 minutes.

KNOWING WHEN FISH IS COOKED

Fish cooks at a lower temperature and more quickly than meat and is therefore easier to overcook. Cooked fish is best eaten when the flesh is still moist and tender and is just opaque. Fish that is fully opaque is overcooked and likely to taste coarse and dry, so look for these signs:
- Whole fish are cooked through when the eyes turn white and the dorsal fin comes away from the body cleanly and easily when pulled.
- When portions of fish are cooked through, the flesh is almost opaque and starts to separate into large flakes when pressed with the index and middle fingers.

BAKING VEGETABLES

One of the simplest foods is the baked potato, turned in a little oil and salt and baked until soft and fluffy inside and crisp on the outside. Root vegetables, onions, squashes, zucchini, eggplant, tomatoes, and fennel are also delicious sprinkled with oil and herbs and seasoning and baked until soft inside and brown and crisp around the edges.

HONEY-BAKED SAUSAGES

Children love sausages cooked in this way. Serve 2 to 3 large sausages per child. Sausages often contain toasted bread crumbs and are not suitable for a gluten-free diet—see the gluten-free recipe for Homemade Pork and Apple Sausages on page 94. **Serves 4**

INGREDIENTS

12 good-quality pork sausages

● **GLUTEN**   check label for gluten
● **DAIRY**   check label for dairy
● **EGG**   check label for egg

2 Tbsp. honey

1 Tbsp. sunflower or corn oil

1 Preheat the oven to 350°F/180°C/gas mark 4.

2 Place the sausages in a single layer in a roasting pan and drizzle with oil. Bake for 15 minutes, or until they start to brown.

3 Remove from the oven and drizzle with the honey. Turn the sausages over in the honey until evenly coated, then return to the oven for another 10 minutes, or until the sausages are golden brown. Serve immediately or the sausages will stick to the bottom of the roasting pan.

BAKED FILLET OF SALMON WITH SHALLOTS, TARRAGON, AND LEMON

This recipe features a quick and simple method for cooking salmon. It is delicious served with brown rice or boiled new potatoes, and steamed green vegetables. Alternatively, serve cold with mayonnaise (page 83) and lemon wedges. **Serves 4**

INGREDIENTS

4 (6½-oz./180-g-thick) salmon fillets, with skin

2 shallots, thinly sliced across

salt and freshly ground black pepper

4 sprigs tarragon

½ lemon, sliced across into 4 rounds

1 Tbsp. extra virgin olive oil

1 Tbsp. white wine

1 Preheat the oven to 350°F/180°C/gas mark 4.

2 Place the salmon fillets skin down in an ovenproof dish. Sprinkle the shallots over each fillet, and season with salt and pepper. Arrange 1 sprig tarragon and 1 slice lemon on each salmon fillet. Drizzle the olive oil and white wine over the salmon.

3 Cover the dish with aluminum foil and bake on the middle rack of the oven for 25–30 minutes, until the salmon is cooked and firm in the thickest part of the fillet.

4 To serve, lift the salmon fillets onto plates and spoon over the cooking juices. Add a lemon slice to each plate and serve.

BAKED MOROCCAN CHICKEN WITH FENNEL, OLIVES, AND APRICOTS

A simply made, very attractive, and tasty dish, this is particularly good served hot or cold with couscous or cold with Rice Salad with Pistachio Nuts and Pomegranate Seeds (page 144). **Serves 4**

INGREDIENTS

4 boneless, skinless chicken breasts, cut across into ¾-in./2-cm slices

1 garlic clove, finely chopped

1 fennel bulb, outer leaves discarded, sliced lengthwise into 8 wedges

1 handful dried apricots, cut in half

1 handful good-quality black olives

juice and finely grated zest of 1 orange

juice and finely grated zest of 1 lemon

2 Tbsp. olive oil

1 Tbsp. brown sugar

salt and freshly ground black pepper

1 Combine the chicken, garlic, fennel, apricots, olives, juice and zest of the orange and lemon and olive oil in a bowl. Cover and leave to marinate overnight in the refrigerator.

2 Preheat the oven to 400°C/200°C/gas mark 6.

3 Spread the chicken mixture in the roasting pan in one layer. Sprinkle the brown sugar over the chicken and season with salt and pepper.

4 Bake on the middle rack of the oven for 20–30 minutes, until the chicken is firm when pressed between thumb and index finger and the ingredients have turned an even golden brown. Turn the ingredients over halfway through cooking so that they brown evenly.

5 Spoon onto plates and serve.

LASAGNA AL FORNO

Lasagna is a well-loved dish for family meals and informal suppers and one that can be adapted for gluten-, egg- and dairy-free diets. Serve with a lightly dressed green salad or tomato salad. **Serves 4–6**

INGREDIENTS

Double recipe béchamel sauce made with flour or cornstarch (page 74)

8 oz./225 g fresh or dried lasagna noodles

● GLUTEN · gluten-free lasagna noodles

● EGG · fresh pasta usually contains eggs

● NUTS · check label for traces of nuts

1 Tbsp. chopped fresh oregano or thyme

BOLOGNAISE SAUCE

sunflower oil or olive oil

18 oz./500 g lean ground beef or lamb

salt and freshly ground black pepper

2 large carrots, diced

1 large onion, diced

1 garlic clove, finely chopped

2 (15-oz./400-g) cans tomatoes with juice

1¼ cups/290 ml White Chicken Stock, plus more as needed (page 64)

1¼ cups/290 ml water

1 bay leaf

1 sprig thyme

FOR THE TOPPING

3 Tbsp. freshly grated Parmigiano-Reggiano cheese

● DAIRY · 3 Tbsp. dried bread crumbs mixed with 1 tsp. dried mixed herbs, ½ tsp. salt, and 3 grinds black pepper

2 Tbsp. olive oil

1 First, make the Bolognaise sauce. Heat 2 Tbsp. oil in a large pan. When the oil is hot enough to make the meat sizzle, add half the meat, season it with ½ tsp. salt and several generous grinds of pepper. Break up any lumps as the meat browns. Once the meat is well browned, remove it and loosen the browned juices on the base of the pan with a large splash of water. Add the loosened juices to the browned meat. Add another 2 Tbsp. oil to the pan and when it is hot, cook and season the next batch of meat. Remove the meat and loosen the browned juices from the pan again.

2 Turn the heat down and add the carrots and onions, adding a little more oil if necessary. Season with salt and pepper, cover with a lid, and allow to fry gently until soft. Remove the lid and continue to fry, stirring regularly, until the vegetables are lightly browned. Add the garlic and gently fry for another minute, stirring continuously.

3 Return the meat to the pan, add the tomatoes, stock, water, and herbs and stir well. If necessary, add more stock or cold water to cover the ingredients by ¼ in./5 mm and bring to a gentle simmer. Cook, uncovered, for 1½ hours, or until the meat is tender. As the sauce cooks, skim the fat from the surface. Keep the liquid topped up with water to at least ¼ in./5 mm above the ingredients. For the last 30 minutes of cooking, allow the liquid to reduce in volume so that it is level with the meat in the sauce. Taste and season.

Meanwhile, make the béchamel sauce and season with oregano. Preheat the oven to 350°F/180°C/gas mark 4.

5 To assemble the lasagna, cover the bottom of a 9 by 12 by 3-inch/24 by 30 by 8-cm ovenproof greased baking dish with one layer of pasta. Spread a generous layer of Bolognaise sauce over the pasta, then spoon béchamel sauce over the meat. Add another layer of pasta and continue to layer the sauces

as before. Continue to layer the lasagna until the lasagna is ¾ in./2 cm below the rim of the dish. Pour over the remaining sauce.

6 Sprinkle the grated Parmesan over the lasagna. (Or for the dairy-free version, mix the bread crumbs, herbs, and seasoning together, and sprinkle over the lasagna). Lightly drizzle with olive oil.

7 Bake for 30–35 minutes, or until it is bubbling, warm, and golden brown.

STICKY FINGER CHICKEN DRUMSTICKS

A very popular dish for informal meals and children's parties, this is great served with brown rice and salad. **Serves 4**

INGREDIENTS

8 chicken drumsticks, trimmed of excess skin

FOR THE MARINADE

2 Tbsp. sunflower or corn oil

2 Tbsp. brown sugar

1 garlic clove, finely chopped

1 tsp. ground paprika

1 Tbsp. white wine vinegar

2 Tbsp. tomato ketchup

- **GLUTEN** check label for wheat
- **NUTS** check label for traces of nuts
- **SOY** check label for soy
- **DAIRY** check label for milk products

pinch of cayenne pepper or red chile flakes, optional

salt and freshly ground black pepper

1 The night before the chicken is to be eaten, place the chicken in a large bowl. Mix the marinade ingredients together and pour over the chicken. Turn the

chicken to ensure the pieces are thoroughly coated in marinade. Cover and marinate overnight in the refrigerator.

2 Preheat the oven to 350°F/180°C/ gas mark 4.

3 Arrange the chicken in its marinade in a roasting pan and bake for 30–40 minutes, basting and turning the chicken two or three times.

4 Remove the chicken from the oven when it is golden brown and the marinade is reduced and sticky. Check that the meat is firm and is no longer pink in the center. If it requires longer in the oven, add 2 or 3 Tbsp. water to the pan and cover the chicken with foil. Bake for another 10 minutes or until the chicken is cooked through.

5 Remove from the oven, turn the chicken over in the sauce, and serve either hot or cold.

| # POACHING AND STEWING

POACHING

Poaching is a method for cooking meat, poultry, fish, and eggs slowly and gently in barely simmering liquid. It is mainly used to cook delicate foods, including tender cuts of meat, fish, and poultry, which have a tendency to dry out and toughen when cooked at high temperatures. The cooking method referred to as "boiling" is, in fact, prolonged poaching and is mainly used for tenderizing large cuts of meat, such as ham, in water or stock flavored with vegetables, herbs, and seasoning. Because the cooking liquid is enriched with the nutrients and flavor from the ingredients cooked in it, it is used as the base for an accompanying sauce or for richly flavored soup.

HOW TO POACH

- Food is poached in a large pan on top of the stove, where the temperature of the poaching liquid can be watched closely and controlled, or in a low oven.
- To poach small portions of food on top of the stove, choose a wide shallow pan with a heavy bottom—such as a frying pan—so that the portions can lie side by side. Don't pile them on top of one another because they will be difficult to remove and may break up.
- Check food regularly as it poaches, ensuring that it remains covered with liquid and is maintained at a slow simmer. Do not allow the poaching liquid to boil or the meat or fish will toughen and dry out.
- To poach small pieces of tender meat, fish, or poultry cut into strips or dice, add them to barely simmering poaching liquid to gently cook through. Lift them out with a slotted spoon when they feel firm between thumb and index finger.

POACHING FISH

Fresh fish is either poached in fish stock, in milk mixed with an equal quantity of water, or a strongly flavored liquid called court bouillon. Smoked fish is always poached in milk because water-based poaching liquid darkens and toughens the flesh. In contrast, the proteins in the milk soften the flavor and texture and lighten the color of smoked fish.

Whole fish

To poach a whole fish, submerge it in cold poaching liquid and slowly heat to a gentle simmer to prevent the flesh from shrinking. If the fish is large, you'll need a long, narrow pan called a fish poacher. If the fish is to be eaten hot, cook it for 5 minutes per 1 lb./450 g of fish. If it is to be eaten cold, remove the pan from the heat when the poaching liquid starts to simmer and leave to cool. When the poaching liquid is lukewarm, the fish is cooked and can be lifted out of the pan.

Fillets of fish

If possible, buy fish fillets with the skin intact, because it holds the flesh together while the fish cooks and when it is lifted out of the pan. When poaching fish fillets on top of the stove, place them skin side down in the pan, to protect them from the hot pan bottom. In the oven, place the fish fillets skin side up, to protect them from the dry heat of the oven. In both cases, make sure the fillets are completely covered in poaching liquid.

The fillets are cooked when the flesh is almost opaque in the thickest part of the fillet and it parts into moist flakes when gently pressed with a finger. The fish will continue to cook in its own heat even when it is removed from the pan, so be careful not to over-cook it.

POACHING POULTRY AND MEAT

White meats, such as pork, veal, and poultry, are left whole—or cut into strips, dice, or individual portions—and poached in stock or water flavored with vegetables and herbs. Asian dishes, such as Thai curries, often use coconut milk for the same purpose (see Thai Green Chicken Curry, page 130). To prevent pieces and individual portions of poultry and meat from drying out, they are added to gently simmering liquid and poached until just cooked through. Always be sure pork and chicken are adequately cooked—the flesh should feel firm under the fingers.

Poaching whole birds and large cuts of meat

Poaching is an ideal method for gently cooking tender whole birds and large cuts of meat, such as ham (see Chicken and Mushroom Pie. page 128, and Boiled Ham, page 129) or slowly breaking down and dissolving the connective tissue in sinewy game birds and tougher cuts of meat, such as bottom round of beef. To cook a whole bird or large cut of meat, submerge it in cold water or stock and bring slowly to simmering point. This encourages fat and other impurities to collect on the surface of the liquid, where they can be skimmed off. This way the poaching liquid remains clear and pure in flavor—essential for the taste and appearance of a soup or sauce made with it.

Whole birds are poached until the meat is just beginning to separate from the carcass, and the legs feel loose when moved from side to side. Tender meat is cooked when the meat has reached 175°F/80°C (see Using an Instant-Read Thermometer, page 112). Tougher meats are poached until the connective tissue holding the muscle fibers together has broken down and dissolved into the poaching liquid. The meat is ready when the coarse muscle fibers start to separate, and the meat is soft and tender in the mouth.

NOTES FOR FOOD ALLERGY SUFFERERS

Poached foods are cooked in water-based or milk-based poaching liquids.

DAIRY-FREE DIET: Soy milk is a very good substitute for cows' milk when poaching fresh and smoked fish, white meat, and poultry, and makes a very good base for parsley sauce, served with poached white fish and boiled ham. Rice milk can also be used for poaching, although white sauces made with it are thinner.

GLUTEN-FREE DIET: Milk-based, water-based, and stock-based poaching liquids are often thickened with flour to make an accompanying sauce, such as the sauce for Chicken and Mushroom Pie (page 128). Substitute an equal quantity of cornstarch for wheat flour to make a smooth, fine-textured sauce.

EGG-, NUT-, AND SOY-FREE DIETS: Either omit egg, nuts, and soy from the recipe or choose another dish.

PROVENÇAL FISH STEW
WITH FENNEL AND POTATOES

The ingredients in this dish are poached but I tend to think of it more as a stew. A hearty meal in a bowl, it is best served with a suitable crusty bread and lightly dressed salad. **Serves 4**

FOR THE STEW

1 lb./450 g new potatoes

extra virgin olive oil

1 bulb Florence fennel, tough outer leaves removed, sliced into 8 wedges

salt and freshly ground black pepper

3 garlic cloves, finely chopped

2 tsp. ground coriander

1 (15-oz./400-g) can diced tomatoes with juice

1 cup/250 ml dry white wine

1 lb./450 g mussels, cleaned under running water, beards pulled away, and any shells that remain open when tapped, discarded

2 large sea bass, filleted and the 4 fillets cut diagonally into thirds (keep the bones for the stock)

1 Tbsp. chopped fresh mint

1 Tbsp. chopped fresh flat-leaf parsley

1 lemon, cut into 4 wedges

FOR THE STOCK

bones from the sea bass, chopped into pieces

2 bay leaves

2 garlic cloves

4 parsley stems

2 sprigs mint

1 fresh red chile, halved lengthwise and stems removed

1 Tbsp. fennel seeds

⅔ cup/150 ml dry white wine

salt and freshly ground black pepper

1 Boil the potatoes until just tender. Drain and allow to cool. Cut into thick slices lengthwise.

2 Meanwhile, combine all the stock ingredients in a pan, cover with water, and season well. Slowly bring to a boil and turn the heat down to a simmer. Simmer for 15 minutes, removing any scum that collects on the surface. Do not simmer for longer or the stock will start to taste bitter. Strain through a sieve into a bowl and set aside.

3 Heat 2 Tbsp. olive oil in a large pan, add the fennel, season with salt and pepper, and fry gently until tender and golden brown. Remove from the pan with a slotted spoon and set aside.

4 Add the garlic to the pan, fry for 30 seconds, then stir in the coriander and tomatoes. Simmer gently until the tomatoes start to disintegrate. Remove the pan from the heat and process the tomato mixture to a smooth puree in a food processor or with a hand-held blender.

5 Pour the pureed tomato mixture back into the pan, add the stock and wine, and bring to a boil. Simmer for 2 minutes to boil off the alcohol in the wine, then add the fennel, mussels, sea bass fillets, and potatoes. Cover, bring the stew to a gentle simmer, and cook for 5 minutes, or until the mussel shells have opened wide. Discard any mussels that remain closed, because they are not safe to eat. Taste and add salt and pepper as necessary.

6 To serve, ladle into bowls, sprinkle with mint and parsley, drizzle with olive oil, and top with a lemon wedge to squeeze over the stew.

CHICKEN AND MUSHROOM PIE

This may seem like a rather lengthy recipe but the chicken can poach while you do other things—and the wait is worth it. The meat will be beautifully tender and the stock full of flavor. This recipe is easy to adapt for dairy-, egg-, gluten- and soy-free diets and does not contain nuts. **Serves 4–6**

FOR THE CHICKEN

4½-lb./2-kg roasting chicken

1 onion, thickly sliced

2 carrots, thickly sliced

2 celery ribs, thickly sliced

1 handful mushroom stems

2 bay leaves

1 sprig thyme

5 parsley stems

3 grinds black pepper

FOR THE SAUCE

1 onion, thinly sliced

6 oz./180 g mushrooms, thickly sliced

1 sprig thyme

● DAIRY

6 Tbsp./85 g butter

3 Tbsp. vegetable oil

● GLUTEN

6 Tbsp./85 g all-purpose flour

3 Tbsp. cornstarch

1 bay leaf

salt and pepper

FOR THE PASTRY

Basic or Whole-wheat Shortcrust Pastry (see box, page 153), using 2 cups flour, 10 Tbsp. butter, and 3 Tbsp. water

● GLUTEN

1½ recipes Cornmeal and Potato Pastry (page 157)

1 beaten egg

● EGG

⅓ cup/100 ml milk or soy milk

1 Trim off any excess fat from the chicken. Place the chicken in a large pan and add the vegetables, herbs, and pepper. Cover the ingredients to a depth of ¾ in./2 cm with cold water. Cover with a lid and bring to the boil over medium heat.

2 Once the liquid starts to boil, remove the lid, reduce the heat to a simmer, and skim off any scum and fat that collects on the surface. Poach the chicken in barely simmering water for about 1½ hours (20 minutes per 1 lb./450 g), skimming off any scum and fat on the surface and replenishing the water so the chicken remains submerged. The chicken is cooked when the meat begins to separate from the bone and the legs move easily from side to side. Lift the cooked chicken out of the stock and allow to cool.

3 Strain the stock into a pan. Bring to a boil and reduce by a third to strengthen its flavor. Reserve 3¾ cups/860 ml of the reduced stock for the sauce.

4 Meanwhile, make the sauce. Combine the onion, mushrooms, thyme, and butter (or oil) in a saucepan and season well. Cover with a lid and cook gently over low heat, until the onion is very soft but not colored.

5 Stir the flour (or cornstarch) into the onion mixture and cook over low heat for 1 minute, stirring continuously. Add the bay leaf and a splash of stock to the pan and stir well until all the liquid has been absorbed. Add the remaining stock, little by little, stirring well between each addition. Bring the sauce slowly to boil, stirring constantly. Simmer for 1 minute, taste, and if necessary, season with more salt and pepper; set aside.

6 To prepare the chicken, discard the skin, remove the meat, and cut it into 1½-in./3.5-cm dice.

7 Mix the sauce and diced chicken together, then spoon into a 9 by 12-in./ 23 by 30-cm ovenproof baking dish.

Remove the thyme and bay leaf.

8 Preheat the oven to 350°F/180°C/ gas mark 4.

9 Roll out the pastry and assemble the pie using techniques described on pages 150–54.

10 Brush the pastry lid with beaten egg (or milk) and bake the pie for about 30 minutes, or until the filling is bubbling and the pastry lid is golden brown.

CORNED BEEF AND CABBAGE

The corned beef is poached in barely simmering water to keep it moist and tender. The addition of potatoes, carrots, and cabbage make it a one-dish meal. **Serves 4**

INGREDIENTS

4½ lb./2 kg corned beef brisket

2 Tbsp. mixed pickling spices

4 potatoes, peeled and quartered

3 carrots, peeled and quartered

1 head cabbage, cut into wedges

1 bay leaf, crumpled

3 cloves

10 peppercorns

5 allspice berries

2 cloves garlic, chopped

1 onion, sliced

Place the corned beef in a pan large enough to hold all the ingredients comfortably. Cover with cold water, add the pickling spices, and cover with a lid.

Bring the cooking liquid slowly to a

boil, remove the lid, and lower the heat to that the corned beef is poaching in barely simmering water. Poach for 20 minutes per pound (½ kg). Add water as necessary to ensure the meat remains submerged (so that it cooks evenly). Do not overcook (see Knowing When Meat is Cooked, page 112).

Let the meat cool in the cooking liquid for 15 minutes. Remove to a platter and cover with a tent of foil.

Return the cooking liquid to a boil. Add the potatoes and carrots and simmer for 20 minutes. Add the cabbage and simmer for 10 minutes, until all the vegetables are tender. Slice the meat against the grain and serve with the vegetables.

THAI GREEN CHICKEN CURRY

For this vibrant curry, the chicken and vegetables are gently poached in coconut milk flavored with green curry paste. The curry paste can be made the day before and stored, covered, in the refrigerator. **Serves 4**

FOR THE GREEN CURRY PASTE

4–6 fresh green chiles (depending on how spicy you like your curry), roughly chopped

½ onion, roughly chopped

5 garlic cloves

2-in./5-cm piece fresh ginger, roughly chopped

2 lemongrass stalks, outer leaves discarded, sliced into short lengths

2 tsp. ground coriander

1 tsp. ground cumin

stems from 1 bunch fresh cilantro, roughly chopped (save the leaves to garnish the curry)

2 tsp. Thai shrimp paste

finely grated zest of 2 limes

1 Tbsp. sunflower or corn oil

1 Tbsp. water

6 grinds fresh black pepper

½ tsp. salt

FOR THE CURRY

3 (14-oz./400-ml) cans coconut milk

2½ Tbsp. Asian fish sauce, plus more as needed

1 Tbsp. superfine sugar, plus more as needed

1 eggplant, cut into ¾-in./2-cm dice

2¼ lb./1 kg boneless, skinless chicken breasts, sliced across into ¾-in./2-cm strips

20 baby corn, cut in half lengthwise

2 fresh red chiles, seeded and quartered lengthwise

1 bunch cilantro leaves, roughly chopped

2 tsp. salt and freshly ground black pepper

lime juice, optional

1 Combine all the curry paste ingredients in a food processor and process until they form a fine paste.

2 Transfer the curry paste into a large saucepan and gently fry in its own oil for 1 minute, stirring continuously. Add 1 cup coconut milk and boil for 2 minutes.

3 Add the remaining coconut milk, the fish sauce, superfine sugar, and eggplant and simmer for 5 minutes.

4 Add the chicken and poach at a gentle simmer for 5 minutes.

5 Add the baby corn and red chiles and cook for 2 minutes. Check that the chicken strips are cooked. They should feel firm when pressed between thumb and index finger.

6 Remove the pan from the heat, stir in half of the chopped cilantro leaves and season with salt and pepper. Taste and balance the flavor the curry with salt, sugar, Asian fish sauce and lime juice as necessary.

7 Ladle the curry onto plates and sprinkle with the remaining cilantro leaves.

STEWING

Stewing involves slowly cooking poultry parts or small pieces of meat and vegetables in simmering liquid until very tender. Some varieties of seafood, such as squid and octopus, also benefit from slow stewing. Before the meat, poultry, or seafood and vegetables are immersed in liquid and stewed, they are usually browned in hot oil to add color and a rich flavor to the dish. Once the meat, poultry, or fish is tender and ready to eat, the richly flavored sauce is often reduced by half by boiling, to concentrate its flavor, and thickened with flour.

Many Asian curries and Moroccan tagines are also prepared by stewing meat, poultry, or fish in a liquid, flavored with spices, vegetables, and herbs (see Lamb Rogan Josh, page 134 and Moroccan Chicken Tagine, page 132).

HOW TO STEW MEAT AND POULTRY

- Trim excess fat and cut meat into pieces measuring no less than 1 by 2 in./2.5 by 5 cm (any smaller and the meat may break up during cooking).
- Season and brown the meat, poultry, or fish and any vegetables, a handful at a time, in hot oil, loosening the browned cooking juices on the bottom of the pan with water or other liquid (see How to Pan-fry on pages 86–87). If the bottom of the pan seems burned, loosen the burned bits with water and throw the liquid away because it would spoil the flavor of the stew.
- You can stir flour or cornstarch into the browned vegetables at this stage to thicken and deepen the color of the sauce. The liquid then can be added gradually.
- Bring slowly to a gentle simmer. As the liquid warms up, fat will rise to the surface. Skim it off with a metal spoon.
- Once the stew has begun to simmer, cover with a tight-fitting lid and continue to simmer the stew on top of the stove or place in an oven preheated to 300°F/150°C/ gas mark 2.
- Stews made with poultry are generally cooked for up to 1½ hours and are ready when the meat is just beginning to fall away from the bone. Stews made with meat, pork, or lamb will take longer (2–2½ hours because the muscle fibers are coarser, contain more connective tissue, and take longer to soften). Stewed meat is cooked when it can be cut in two easily with a fork. Overcooked meat falls apart into fine shreds.
- If the sauce is thin or very fatty, strain it into a clean pan, skim any remaining fat, and boil the sauce to reduce to a syrupy consistency before you serve the stew. Taste and season as necessary.

NOTES FOR FOOD ALLERGY SUFFERERS

Stews are largely safe for egg-, soy-, and nut-free diets but need some adjustment for those with a dairy or gluten allergy.

DAIRY-FREE DIET: Butter is often added to the oil used to brown meat before the stew is assembled, to enrich the flavor of the stew. Simply omit the butter and use a little more oil in its place.

GLUTEN-FREE DIET: Before browning, pieces of meat, poultry, or seafood are often rolled in seasoned flour, to thicken the cooking liquid. Alternatively, flour is added to vegetables as they are browned, to color and to thicken the sauce. Replace wheat flour with cornstarch.

MORROCAN CHICKEN TAGINE

A wonderfully rich and aromatic stew made with browned pieces of chicken or lamb (see variation opposite). It is free of dairy, gluten, eggs, nuts, and soy. Serve with Tabbouleh (page 140), couscous, bulgur, or brown rice and green beans. Make the day before it is due to be eaten because its flavor improves overnight. **Serves 4**

INGREDIENTS

sunflower or corn oil

3-lb./1.5-kg roasting chicken, cut into 8 pieces or 4 drumsticks and 4 thighs

salt and freshly ground black pepper

⅔ cup/150 ml dry white wine

1 large onion, halved from shoot to root and sliced thickly

1 red bell pepper, cored, seeded, and cut lengthwise into thick slices

4 garlic cloves, finely chopped

1-in./2.5-cm piece fresh ginger, finely chopped

2 tsp. cumin seeds

2 tsp. ground coriander

2 bay leaves

1 cinnamon stick

1 (15 oz./400 g) can diced tomatoes with juice

1 lemon, cut into thin wedges

1 pinch saffron

1 bunch cilantro, stems finely sliced and leaves chopped

2½ cups/570 ml White Chicken Stock (page 64)

4 oz./110 g dried apricots, cut in half

1 (15-oz./400-g) can chickpeas, rinsed and drained

1 heaped Tbsp. good-quality green olives

1 heaped Tbsp. good-quality black olives

1 Preheat the oven to 300°F/150°C/ gas mark 3.

2 Heat 2 Tbsp. of oil in a large Dutch oven. Season the skin side of each chicken piece and place half the pieces, in the Dutch oven. Gently fry the chicken until the skin is crisp and golden brown, then turn and brown the flesh side. Set aside. Brown the remaining chicken in the same way.

3 Using a wooden spoon, loosen any browned cooking juices on the bottom of the pan with the wine and pour over the browned chicken.

4 Heat 1 Tbsp. oil in the pan and add the onion and red pepper. Fry gently, stirring frequently, until soft and golden brown. Add the garlic, ginger, cumin, coriander, bay leaves, and cinnamon. Fry for another 30 seconds, stirring continuously.

5 Return the chicken and cooking juices to the pan and add the tomatoes, lemon, saffron, cilantro stems, stock, and enough water to cover the ingredients. Bring to the simmering point, skimming off any fat and scum that floats to the surface.

6 Cover and bake in the oven for 1 hour. Remove the pan from the oven and stir in the apricots, chickpeas, and olives. Cover and return to the oven for another 30 minutes, or until the chicken meat is just beginning to fall from the bone.

7 To thicken the sauce, lift out the chicken and vegetables and boil the sauce until it coats the back of a spoon.

Return the chicken and vegetables to the pan and bring back to a simmer. Taste and season as necessary.

8 Roughly chop the cilantro leaves. To serve, spoon the tagine onto plates and sprinkle with chopped cilantro.

VARIATION
LAMB TAGINE
In place of chicken use 1½ lb./600 g stewing lamb from the neck or shoulder, cut into 1-in./2.5-cm cubes. Brown the lamb in a pan, then bake for 2 hours in the oven or until the meat is easily cut with a fork. Add the chickpeas, apricots, and olives in the last 30 minutes of cooking.

LAMB ROGAN JOSH

This rich, aromatic curry has lots of deep red sauce. Serve with basmati rice to soak up the sauce and accompany with yogurt or soy yogurt flavored with chopped mint. Make the curry the day before serving, because its flavor improves overnight. **Serves 4**

INGREDIENTS

sunflower or corn oil

2¼ lb./1 kg stewing lamb, trimmed of fat and cut into 1 by 2 in./2.5 by 5 cm pieces

salt and freshly ground black pepper

2½ cups/570 ml White Chicken Stock (page 64) or water

2 large onions, finely diced

2 green bell peppers, cut into strips

6 garlic cloves, finely chopped

2-in./5-cm piece ginger, finely chopped

3–5 fresh red chiles , seeded and finely diced

6 cardamom pods

6 cloves

3 bay leaves

1 cinnamon stick

1 Tbsp. ground coriander

1 Tbsp. cumin seeds

2 Tbsp. paprika

1 (15-oz./400-g) can dried tomatoes

1 bunch cilantro stems, finely sliced

1 tsp. sugar

2 tsp. garam masala

● GLUTEN check label for wheat

1 bunch leaves from cilantro, chopped

1 Preheat the oven to 300°F/150°C/ gas mark 2.

2 Heat 1 Tbsp. oil in a Dutch oven over medium heat. Add a handful of lamb to the pan, season, and leave to stick to the pan to brown. Turn and brown the other side only when the meat releases itself from the bottom of the pan.

3 Repeat this process until all the lamb is cooked, loosening the browned cooking juices in the pan between batches with a splash of stock. Add this to the browned meat. Add a little oil to the pan between batches.

4 Season and fry the onions and peppers in 1 Tbsp. oil until golden brown. Add the garlic, ginger, chiles, cardamom, cloves, bay leaves, cinnamon, coriander, cumin, and paprika and gently fry for 30 seconds. Return the meat and the cooking juices to the pan. Over low heat, stir in the tomatoes, cilantro stems, and sugar. Add stock so the meat is covered. Cover with a lid and return to a boil.

5 Remove the lid and skim off any fat or scum on the surface. Replace the lid and and cook the curry in the oven for 1½ hours, or until a piece of lamb can be cut easily with a fork. Remove the curry from the oven every 30 minutes to skim off any fat and add water as necessary, so that the meat is just covered.

6 When the meat is cooked, stir in the garam masala, taste the sauce, and season as necessary. Spoon onto plates and sprinkle with the coriander leaves.

Chapter 14

POTATOES

Potatoes are starchy tubers, valued for their versatility in cooking and as a source of carbohydrate, fiber, minerals, and vitamin C. Potatoes also provide a starchy alternative in gluten-free diets in place of bread, pasta, and couscous.

Potatoes are available as small, new potatoes—which have a firm, waxy texture when cooked—and older, baking potatoes, which become soft and fluffy when cooked. New potatoes are best boiled and used in salads, simply tossed in olive oil or butter, lightly crushed with oil and seasoning (see Crushed New Potatoes on page 137), or gently fried. Baking potato varieties are suited to a wider variety of cooking methods including boiling, mashing, deep-frying, roasting, and sautéing. The potato dishes in this section make ideal accompaniments to many of the recipes in this book.

ROAST POTATOES

Potatoes are often served with a roast meat and roast very well in the top third of the oven at 350–400°F/180–200°C/gas mark 4–6, the standard temperature required to roast a meat or bird. Allow more time for them to brown and crisp up at the lower temperature. **Serves 4**

INGREDIENTS

2¼ lb./1 kg baking potatoes, peeled

sunflower or corn oil

salt

1 Cut the potatoes into 2-in./5-cm pieces. Place in a large saucepan, cover with cold salted water, put the lid on, and bring to a gentle simmer.

2 Cook until the potatoes can be pierced through with a table knife, then drain them in a colander, and allow them to steam dry for a few minutes.

3 Meanwhile, preheat the oven to 400°F/200°C/gas mark 6. Pour the oil into a roasting pan to a depth of

¼ in./1 cm and place in the oven.

4 Once the oil is hot enough to gently sizzle when a potato is added, carefully arrange the potatoes in one layer in the roasting pan. Quickly rough up the surfaces of the potatoes with a fork to help them crisp up, spoon oil over them, and place in the top third of the oven.

5 Roast the potatoes for 60–75 minutes, turning the potatoes every 20 minutes to help them brown and crisp up evenly.

6 When the potatoes are crisp and golden, use a slotted spoon to transfer them to a serving dish.

OVEN-BAKED FRIES

Golden and crispy and made with very little oil, these fries are much healthier—but just as tasty—as the deep-fried variety. **Serves 4**

INGREDIENTS

2¼ lb./1 kg large potatoes

3 Tbsp. sunflower or olive oil

sea salt and freshly ground black pepper

1 Preheat the oven to 400°F/200°C/ gas mark 6.

2 Scrub the potatoes, cut them in half lengthwise then slice each half into long wedges approximately ¾ in./2 cm thick.

Arrange in a single layer on the roasting pan.

3 Drizzle the potato wedges with oil, sprinkle with a large pinch of salt, and season lightly with black pepper. Turn the wedges over a few times to coat evenly with oil and seasoning.

4 Bake the potatoes for 30 minutes, turning after 15 minutes to allow them to brown and crisp evenly on all sides. Serve immediately.

MASHED POTATOES

Hot and fluffy mashed potatoes are traditionally served with stews and as a topping on oven-baked dishes. Use baking potatoes; waxy, new potatoes become gluey when mashed. **Serves 4**

INGREDIENTS

2 lb./900 g baking potatoes, peeled

● **DAIRY** 2½ Tbsp./40 g butter
dairy-free spread or 1 Tbsp. olive oil

● **DAIRY** ⅔ cup/150 ml milk
soy or rice milk

salt and freshly ground black pepper

1 Cut the potatoes into even size pieces, place in a pan of cold salted water, cover with a lid, and simmer gently for 25 minutes, or until you can push a table knife into them easily. Do not overcook.

2 Drain the potatoes and leave in the colander to steam dry for a minute or so.

3 Return the potatoes to the pan, add the butter, milk, and seasoning. Mash the potatoes until lump free and fluffy. Taste and season again if necessary.

VARIATION
CHAMP
Add a handful of thinly sliced scallions to the milk and simmer for 5 minutes. Add to the potatoes before mashing.

CRUSHED NEW POTATOES

New potatoes taste wonderful flavored with garlic and good-quality olive oil. Serve with pan-fried or grilled meat, poultry, or fish. **Serves 4**

INGREDIENTS

1½ lb./675 g new potatoes

sea salt and freshly ground black pepper

2 unpeeled garlic cloves

2 Tbsp. olive oil

2 Tbsp. chopped chives

1 Place the potatoes in a pan with ½ tsp. salt and the garlic, and cover with cold water. Cover with a lid and bring to a boil.

2 Remove the lid and cook the potatoes at a lively simmer for 15–20 minutes, until the potatoes feel tender when a knife is inserted into them. Do not overcook the potatoes.

3 Drain in a colander and leave the potatoes to dry for a few minutes.

4 Return the potatoes to the pan. Squeeze the softened garlic out of its skin onto the potatoes and add the olive oil, 1 tsp. salt, and 3 grinds of black pepper.

5 Gently press down on the cooked potatoes with a potato masher a few times to break them into small pieces. Do not mash the potatoes or they will become sticky. Gently stir the chives into the potatoes. Taste and add a little more salt and pepper, if necessary.

Chapter 15 | GRAINS, RICE, AND PASTA

GRAINS

In cooking, the term grain refers to the edible seeds of plants, mainly from the grass family. Wheat and its close relatives, barley and rye, produce grains rich in the protein gluten. Other plants from the grass family produce gluten-free grains, such as rice, millet, and corn. Quinoa, the seeds of a plant related to spinach, and buckwheat, the seeds of a plant related to rhubarb, are also ideal gluten-free substitutes for grains containing gluten.

GRAINS CONTAINING GLUTEN

BARLEY At one time barley held a similar position to that of wheat in today's Western diet. However, it is now mainly used to add thickness and texture to winter soups and stews. It fulfills this role admirably, but it can easily be replaced by lentils, beans, or brown rice. Pearl barley, which is the type used in most recipes, needs to be simmered for 45–60 minutes—on its own or in a soup or stew.

RYE Rye is mainly used to make dense, richly flavored rye bread and crackers but can also be eaten as a whole grain in stews and breads or rolled to form flakes for use in muesli.

WHEAT Because wheat berries are very hard, it is first parboiled, then crushed or cracked into varying sizes.
Bulgur or cracked wheat: Bulgur is a traditional ingredient in Middle Eastern cooking and is served hot with meat and vegetables or cold in salads. Its tender but chewy consistency makes it a great base for meat-free stuffing. To cook bulgur, see the recipe for Tabbouleh, page 140.
Couscous: Couscous is a staple of North Africa where it is eaten with savory dishes, such as tagines. Semolina (roughly ground durum wheat) is steamed, then dried to form fine, pale yellow granules. Couscous grains are much finer than bulgur and cook more quickly. Simply place the couscous in a bowl, cover with boiling water to a depth of 1 in./2.5 cm, stir in a pinch of salt and a Tbsp. of olive oil, cover with plastic wrap or a plate, and leave to stand for 10–15 minutes.

Oats

Oats are a valuable breakfast cereal and baking ingredient but they contain a protein similar to gluten and should be avoided by those on a gluten-free diet (also, oats are often processed in factories that process wheat). Buckwheat flakes have a very similar texture to rolled oats and can be used in place of them to make muesli (see page 141). Millet and Rice Flake Porridge also stands in very well for porridge made with oatmeal (see Breakfast Cereals, page 141).

BUCKWHEAT   GLUTEN-FREE GRAINS

Buckwheat produces dark, triangular-shaped seeds and is used widely in Chinese and Eastern European cooking. Buckwheat grain is either roasted to develop its characteristic flavor before being ground into flour or is dried for a milder taste. Buckwheat flour has a strong flavor that is a particularly good foil for contrasting flavors (see Buckwheat Pancakes, page 196). Steamed and rolled buckwheat flakes are mild in flavor and similar to oats in texture so they are a useful oat substitute in breakfast cereals. They can also be used to add texture to gluten-free bread.

CORN   Corn, also called maize, is a cereal grass, related to wheat, rice, oats, and barley. As well as eaten fresh from the cob, it is dried and ground into coarse cornmeal, a staple in some parts of the world, or formulated into the fine powder known as cornstarch.

Cornmeal: Cornmeal, also known as polenta, is ground either to a coarse powder with a gritty texture or more finely into a softer-textured flour used in baking. Cornmeal tastes of corn and gives a coarse, crumbly texture to baked goods. Due to its coarse texture, it is usually blended with other flours for baking.

Cornstarch: A flavorless, fine white powder with a smooth consistency, cornstarch is made from the dried white center of corn kernels. Cornstarch is traditionally used to thicken sauces in Chinese cooking and is a very good gluten-free thickening agent and substitute for wheat flour, for savory and sweet flour-thickened sauces. Cornstarch also adds lightness to gluten-free pastry, cookies and cakes—which can be rather heavy. Used alone, cornstarch produces light but very dry baked products, so is best blended with other gluten-free flours.

MILLET   This nutritious, ancient grain, originally eaten by the Egyptians, is finely ground and used to make flat bread in North Africa and India. Millet grain is tiny, round, and either yellow, white, or red. It is eaten as a whole grain or hulled. Boiled millet has a light, delicate flavor with a firm bite and makes a great gluten-free substitute for couscous and bulgur. Fine-textured millet flakes are a good substitute for oatmeal in hot cereal and can add fiber and texture to gluten-free bread. Millet flour has a grainy texture rather like cornmeal and is best used for coating meat, poultry, and fish before frying to form a crispy coating. It is also used to make gluten-free pasta (see page 147).

QUINOA   Quinoa, pronounced "keen-wa," was a staple of the Incas in South America. The grains are small and round with a subtle nutty flavor and provide one of the best sources of protein of any vegetable. It can be bought in health food stores and good supermarkets and is a valuable alternative grain to rice, bulgur, and couscous. It is also great used in stuffing to add bulk and texture.

When boiled, quinoa expands to four times its original size and cooks in approximately 15 minutes (see Quinoa Tabbouleh, page 140).

TABBOULEH

Bulgur is traditionally the main ingredient, but brown rice, millet, and quinoa make very good gluten-free alternatives (see Variations below). Tabbouleh is full of color and aromatic flavor and is a great accompaniment to Baked Moroccan Chicken with Fennel (page 121). **Serves 4**

INGREDIENTS

1 cup/170 g bulgur

½ tsp. salt, plus more as needed

¼ cup extra virgin olive oil

finely grated zest and juice of 2 lemons

freshly ground black pepper

1 bunch flat-leaved parsley, finely chopped

1 handful mint leaves, finely chopped

1 handful cilantro leaves, finely chopped

4 scallions, finely sliced

4 ripe tomatoes, seeded and diced

½ cucumber, halved, seeded, and diced

1 tsp. superfine sugar

1 Place the bulgur in a medium-sized bowl and cover with boiling water to a depth of 1 in./2.5 cm. Stir in the salt and 1 Tbsp. olive oil. Cover and leave for 15–20 minutes, until the grains are chewy, not hard.

2 Drain the bulgur in a sieve, then spread out to dry and cool on a tray lined with paper towels.

3 Whisk the remaining 3 Tbsp. oil with the lemon juice and black pepper.

4 Transfer the bulgur to a bowl. Stir in the parsley, mint, cilantro, scallions, tomatoes, cucumber, and sugar. Taste and add more seasoning as necessary. Cover with plastic wrap and chill for 30 minutes before serving.

VARIATIONS

BROWN RICE TABBOULEH

Rinse 1 cup/225 g brown rice under cold running water and add to a pan of boiling salted water. Bring back to a simmer and cook the rice for 30–35 minutes, until tender. Drain, then rinse the rice under cold running water to cool quickly. Follow the recipe above from step 3.

MILLET TABBOULEH

Combine ¾ cup/170 g millet, 2⅔ cups/ 600 ml water, and ½ tsp. salt in a pan. Cover and bring to a boil. Reduce the heat and simmer for 20–30 minutes, until the millet is tender and fluffy. Follow the recipe from step 3.

QUINOA TABBOULEH

Rinse ¾ cup/170 g quinoa under cold running water and add it to 1½ cups/ 340 ml salted boiling water. Bring back to a simmer and cook for 10 minutes, until the circular germ begins to separate from the seed. Remove the quinoa from the heat, cover with a tight-fitting lid, and leave it to absorb the remaining water. The quinoa will increase by three to four times in volume and should be light and fluffy in texture. Spread out on paper towels to cool, then follow the recipe from step 3.

BREAKFAST CEREALS

A good breakfast is a vital part of a healthy, varied diet. Too often people automatically eat the same old cereal every morning. Here are some ideas for home-cooked or home-mixed cereals—some are suitable for those with a gluten allergy, some are not, but they are all delicious.

CREAMY OATMEAL

This recipe isn't suitable for those with a gluten allergy (for gluten-free cereal, try the Creamy Rice Pudding or Millet and Rice Flake Porridge recipes below), but it is suitable for dairy-free diets if you use soy, rice, or oat milk. This recipe serves 4.

Place 2 cups/200 g rolled oats, 2½ cups/570 ml milk, and ½ tsp. salt in a pan. Slowly bring the cereal to a gentle simmer over low heat, stirring slowly and continuously for 2–3 minutes, until the oats have softened and the cereal is thick and creamy (add a little more milk if it is too stiff and thick). Stir in 1 Tbsp. honey, maple syrup, or sugar. Spoon into bowls, pour over a little milk, and serve immediately.

CREAMY RICE PUDDING

This gluten-free pudding is also delicious served as "porridge" for breakfast. It takes an hour to cook, so it is best made the night before. Reheat by adding a splash of milk and stirring it over a low heat until it starts to simmer. This recipe serves 4.

Slowly bring 4 cups/1.2 litres of milk (cows' or dairy-free) to boil. Add 1 cup/170 g arborio rice, ½ tsp. salt, 1 Tbsp. honey, and 1 cinnamon stick or ½ tsp. ground cinnamon. Cover and simmer gently for 1 hour, or until the rice is soft. Serve immediately or allow to cool and store covered in the refrigerator until required.

MILLET AND RICE FLAKE PORRIDGE

This smooth, gluten-free hot cereal has a delicate flavor similar to semolina pudding. The rice flakes are included in the recipe to add a soft, chewy texture similar to oatmeal. This recipe serves 4.

Combine 1½ cups/150 g millet flakes, ⅓ cup/55 g rice flakes, ½ tsp. ground cinnamon, and ½ tsp. salt in a pan. Stir in 3 cups/860 ml milk and slowly bring the mixture to a simmer over low heat, stirring continuously. Simmer for 15 minutes, or until the millet flakes are no longer gritty and the rice flakes have softened but are still slightly chewy. Stir in 2 Tbsp.s honey, spoon into bowls, pour over a little milk, and serve immediately.

GLUTEN-FREE MUESLI

This muesli is full of texture and flavor and is delicious served with dairy or soy yogurt, honey, and fresh fruit. Experiment with different dried fruit and nuts, or for a nut- and seed-free diet, substitute an equal amount of gluten-free flakes. Brown rice flakes, buckwheat flakes, and millet flakes, are all available from health food stores. This recipe makes 4 servings.

In a medium-sized bowl, mix ½ cup/60 g each of brown rice flakes, buckwheat flakes, millet flakes, roughly chopped Brazil nuts, flaked almonds, and chopped dried apricots with 2 Tbsp. rice bran, ¼ cup/30 g golden raisins, ¼ cup/30 g dried cherries, 1 Tbsp./15 g flaxseed, 1 Tbsp./15 g sunflower seeds, and 1 Tbsp. brown sugar (optional). Use as required.

RICE

Rice is eaten as a staple grain by half of the world's population—and is much loved the world over for its taste and versatility. Before it can be eaten, the tough outer hull is removed to produce brown rice. The husk and germ, left intact on brown rice grains, is extremely nutritious because it is high in fiber and minerals, including potassium, magnesium, iron, calcium, and zinc. Brown rice is also rich in carbohydrate, vitamin E, thiamine, riboflavin, niacin, and folic acid. Brown rice has a mild, nutty flavor and a chewy texture and is altogether a superior grain to white rice in flavor and nutritional value.

Rice is classified into long-grain, medium-grain, and short-grain varieties, all of which are available as brown or white rice.

LONG-GRAIN RICE

Long-grain varieties include basmati rice and jasmine rice. Long-grain rice has a firm but delicate texture and is normally served plain or fried with other ingredients to make rice dishes such as pilau rice or Chinese stir-fried rice. It is also eaten cold in salads.

Cooking long-grain rice

Two cooking methods are used to cook long-grain rice—the boiling method and the absorption method. Brown rice requires more cooking than white rice and is best cooked by the boiling method. Boiling is also suitable for white rice, but the absorption method produces dry, light fluffy grains and is used widely in Asian and Middle Eastern cooking.

The boiling method

- Fill a large pan two-thirds full of water. Add salt and bring to a rolling boil.
- Allow ⅓ cup/55–85 g uncooked rice per person. Rinse the rice under cold running water to remove starch, which keeps the grains from sticking to each other.
- Pour the rice into the boiling water and cook, uncovered, at a gentle simmer for

approximately 15 minutes for white rice and 30 minutes for brown rice. White rice is cooked when the grains are tender and no longer chalky in the center: brown rice is cooked when the grain is soft in the center but still chewy.
- Drain the rice in a fine-mesh sieve. Pour boiling water through it and allow the rice to steam-dry for a minute. Fluff up with a fork and use as required.

The absorption method

This method is used for plain rice and for complete rice dishes cooked in the pot. Stock is often used in place of water to add extra flavor to the rice.
- Allow ⅓ cup/55–85 g uncooked rice per person. Rinse

Rice products

Rice is used to make a wide variety of products that are common in Asian cooking. These are tasty in their own right, but are also useful gluten-free ingredients.

Rice noodles: White and translucent in appearance, rice noodles are made from ground rice and water. They are cut into wide ribbons, thick strands, or very thin thread-like noodles known as "glass noodles," because they become clear when cooked. Rice noodles are soaked in hot water for hot dishes, in cold water for use in salads, lightly cooked in stock-based soups, or deep-fried and used as a crispy garnish.

Rice pasta: Rice is usually mixed with millet to make gluten-free pasta (see Gluten-Free Pasta, page 147).

Rice flour: This is made from brown or white rice ground to a fine powder. Brown rice flour is high in fiber and far more nutritious than white rice flour. They both have a mild flavor, creamy color, and are used in mainstream cooking to make short, crumbly cookies and very light cakes. For gluten-free cooking, rice flour is invaluable and is used in cakes, bread, cookies and pastry (see Chapter 16).

Ground rice: Ground rice has a gritty texture because it is more coarsely ground than rice flour. Its grittiness limits its uses to producing a very short, crumbly texture in some baked foods.

Rice bran: The bran lies between the husk and starchy center of rice grain and is very high in fiber. It is brown in color with a mild, malty flavor. It is ideal for adding fiber, color, and flavor to gluten-free baked foods, such as bread (see Gluten-free Brown Bread, page 187) and pastry (see Gluten-free Whole-Grain Rice and Almond Pastry, page 155).

the rice under cold running water to remove the starch, to keep the grains from sticking to each other.
- Place the rice in a pan, pour over double the volume of boiling water or stock, and season with salt. Place a close-fitting lid on the pan and gently simmer for 10–15 minutes, until the water has almost been absorbed and little pits appear on the surface of the rice.
- Remove the pan from the heat and leave the rice, with the lid firmly on, to finish cooking in its own steam for another 10 minutes, until tender. Fluff up with a fork and use as required.

MEDIUM-GRAIN RICE

Medium-grain rice includes Italian arborio rice, Spanish paella rice, and red Camargue rice.

Cooking medium-grain rice

Medium-grain rice are versatile grains used to make Italian risotto and Spanish paella. Neither is suited to the cooking methods used for long-grain rice because the grains become mushy. First lightly pan-fry in butter or olive oil, to prevent them from sticking together, then gradually stir hot stock into the rice over a low heat, until the stock is absorbed and the rice is tender (see Seafood Risotto, page 146). Constant stirring also helps to mix the starch on the surface of the rice grains with the liquid to give the creamy consistency of risottos and paellas.

SHORT-GRAIN RICE Almost round in shape, short-grained rice varieties include carnaroli, used to make risottos; glutinous rice, used widely in Asian cooking; and pudding rice, used to make rice pudding.

Cooking short-grain rice

Short-grain rice must be cooked very gently to prevent it from becoming mushy. Carnaroli rice is cooked in the same way as the medium-grain rice arborio.

Glutinous rice is cooked by the absorption method (see above). Because it is high in starch, the cooked grains of rice stick lightly to one another, which makes it easy to eat with chopsticks and to mold into sushi.

Pudding rice is gently simmered in milk flavored with sugar, citrus zest, or cinnamon (see Creamy Rice Pudding, page 141). For dairy-free rice pudding, use rice milk or soy milk.

RICE SALAD WITH PISTACHIO AND POMEGRANATE SEEDS

Not your average rice salad, this recipe will surprise your guests with its interesting ingredients, colorful appearance and light, fragrant flavor. It's a great dish to serve at a summer lunch or as part of a buffet with barbecued or grilled meat and fish. **Serves 4**

INGREDIENTS

1¼ cups/225 g basmati rice

2 Tbsp. freshly squeezed lemon juice

1 tsp. superfine sugar

salt

freshly ground black pepper

5 Tbsp. extra virgin olive oil

½ red onion, finely sliced

1 ripe pomegranate

finely grated zest of ½ lemon

½ cup/55 g roasted, shelled pistachios,

diced cucumber

1 bunch flat-leaved parsley, roughly chopped

● NUTS

1 Rinse the rice in a sieve under cold running water. Bring a large pan of salted water to boil, then pour in the rinsed rice and simmer gently, uncovered, for approximately 15 minutes, or until the rice grains are tender. Do not allow the water to boil too hard because the surface of the grains is liable to become mushy before the center is properly cooked.

2 Meanwhile, pour the lemon juice into a small bowl, add the sugar, ½ tsp. salt, and 3 grinds black pepper. Whisk until the sugar and salt have dissolved. Whisk in the oil, 1 Tbsp. at a time to form an emulsion. Stir in the finely sliced red onion and leave to soften while the rice is cooking.

3 Drain the cooked rice in a large sieve or colander and place under cold running water until the rice is thoroughly cooled. Leave to drain for 10 minutes.

4 To remove the seeds from the pomegranate, cut it in half across the middle and, using a teaspoon, scrape out the seeds into a bowl and remove any white membrane. (Wear an apron because pomegranate juice stains.)

5 In a large bowl, mix the rice with the lemon and onion dressing, the lemon zest, pistachios, parsley, and pomegranate seeds.

6 Cover and chill the salad for at least 3 hours before serving, to allow the rice to absorb the flavors of the other ingredients. Taste and season as necessary.

TOMATO AND GARLICKY PASTA WITH SHRIMP AND LEMON

This easy-to-prepare dish is so delicious it has become a strong favorite with my family. Its lively, aromatic flavors rely on good-quality, fresh ingredients prepared just before cooking. The flat, ribbon shape of linguine goes particularly well with seafood, but gluten-free rice and millet fusilli also works well. The quantities are generous because your guests are very likely to ask for a second helping. **Serves 4**

INGREDIENTS

1 lb./500 g linguine

● **GLUTEN**
rice and millet pasta or corn pasta

● **EGG**
most fresh and some dried pasta uses egg—check the package

extra virgin olive oil

4 large ripe tomatoes, roughly chopped

2 large garlic cloves, finely chopped

sea salt and freshly ground black pepper

1½ lb./500 g shrimp, cooked and peeled

finely grated zest of 1 lemon

finely chopped parsley or torn basil leaves

1 Cook the pasta in boiling salted water (see Cooking Pasta, page 147). Dried pasta will take approximately 12 minutes to cook; fresh pasta 4–5 minutes.

2 Meanwhile, pour enough olive oil into a medium-sized pan to cover the bottom to a depth of ¼ in./1 cm. Place the pan over medium heat. Once the oil is hot, add the tomatoes, garlic, a generous pinch of sea salt, and a grind of pepper. Bring slowly to a gentle simmer.

3 When the tomatoes are soft, stir in the shrimp. Bring the sauce back to a simmer, remove from the heat, and cover with a lid. Do not overcook the shrimp because they will become dry and tough.

4 Thoroughly drain the pasta in a colander and pour it back into the pan.

5 Stir the lemon zest into the sauce. Mix the sauce with the pasta so that the pasta is evenly coated. Taste and season with sea salt to bring out the flavors. Sprinkle with parsley before serving.

Chapter 16 | HOME BAKING

PASTRY

Of the many styles of pastry, shortcrust is the most versatile. Not only does it have a neutral flavor that makes it ideal for a wide variety of sweet and savory fillings, but it can be adapted easily—enriched with egg, sweetened with sugar, flavored with cheese and finely ground nuts, or made with whole-wheat flour. It is also the most adaptable pastry for food-allergy sufferers.

Although it is traditionally made with flour, butter, water, or egg, shortcrust pastry can be made just as well with gluten-free flours, dairy-free margarine, and water. However,

NOTES FOR FOOD ALLERGY SUFFERERS

DAIRY-FREE DIET: Butter is used to add flavor, richness, and color, and to make a pastry that is easy to handle. Hard dairy-free baking margarine is a perfectly good alternative. Its flavor is not as rich and buttery, but it makes pastry dough that is easy to handle and is just as light and crumbly when baked. Soft margarine is not suitable because it produces a dough that is too soft to handle.

GLUTEN-FREE DIET: Most fine-textured gluten-free flours are suitable for making shortcrust pastry, but they are best blended in specific proportions to closely imitate the properties of wheat. For example, rice flour, when used alone, produces a dry, gritty-textured pastry. However, when it is blended with cornstarch, which adds lightness, and ground almonds, which add moisture and richness, the result is a gluten-free pastry to rival wheat flour pastry in flavor, texture, and appearance. Stronger flavored flours, such as buckwheat, cornmeal, and soy flour, are also suitable for pastry making, provided they are blended with blander flavored flours to prevent the pastry from overpowering the flavor of the overall dish.

EGG-FREE DIET: Cold beaten egg, mixed with a small quantity of water, is often used to bind pastry ingredients, because it adds color and richness and softens the texture of pastry. For egg-free pastry, use chilled water only (this simply gives a paler and crisper pastry than one bound with egg). Mashed potato can also be used instead of egg to bind savory pastry (see Cornmeal and Potato Pastry, page 157).

NUT-FREE DIET: Ground almonds, walnuts, and hazelnuts are sometimes used to add flavor, richness, and texture to shortcrust pastry. Instead, simply use a basic savory or sweet shortcrust pastry or, for a nutty flavor, whole-wheat pastry. Many of the gluten-free pastry recipes that follow use ground almonds. Replace these with soy flour for a rich, soft crumbly pastry or cornmeal for a crisp-textured pastry.

SOY-FREE DIET: Pastry is suitable for soy-free diets provided soy flour and margarine containing soybean oil is not used to make it.

due to the lack of gluten, which helps bind the ingredients, gluten-free shortcrust pastry is made differently from that made with wheat flour. You'll find recipes for both versions in this chapter.

GUIDELINES FOR
MAKING
SHORTCRUST
PASTRY

The presence of gluten in wheat flour is both an advantage and disadvantage in pastry making. Gluten lightly binds dough together so that it does not fall to pieces when handled and is firm but crumbly when baked. However, when too much water is added to the dough or it is kneaded or rolled too much, the gluten strands develop, toughening the pastry and causing it to harden and shrink as it cooks. Follow these steps to ensure perfect pastry:

Preparing the dough
- Keep the ingredients cool and use very cold water or a chilled beaten egg to bind. Warm ingredients produce a greasy, tough pastry.
- Measure your ingredients accurately. Too much or too little flour, fat, or liquid may result in dry, greasy, or tough pastry.
- To rub flour and fat together, use the fingertips of both hands, letting the rubbed mixture fall back into the bowl. Continue a bit at a time until the mixture resembles fine bread crumbs. If your hands are warm, cut the flour and butter together using a scissorlike action with two table knives. This way the fat will not melt into the flour and toughen the pastry.
- Stir the liquid into the flour and butter crumbs, tablespoon by tablespoon, until the mixture is sufficiently damp to clump together and form a ball of dough. Do not add too much liquid—wet dough is hard to handle and produces tough, shrunken pastry.

Rolling the pastry
- Sprinkle the work surface lightly with flour to keep the pastry from sticking.
- Place the ball of dough on the floured work surface and, using a lightly floured rolling pin, flatten it into a rough circle, approximately 1 in./2.5 cm thick.
- With firm strokes away from your body, roll the pastry out into a circle at least 1 in./2.5 cm larger than the pan. Turn the pastry a quarter turn every four rolls to ensure it is rolled evenly and to prevent it from sticking to the work surface. Pastry used to line a tart pan or pie dish should be no thicker than ⅛ in./3 mm. Pastry for small individual tarts and pies should be slightly thinner.
- Before moving the pastry, run a palette knife under it to free any patches that may have stuck to the work surface.

Lining a pan
- Wrap the pastry around the rolling pin, then lift it above the pan. Unwind the pastry into the pan or pie dish and gently press the pastry into place on the bottom, sides, and corners with your fingers. If the pastry breaks, don't worry; it can be patched up with trimmings afterwards.
- Roll the rolling pin over the rim to remove the excess pastry.

Patching cracked pastry shells

Pastry shells sometimes crack as they bake and must be patched up before the filling is added, to prevent leakage. Brush fine cracks with beaten egg or patch up wider cracks or holes with a small amount of leftover pastry. Return the pastry shell to the oven to set the egg or to lightly bake any pastry used for patching.

- Repair any holes by pressing the dough back together or using a little of the excess dough to fill large holes.
- Place the lined tart pan in the refrigerator for 30 minutes, to firm up the pastry before baking. This reduces the likelihood of the pastry shrinking and losing its shape in the oven.

Baking blind

To prevent pastry shells that contain moist fillings from becoming heavy and soggy when baked, they are often "baked blind" until crisp before they are filled.

- Cut out a large circle of parchment paper and crumple it into a ball (to soften it so that it fits tightly into the corners). Open the paper out and line the pastry, then weight it down with 2–3 Tbsp. of ceramic baking beans or dried beans or rice.
- Preheat the oven to 400°F/200°C/gas mark 6. Do not put the pastry in the oven until it has reached the correct temperature (otherwise it may collapse and become very greasy).
- Bake the pastry for 15–20 minutes, until it is dry and firm. Remove the paper and beans and bake for another 10 minutes, or until the pastry shell is an even light golden color and dry and crisp to touch. Watch sweetened pastry carefully because it burns easily. If the rim of the pastry is browning too quickly, reduce the oven temperature and cover the top edge and sides of the tart shell with foil.
- Leave the pastry to cool on a wire rack before adding the filling.

Assembling a single-crust pie

Single-crust pies consist of a pie filling covered with a pastry lid. They're a great way to turn the simplest filling into something a little more special.

- Spoon the filling into the pie dish and roll out the pastry lid to ⅛ in./3 mm thick and 2 in./5 cm larger than the dish.

- From the edge of the rolled pastry, cut long strips slightly thicker than the rim of the dish. Brush the rim of the dish with water and stick the strips of pastry to it, trimming away any excess pastry with a sharp knife. This forms a firm base for attaching the pie lid.

- Brush the pastry rim with water and lay the rolled-out pastry over the dish, using your rolling pin to lift and support it. Gently press the edges of the pastry lid down onto the pastry-covered rim to seal in the filling. Cut away any excess pastry. Scallop the edges with the tips of your fingers, if you wish.

- Make a small hole in the center of the pastry lid to allow steam to escape. Decorate the pie by sticking leaf-shaped pieces of pastry onto the lid with a little water.

- To glaze the pie, brush all over with beaten egg or milk and chill for 20 minutes in the refrigerator, to set the pastry. Bake the pie in a preheated oven.

BASIC SHORTCRUST PASTRY

Before making this pastry, read about Making Shortcrust Pastry, page 150.

This versatile pastry has a delicate flavor and crumbly texture that is perfect for pastry cases and pie shells for savory or sweet fillings. It is egg free and easily adapted for dairy-free diets, but it contains wheat flour—for gluten-free pastry, see pages 155–57. This recipe makes one 10–12-inch/25–30-cm tart. **Serves 8–10**

INGREDIENTS

1¾ cups/225 g all-purpose flour

¼ tsp. salt

½ cup/110 g chilled butter, cut into ⅓-in./1-cm dice

dairy-free hard baking margarine

2–3 Tbsp. cold water

● **DAIRY**

1 Sift the flour and salt into a mixing bowl and add the diced butter. Rub the flour and butter together with your fingertips until they resemble coarse crumbs.

2 Using a table knife and then your fingertips, stir in 2 Tbsp. water to bind. The dough should be just damp enough to form a ball. If the mixture is too dry to clump together, stir in another 1 Tbsp. cold water.

3 Wrap the pastry dough in plastic wrap and chill for 30 minutes. Preheat the oven to 400°F/200°C/gas mark 6.

4 Roll the pastry to the correct thickness and use as required. If the pastry is soft after being handled, rest it once more in the refrigerator until cold and firm.

VARIATIONS

SAVORY RICH SHORTCRUST PASTRY
Egg enriches the flavor and softens the crumb of shortcrust pastry, making it perfect for rich-flavored fillings. To adapt the basic recipe above, mix 2 chilled egg yolks with 2 Tbsp. cold water and use as per the instructions for step 2.

SWEET SHORTCRUST PASTRY
With its delicate flavor and crisp texture, this pastry is mainly used to make sweet tarts and fruit pies. It can also be used in place of sweet rich shortcrust pastry for an egg-free diet. To adapt the Basic Shortcrust Pastry recipe above, stir 6 Tbsp./70 g superfine sugar into the butter and flour crumbs, then bind the pastry with 2–3 Tbsp. cold water, as above.

SWEET RICH SHORTCRUST PASTRY
This recipe is ideal for making tart shells and rich pies. To adapt the Basic Shortcrust Pastry recipe above, stir 6 Tbsp./70 g superfine sugar into the butter and flour crumbs, then mix 2 chilled egg yolks with 2 Tbsp. cold water and mix into the flour, butter, and sugar mixture, to form the dough.

WHOLE-WHEAT PASTRY
Whole-wheat flour gives a nutty flavor, making it ideal for hearty sweet and savory pies and tarts. For savory pastry, substitute 1 cup/110 g all-purpose flour with plain whole-wheat flour and continue as above. To make sweet whole-wheat pastry, substitute 1 cup./110 g all-purpose flour with all-purpose whole-wheat flour and stir in 6 Tbsp./ 70 g superfine sugar at step 2.

Pastry quantities

This useful guide indicates what size tart pan or pie dish is required to feed a certain number of people and how much pastry you need for it.

Tart shells

To serve 2–4: line a 6-in./15-cm tart pan with pastry made with 14 Tbsp./110 g flour; ¼ cup/55 g butter or dairy-free hard baking margarine, diced; and 1–2 Tbsp. cold water. For rich shortcrust pastry, mix 1 egg yolk with 1 Tbsp. cold water. For sweet shortcrust pastry, add 2 tsp. superfine sugar to the flour and butter.

To serve 4–6: line a 7–8-in./18–20-cm tart pan with pastry made with 1⅓ cups/170 g flour; 6 Tbsp./85 g butter or dairy-free hard baking margarine, diced; and 1–2 Tbsp. cold water. For rich shortcrust pastry, mix 1 egg yolk with 1–2 Tbsp. cold water. For sweet shortcrust pastry, add 4 Tbsp./55 g superfine sugar to the flour and butter.

To serve 8–10: line a 10–12-in./25–30 cm tart pan with pastry made with 1¾ cups/225 g flour; ½ cup/110 g butter or dairy-free hard baking margarine, diced; and 2–3 Tbsp. cold water. For rich shortcrust pastry, mix 2 egg yolks with 2 Tbsp. cold water. For sweet shortcrust pastry, add 6 Tbsp./70 g superfine sugar to the flour and butter.

To make twenty 2½-in./6-cm tarts: make the pastry using the quantities given in "To serve 8–10" above.

Pie crusts

To make twelve 2½-in./6-cm pies with lids: make the pastry using the quantities given in "To serve 8–10" above.

To make a single-crusted pie to serve 4–6: use a 9-in./1.5-l pie dish and make the pastry lid with 2⅓ cups/300 g flour, 10 Tbsp./140 g butter and 3 Tbsp. cold water. For rich shortcrust pastry, mix 2 egg yolks with 2 Tbsp. cold water. For sweet shortcrust pastry, add 7 Tbsp./85 g superfine sugar to the flour and butter.

To make a double-crusted pie to serve 4–6: use a 9-in./1.5-l pie dish or a 9–10-in./23–25-cm round pie plate and make the pastry with double the quantities given in "To serve 4–6" above.

MAKING GLUTEN-FREE SHORTCRUST PASTRY

Preparing the dough

The absence of gluten means that gluten-free pastry requires more water for binding than its wheat flour counterpart. Where egg is used to bind, whole egg—rather than egg yolk—is used.

In addition, gluten-free dough must be kneaded lightly with the fingertips for 2–3 minutes until soft and smooth. This encourages the gluten-free flours to absorb liquid so the pastry is not overly crumbly. If the dough starts to crack while it is being kneaded it requires more liquid: crumble the dough back into the bowl, stir in more water, 1 tablespoon at a time, and knead again.

Rolling it out

Gluten-free pastry is very delicate and requires careful handling.
- To hold the pastry dough together, place it between two sheets of plastic wrap.
- With the rolling pin, press and flatten the ball of pastry into a rough circle, approximately 1 in./2.5 cm thick.

• With firm strokes away from your body, roll the pastry out into a large circle to the required thickness (no thicker than ⅛ in./3 mm for lining a tart pan or pie dish and slightly thinner for small individual tarts and pies), turning the pastry a quarter turn every four rolls to ensure it is rolled evenly.

For a single-crust pie, consisting of a filling covered with a pastry lid, follow the instructions for Assembling a Single-Crust Pie on page 151, but roll the gluten-free pastry between two sheets of plastic wrap (see below) and use the bottom sheet to support the pastry lid as you lift and turn it onto the pie dish.

Lining a pan
• Peel off the top sheet of plastic wrap and transfer the rolled pastry to the pan with the remaining sheet of plastic wrap on top.
• Gently press the pastry into the pan so that the pastry hugs the bottom, corners, and sides, then carefully peel away the second layer of plastic wrap.
• Roll the rolling pin over the rim of the pan to remove the excess pastry.
• Repair any holes by pressing the dough back together or using a little of the excess dough to fill large holes. Don't worry if the shell looks patchy because the pastry will even out in the oven. Reserve a little of the dough to patch any holes that appear as the pastry bakes.
• Place the tart shell in the refrigerator to firm up for 30 minutes before baking. Cold, firm pastry is less likely to lose its shape in the oven.

Baking
Gluten-free pastry is prone to losing its shape in the oven unless it is baked blind first (see page 151). Like wheat-based pastry, gluten-free pastry requires a hot oven so that it quickly hardens and holds its shape. If the oven temperature is too low, the pastry will melt, lose its shape, and become tough and greasy.

RICE AND ALMOND SHORTCRUST PASTRY

Before making this pastry, read Making Gluten-free Shortcrust Pastry, page 153.

This versatile gluten-free pastry is for those who are able to eat nuts. It is crisp, delicately flavored, and ideal for savory tart shells. This recipe makes enough for one 10–12-in./25–30-cm tart pan. **Serves 8–10**

INGREDIENTS

1 cup/110 g brown rice flour

½ cup/55 g cornstarch

½ tsp. salt

½ cup/55 g ground almonds

½ cup/110 g cold butter

DAIRY
dairy-free hard baking margarine, diced

1 large egg, beaten with 1 Tbsp. water

EGG
2 Tbsp. water

1 Sift the flour, cornstarch, and salt into a large mixing bowl and stir in the ground almonds.

2 Rub the butter into the flour mixture with your fingertips until the mixture resembles bread crumbs.

3 Using a table knife, stir in 1 Tbsp. of the liquid until the flour and butter crumbs clump together. Add another 1 Tbsp. of liquid if the mixture is still too dry and crumbly.

4 Bring the dough together into a ball. Knead the dough lightly until it is smooth and soft on a work surface lightly dusted with rice flour. If it starts to crack, it requires more water. Wrap in plastic wrap and chill for 30 minutes.

5 Roll thinly between two sheets of plastic wrap and use as required.

VARIATIONS

SWEET RICE AND ALMOND PASTRY

This crisp, sweet pastry is for those who can eat nuts. It is ideal for making sweet tarts, such as French Apple Tart, page 164. For the sweet version of the above recipe, simply stir 6 Tbsp./70 g superfine sugar into the flour and butter crumbs in step 2.

WHOLE-WHEAT RICE AND ALMOND PASTRY

This light-textured yet hearty pastry is great for pies and tarts. For the whole-wheat version of the main recipe, simply substitute the ground almonds with 2 oz./55 g whole almonds, finely ground, and add 1 Tbsp. rice bran. Follow the recipe above, adding the rice bran to the bowl with the almonds in step 1.

TARTE NIÇOISE

This tart is full of flavor, color, and texture and is simple to make. It is also free of gluten, dairy products, egg, soy, and nuts. The combination of tomato, black olives, tuna, onion, and herbs on the cornmeal and potato base is truly delicious. Eat it hot or cold with new potatoes and lightly dressed salad. **Serves 6–8**

FOR THE PASTRY

Double recipe Cornmeal and Potato Pastry (page 157)

FOR THE FILLING

½ recipe Rich Italian Tomato Sauce (page 80)

2 (7-oz./210-g) cans tuna, broken into chunks

2 handfuls good-quality pitted black olives

½ red onion, thinly sliced

2 tsp. fresh thyme leaves

1 (2-oz./50-g) can anchovies

2 Tbsp. extra virgin olive oil

freshly ground black pepper

1 Preheat the oven to 400°F/200°C/ gas mark 6. Roll the pastry to fit a shallow rectangular baking sheet approximately 11 by 15 in./30 by 42 cm. Remove the top sheet of plastic wrap and transfer the pastry to the baking sheet, pastry side down. Press the pastry against the sides and into the corners of the baking sheet, then peel away the top sheet of plastic wrap. Using a sharp knife, cut away any excess pastry that rises above the edges of the pan. Chill for 15 minutes.

2 Prick the bottom of the pastry shell with a fork and bake for 20 minutes, or until light golden.

3 Spread the tomato sauce evenly over the pastry and evenly scatter the tuna, olives, onion, and thyme leaves over the tart. Lay the anchovies over the ingredients and drizzle the tart with olive oil. Season with pepper (there should be no need for salt).

4 Bake the tart for 20 minutes, or until the edge is crisp and golden brown. Remove from the oven and check that the pastry has evenly browned underneath by lifting a corner with a spatula. If not, return the tart to the oven for another 5 minutes. Lower the temperature to 325°F/170°C/gas mark 3 if the tart filling is beginning to brown. Serve warm or cold.

TOMATO, RED ONION, AND BASIL TART

The rich, aromatic flavors of ripe tomatoes and basil make this the ideal summer tart. Serve as a starter or for lunch with boiled new potatoes and dressed green salad.
Serves 6–8

FOR THE PASTRY

1 recipe Basic Shortcrust Pastry (page 152)

● GLUTEN

Parmesan and Potato Pastry (page 157) or Rice and Cornmeal Pastry (page 156)

FOR THE FILLING

4 Tbsp. olive oil

3 large red onions, halved from root to shoot and sliced thinly

3 sprigs thyme

sea salt and freshly ground black pepper

3 garlic cloves, finely chopped

2 handfuls torn basil leaves

12 ripe but firm tomatoes, sliced into thin rounds

1 Make the pastry, roll to ⅛ in./3 mm thick, and use to line a 10–12-in./ 25–30-cm tart pan. Chill the pastry for 30 minutes.

2 Preheat the oven to 400°F/200°C/ gas mark 6.

3 Blind-bake the pastry (see page 151) for 20 minutes, or until the pastry shell is set and firm. Remove the paper and beans and return to the oven for another 5 minutes, or until the pastry is crisp and an even pale golden color.

4 Heat 2 Tbsp. of the olive oil in a large frying pan and add the onions, thyme, ½ tsp. salt, and 4 grinds pepper. Cover and fry over low heat for 20 minutes, or until the onions are soft but not colored. Add the garlic and fry over medium heat for 1 minute.

5 Remove the sprigs of thyme and spread the softened onions and garlic over the bottom of the baked tart shell. Scatter a third of the basil leaves on top.

6 Starting at the edge of the pastry shell, loosely overlap half of the tomato slices in one layer, spiraling towards the center. Lightly season the tomatoes with sea salt and black pepper and scatter on half of the remaining basil leaves.

7 Arrange the remaining slices in the same way and season lightly with sea salt and black pepper.

8 Lightly drizzle 2 Tbsp. olive oil over the tart and place on the middle rack of the oven. Reduce the heat to 325°F/170°C/gas mark 3 and bake for 45 minutes, or until the tomatoes have softened and are lightly browned on the top. Scatter with the remaining basil leaves before serving.

APRICOT AND ORANGE TART

This tart looks impressive and tastes wonderful. It is soy free and simple to adapt for dairy-, gluten-, and nut-free diets. For an egg-free tart, see the variation below (this requires a few more substitutions but it is well worth the effort). Serve with Crème Anglaise (page 207) or vanilla ice cream, or on its own with tea or coffee. **Serves 8–10**

FOR THE PASTRY

● GLUTEN

1 recipe Sweet Rich Shortcrust Pastry (page 152)
Rice and Almond Pastry (page 155) or Rice and Cornmeal Pastry (page 156)

FOR THE FILLING

● DAIRY

½ cup/110 g butter, softened
dairy-free margarine

½ cup/110 g superfine sugar

2 eggs, beaten

● NUTS

1 cup/110 g ground almonds
self-rising flour

● GLUTEN

4 Tbsp./30 g all-purpose flour
potato flour

finely grated zest and juice of 1 orange

1½ lb./750 g fresh ripe apricots, halved and pitted

TO GLAZE

3 Tbsp. apricot jam

1 Preheat the oven to 350°F/180°C/gas mark 4.

2 Make the pastry, roll thinly, and use to line a 10-in./25-cm tart pan with a removable bottom. Chill for 30 minutes.

3 To make the filling, whisk the butter, superfine sugar, eggs, almonds, flour, and orange zest and juice in a bowl until light and fluffy (if the mixture curdles, the cooked filling may be slightly denser but

just as delicious). Spread the mixture over the chilled pastry shell and arrange the apricot halves, skin side up, on the top.

4 Bake the tart on the middle rack of the oven for 15 minutes, or until the filling has puffed up and is turning light golden brown. Turn the oven down to 325°F/170°C/gas mark 3 and bake the tart for a another 30 minutes, or until the filling is set in the center.

5 Lift the tart out of the oven, remove the sides of the tart pan, and leave to cool on a wire rack.

6 Meanwhile, melt the jam in a small pan, pass it through a sieve into a bowl to remove any pieces of fruit and leave to cool for 1 minute.

7 With a pastry brush, dab and brush the glaze over the surface of the tart, filling any gaps with glaze. Leave the glaze to set before serving the tart.

VARIATION
EGG-FREE TART

Use Basic Shortcrust Pastry (page 152) for the shell. For the filling, mix together ½ cup/55 g ground almonds, ⅔ cup/85 g self-rising flour, and 1 tsp. baking powder; whisk this mixture with the softened butter, sugar, orange zest, and juice, and 6 Tbsp./100 ml unsweetened applesauce (page 36) until light and fluffy. Spread the filling in the pastry shell as in step 3 above and continue with the recipe.

LEMON TART

This tart is rich, creamy, and very lemony. It is egg-free and can be made with gluten-free shortcrust pastry, but it is not suitable for dairy-free diets because the filling relies on the mild, rich flavor of cream. The tart needs to set in the refrigerator for at least 2 hours before serving. **Serves 8**

FOR THE PASTRY

1 recipe Sweet Shortcrust Pastry (page 152)

● GLUTEN

Rice and Almond Pastry (page 155) or Rice and Cornmeal Pastry (page 156)

FOR THE FILLING

3 lemons

2½ tsp. plain gelatin

5 Tbsp. superfine sugar

2 tsp. custard powder

14 Tbsp./200 ml whole milk

2⅛ cups/500 ml heavy cream

confectioners' sugar for decorating

● GLUTEN

check label for wheat

1 Make the pastry and use to line a 10-in./25-cm tart pan with a removable bottom. Fill any holes or cracks in the pastry and chill for 15 minutes. Blind-bake the pastry (see page 151).

2 When the pastry shell is baked, patch any cracks or holes with a little of the remaining pastry (see Patching Cracked Pastry Shells, page 150). Place the pan on a wire rack to cool.

3 Finely grate the zest of two of the lemons and set aside. Squeeze the juice from the zested lemons and the third lemon and pour into a small pan.

4 Sprinkle the gelatin over the lemon juice and leave to stand for 10 minutes.

5 Meanwhile, combine the lemon zest, superfine sugar, and custard powder in a saucepan and slowly add the milk to form a smooth mixture. Add the cream and, stirring continuously, bring the mixture to a simmer to cook. Remove from the heat.

6 Gently heat the gelatin and lemon juice, continuously swirling the mixture around the pan, until it starts to steam and the gelatin crystals have dissolved. Immediately remove the pan from the heat.

7 Pour the melted gelatin and lemon juice into the cream mixture and stir well. Allow the lemon cream mixture to cool for 10 minutes. If there are any thin cracks or small holes in the pastry base, brush some of the lemon filling over the pastry and leave to set for 5 minutes before pouring in the remaining filling.

8 Place the tart in the refrigerator and leave to set for 2 hours.

9 Remove from the refrigerator 30 minutes before the tart is due to be eaten to allow the filling to soften slightly. Sift confectioners' sugar over the tart and serve.

JAM TARTS

These colorful tarts are fun to make with children, as a treat for tea parties. Use a variety of jams for different colored and flavored jam tarts. **Makes 18–20**

FOR THE PASTRY

1 recipe Basic Shortcrust Pastry (page 152)

Rice and Cornmeal Pastry (page 156) or Rice and Almond Pastry (page 155)

● GLUTEN

FOR THE FILLING

1 cup/340 g raspberry, strawberry, black currant, or apricot jam

1 Preheat the oven to 350°F/180°C/ gas mark 4.

2 Make the pastry and let it chill for 20 minutes.

3 On a lightly floured surface, roll out the chilled pastry to ⅛ in./3 mm thick. Cut out as many rounds as you can using a 3-in./7.5-cm fluted pastry cutter. Bring the remaining pastry together, roll out again, and cut out more rounds.

4 Line two muffin pans with the rounds of pastry and place 1 heaped tsp. of jam in each. Do not overfill with jam.

5 Bake the jam tarts on the middle rack of the oven for 10–15 minutes, until the pastry is crisp and light brown.

6 Run a knife around the hot tarts and lift them out with a palette knife onto a wire rack to cool.

FRENCH APPLE TART

This traditional French tart is easily adapted for dairy-, egg-, and gluten-free diets. Serve with Banana Ice Cream (page 205), Vanilla Cream Sauce (page 208), or heavy cream. **Serves 8–10**

EGG

GLUTEN

FOR THE PASTRY

1 recipe Sweet Rich Shortcrust Pastry (page 152)

Sweet Shortcrust Pastry (page 152)
Sweet Rice and Almond Pastry (page 155) or Sweet Rice and Cornmeal Pastry (page 156)

FOR THE FILLING

2 lb./900 g Granny Smith apples, peeled, cored, quartered, and thinly sliced

1½ Tbsp. lemon juice

1½ Tbsp. superfine sugar

TO GLAZE

½ cup apricot jam

1 Preheat the oven to 350°F/180°C/gas mark 4.

2 Make the pastry, roll to ⅛ in./3 mm thick, and use it to line a 10–12-in./25–30-cm tart pan with a removable bottom.

3 Chill the tart for 15 minutes, then blind bake (see page 151) until light brown and crisp.

4 Toss the apples in lemon juice to prevent them from discoloring.

5 To assemble the tart, pile the apples into the baked pastry shell in even layers, sprinkling each layer with superfine sugar, to just below the rim of the tart shell. Arrange the top layer of apple slices in overlapping concentric circles. Sprinkle with the remaining sugar.

6 Bake on the middle rack of the oven for about 30 minutes, or until the apples are tender and lightly browned on top. The pastry should be golden brown and crisp. If the apples start to brown too quickly, reduce the temperature of the oven to 300°F/150°C/gas mark 2. Place on a wire rack to cool.

7 Melt the apricot jam in a small pan, stirring regularly. Pass it through a sieve into a bowl and leave to cool until it is thick enough to evenly coat the back of a spoon.

8 Using a pastry brush, dab and brush the apricot glaze over the apples, filling the gaps between slices with glaze. The glazed tart should look smooth and shiny. Leave the glaze to set before serving.

CAKES

Everyone loves cake and not being able to indulge is an on-going source of frustration for those suffering from food allergies. However, this does not have to be the case: although store-bought cakes are usually unsuitable for people with food allergies, homemade cake recipes can be adapted easily to suit gluten-, egg-, dairy-, nut-, and soy-free diets. Cakes can still be tender, moist, richly flavored and crumbly when made with ingredients such as gluten-free flour, egg substitutes, or dairy-free margarine. It is important to note that it is not possible to produce a light, moist cake that is both gluten and egg free, because one of these is needed to bind and lighten the mixture. Turn to the "Knowing How to Substitute for" chapters for a comprehensive explanation of the purpose of wheat flour, eggs, dairy products, nuts, and soy in cake making and how they can be replaced.

NOTES FOR FOOD ALLERGY SUFFERERS

DAIRY-FREE DIET: Most cakes can be made with dairy-free margarine instead of butter, and soy or rice milk instead of cows' milk. Buttercream frostings for cakes are also just as good made with dairy-free margarine. All the recipes in this chapter can be made with dairy-free ingredients.

GLUTEN-FREE DIET: Perfectly delicious cakes can be made using gluten-free flours—if you use a mixture of neutral-flavored flours. The best combination is 50 percent rice flour, 25 percent cornstarch, and 25 percent ground almonds. Rice flour provides the neutral-flavored base, ground almonds add richness and moisture, and cornstarch lightens the consistency. Potato flour is an ideal substitute for wheat flour in cakes requiring a moist, soft texture, such as brownies. Eggs and extra baking powder are essential to bind, moisten, and lighten cakes made with gluten-free flours. The general rule is to add 3 eggs for every ⅔ cup/110 g of flour used, to produce a feather-light cake with a spongy texture.

Check the labels of powdery ingredients, such as baking powder, confectioners' sugar, and spices, because they are sometimes mixed with wheat flour to prevent lumps from forming.

EGG-FREE DIET: Egg helps bind the raw ingredients and produces a light, moist cake. It is possible to replace egg in cake mixtures with other ingredients that provide moisture and lightly bind the ingredients, such as fruit purees, mashed banana, custard, and liquids such as milk (see Egg Substitutes, page 166). Self-rising flour plays an important role in egg-free cakes, because it contains gluten, which helps to bind the cake mixture together, and leavening agents that fill the mixture with bubbles. You'll need extra baking powder as well to ensure the baked cake is as light as possible.

NUT-FREE DIET: While cakes based on ground nuts are obviously off limits, those that use nuts in small quantities generally can be easily adapted. When chopped nuts are used to add texture, replace them with an equal quantity of dried fruit. When ground nuts are used to enrich the flavor of cake mixture (see Rich Fruit Cake, page 170), replace them with an equal quantity of the flour used in the recipe and an extra tablespoon of fat. Be wary of margarines—use butter or read the label on margarines to make sure they do not contain nut-based oils.

SOY-FREE DIET: Although soy is prevalent in store-bought cakes, it is only present in homemade cakes if soy flour, soy milk, or margarine made with soybean oil are used. Replace soy flour with another neutral-flavored flour, use butter or soy-free margarine, and rice milk or cows' milk.

EGG SUBSTITUTES

For successful egg-free cakes, it is important to select an egg substitute that enhances but does not overpower the overall flavor of the cake. Apricot puree has a strong fruity flavor and is best used in fruit cakes. Unsweetened applesauce has a more delicate flavor and is perfect for cakes with a mild zesty flavor. Extra mashed banana works well as an egg replacer in cakes already flavored with banana, and thick, cold custard successfully replaces egg in plain sponge cakes.

Some cake mixtures do not require eggs and instead contain a high proportion of self-rising flour, chemical leavening agents, and liquid, normally milk, to bind and lighten the mixture. The following egg substitutes are used in many of the recipes in this chapter.

APRICOT PUREE

Place 6 oz./170 g pitted, dried apricots in a pan and add ⅔ cup/150 ml water. Cover and simmer gently for 15 minutes, or until the apricots are very soft. Using a hand-held blender or food processor, puree until smooth but still thick enough to hold its shape. Allow to cool and use as required. This puree can be covered and stored in the refrigerator for up to 3 days or frozen in an airtight container. Makes approximately 1¼ cups/290 ml.

UNSWEETENED APPLESAUCE

Peel, core, and slice 12 oz./340 g apples and place in a pan with ¼ cup water. Cover and cook over medium heat for 15 minutes, or until soft. Using a wooden spoon, beat until smooth but still thick enough to hold its shape. Allow to cool and use as required. This puree can be covered and stored in the refrigerator for up to 3 days or frozen in an airtight container. Makes approximately 1¼ cups/290 ml.

CUSTARD

Combine 1 tablespoon egg-free, cornstarch-based custard powder, and 1 tablespoon superfine sugar in a pan and mix together. Measure 1¼ cups/290 ml milk or dairy-free milk in a measuring cup. Stir 2 Tbsp. of the milk into the custard powder and sugar until smooth. Gradually stir in the remaining milk and place over medium heat. Bring the custard to a boil, stirring constantly, until thickened and smooth. Remove from the heat, allow to cool, and use as required. Custard can be stored, covered, in the refrigerator for up to 3 days.

REPLACING EGG WITH EGG SUBSTITUTES

In order to adapt your own recipes, use one of the following substitutions to replace each egg called for in a recipe:
• ¼ cup/50 ml fruit puree, custard, or liquid, plus 1 extra teaspoon baking powder per ⅔ cup/110 g self-rising flour
• for banana cakes, 1 extra small banana or ½ a large banana, plus 1 extra teaspoon baking powder per ⅔ cup/110 g self-rising flour.

BANANA HONEY CAKE

This moist, light cake is egg-, soy- and nut-free and is easily adapted for gluten- and dairy-free diets. The gluten-free version requires an egg to help bind the ingredients. This is a good recipe to make with children, and it's great for children's birthday parties.
Serves 8–12

INGREDIENTS

1¾ cups/225 g self-rising flour

● **GLUTEN** 14 Tbsp./110 g rice flour, 7 Tbsp./55 g cornstarch, and ⅓ cup/55 g ground almonds

● **NUTS** 14 Tbsp./110 g rice flour, 7 Tbsp./55 g cornstarch and 7 Tbsp./55 g potato flour

1 tsp. baking powder

● **GLUTEN** 2 tsp. gluten-free baking powder

1 tsp. ground cinnamon

½ cup/110 g butter

● **DAIRY** dairy-free margarine

6 Tbsp./85 g dark brown sugar

2 Tbsp. honey

finely grated zest of 1 orange

5 ripe bananas, mashed with a fork

● **GLUTEN** replace 1 banana with 1 beaten egg

½ cup/85 g golden raisins
milk, as needed

1 Preheat the oven to 325°F/170°C/gas mark 3. Grease a 9 by 5-inch/900-g loaf pan and line it with oiled waxed paper.

2 Sift the flour, baking powder, and cinnamon into a bowl.

3 Add the butter, brown sugar, honey, orange zest, and egg, if using, to the dry ingredients and whisk together until the mixture is smooth.

4 Fold in the mashed bananas and golden raisins. The mixture should be soft enough to fall slowly from a spoon. If the mixture is too firm, stir in 1 Tbsp. milk.

5 Spoon into the prepared pan, level with the back of a spoon, and bake for 45–60 minutes, until springy in the center. Insert a skewer into the center— if it comes out clean the cake is ready.

6 Leave to set for 5 minutes in the pan, then run a knife around the cake to loosen it; turn it out onto a wire rack to cool completely. The cake can be stored for up to 3 days in an airtight container or wrapped well in plastic wrap and frozen.

LEMON AND ORANGE MARMALADE CAKE

This wholesome citrus-flavored cake is egg free, unless it is made with gluten-free flour. The lack of gluten means that egg is required to bind the cake, help it rise and prevent it crumbling. This delicious cake is also easily adapted for a dairy-free diet.
Serves 8–12

INGREDIENTS

1¾ cups/225 g self-rising flour

● GLUTEN 14 Tbsp./110 g rice flour, 7 Tbsp./55 g cornstarch, ⅓ cup/55 g ground almonds, and 2 tsp. gluten-free baking powder

½ cup/110 g butter

● DAIRY dairy-free margarine

½ cup/110 g superfine sugar

grated zest of 1 lemon

grated zest of 1 orange

1 tsp. pumpkin pie spice

● GLUTEN check for wheat flour

⅓ cup/55 g raisins

⅓ cup/55 g glazed mixed peel

½ tsp. salt

1 Tbsp. lemon juice

2 Tbsp. marmalade

¾ cup/175 ml milk

● DAIRY dairy-free milk, plus more as needed
● GLUTEN 3 eggs beaten instead of milk

1 Tbsp. Demerara sugar

confectioners' sugar (optional)

1 Preheat the oven to 350°F/180°C/gas mark 4. Grease a 9 by 5-inch/900 g loaf pan, line with waxed paper and brush with oil.

2 In a mixing bowl, rub the butter (or margarine) into the flour, until the mixture resembles coarse crumbs. Add the superfine sugar, lemon and orange, zest, pumpkin pie spice, raisins, mixed peel, and salt and mix well.

3 In a separate bowl, mix the lemon juice with the marmalade.

4 Working quickly (to make the most of the leavening agents), pour the milk (or beaten eggs) and the lemon juice and marmalade mixture into the flour mixture and stir until all the ingredients are well mixed. The cake mixture should be soft enough to fall slowly from a spoon. Add a little more milk, if necessary.

5 Spoon the cake mixture into the prepared pan. Level the surface with the back of a spoon, sprinkle with the Demerara sugar, and bake for 40 minutes. Reduce the oven temperature to 300°F/160°C/gas mark 3 and bake for another 20 minutes, or until the center of the cake is firm and a skewer inserted into the center comes out clean.

6 Leave the cake to cool for 10 minutes in the pan before turning it out onto a wire rack. If you wish, drizzle the cake with icing (see page 171). The cake can be stored in an airtight container for up to 1 week or frozen.

CHOCOLATE CHIP COOKIES

These deliciously chewy cookies can be adapted very easily for dairy-, gluten-, and egg-free diets. To adapt the recipe for egg-free diets, self-rising flour is used to add lightness and milk is added to provide the liquid necessary for binding the ingredients together. **Makes 18**

INGREDIENTS

● DAIRY
½ cup/110 g butter, softened
dairy-free margarine

9 Tbsp./110 g granulated sugar

½ cup/110 g light brown sugar

● EGG
1 egg, beaten
2 Tbsp./50 ml milk

● GLUTEN
1⅓ cups/170 g all-purpose flour
⅔ cup/85 g rice flour and ⅔ cup/85 g cornmeal or ground almonds

● EGG
1⅓ cups/170 g self-rising flour

● GLUTEN
1 tsp. baking powder
gluten-free baking powder

½ tsp. salt

● DAIRY
1 Tbsp. milk
dairy-free milk

3 oz./85 g good-quality dark chocolate, roughly chopped

● NUTS
check for traces of nuts

● SOY
check for soy lecithin

1 Preheat the oven to 350°F/180°C/gas mark 4. Line 3 baking sheets with oiled waxed paper and shake a spoonful of flour, cornmeal, or rice flour over the baking sheet until the oil is evenly covered. Pour away any excess flour.

2 Beat the butter and sugars with a wooden spoon or electric whisk until pale and fluffy. Add the egg (or milk) and beat well.

3 Sift the flour, baking powder, and salt into the bowl and whisk into the beaten butter mixture. Stir in the milk and the chocolate.

4 Leaving a wide gap between cookies, spoon no more than 6 heaped teaspoons of the mixture onto each lined baking sheet, because the dough spreads as it bakes.

5 Bake for about 15 minutes, or until the cookies are lightly browned and just set in the center. Do not overcook the cookies or they will lose their chewiness.

6 Leave them to set on the baking sheet for 30 seconds, then transfer to a wire rack to cool. The cookies are best served freshly made, but store well for up to 2 days in an airtight container. They can also be frozen, sealed in plastic bags.

GLUTEN-FREE WHITE BREAD

This loaf has a delicate flavor very similar to wheat bread. It is very simple and quick to make because it does not require time to rise before baking. Store and use like conventional bread. This recipe can also be used to make bread rolls, Italian focaccia and pizza dough (see overleaf). **Makes one medium loaf**

INGREDIENTS

14 Tbsp./110 g potato flour

7 Tbsp./55 g tapioca flour and 2 tsp. oil

⅓ cup/55 g rice flour

⅔ cup/110 g cornstarch

2 tsp. salt

2 tsp. sugar

2 tsp. xanthum gum powder

½ oz./14 g or 2 packets dried yeast granules

⅓ cup/55 g ground almonds

⬤ **NUTS** ⅓ cup/55 g rice flour and 2 extra tsp. oil

2 Tbsp. sunflower or olive oil

millet flakes and buckwheat flakes, poppy seeds, or sesame seeds to decorate (optional)

1 Preheat the oven to 400°F/200°C/gas mark 6. Lightly grease and flour a 9 by 5-inch/900-g loaf pan, pouring out any excess flour.

2 Sift the flours, cornstarch, salt, sugar, and xanthum gum powder into a mixing bowl. Stir in the yeast and ground almonds. Make sure the yeast is mixed in properly to avoid pockets of yeast activity and uneven rising.

3 Measure out 1½ cups/350 ml of lukewarm water (it must be no warmer than blood temperature). Add the oil to the water.

4 Pour 1⅛ cups/300 ml water and oil onto the dry ingredients and beat with a wooden spoon until smooth, and firm enough to hold its shape but soft enough to fall slowly from a spoon. If the mixture seems too firm or dry, stir in more water, a tablespoon at a time, until the bread mixture reaches the required consistency. If the bread mixture is too stiff, the bread will not rise. If the mixture is too runny, the dough will not be strong enough to trap the precious bubbles of air that cause it to rise.

5 Spoon the bread mixture into the prepared loaf pan. Dip a tablespoon in water and smooth the surface of the bread mixture with the back of the wet spoon. Sprinkle over the millet and buckwheat flakes and place on the middle rack of the oven.

6 Bake for 45–60 minutes, until the bread is crisp and golden brown on all sides. If the bottom and sides of the bread are pale, place the bread upside down in the pan and return to the oven for 10 minutes. The bread is done when all sides are brown and firm and the underside of the bread sounds hollow when tapped gently with your knuckles.

7 Remove the bread from the pan and place it on a wire rack to cool. Do not slice the loaf until it is completely cooled. Eat really fresh, store for up to 2 days in an airtight container, or slice and freeze in a sealed plastic bag.

WHITE BREAD VARIATIONS

WHITE BREAD ROLLS
Follow the recipe for Gluten-free White Bread but instead of using a loaf pan, using a wet spoon, neatly place tablespoons of the bread mixture onto a greased and floured baking sheet. Smooth the surface of each roll with the back of the wet spoon and sprinkle with millet flakes, buckwheat flakes, poppy seeds, or sesame seeds. Bake in a preheated oven at 400°F/200°C/gas mark 6 for 15–20 minutes, or until crisp and golden brown on all sides.

ITALIAN FOCACCIA WITH ROSEMARY
Follow the recipe for Gluten-free White Bread, using olive oil, and spoon into a greased and floured 8- to 9-inch/20–23 cm round cake pan. With the back of a wet spoon, spread the dough out to fill the pan. Make shallow indents with your fingertips at regular intervals on the surface, drizzle 1 Tbsp. olive oil over the bread mixture, and sprinkle with a large pinch of sea salt crystals and 1 Tbsp. chopped rosemary. Bake in a preheated oven at 400°F/200°C/gas mark 6 for 45 minutes, or until risen and golden brown.

ONION FOCACCIA
Peel and halve an onion and cut across into thin slices. Follow the recipe for Gluten-free White Bread, using olive oil, and spoon into a greased and floured 8- to 9-inch/20–23-cm round cake pan. With the back of a wet spoon, spread the dough out to fill the pan and make shallow indents at regular intervals on the surface. Spread the sliced onions over the top of the bread mixture, drizzle with 1 Tbsp. olive oil, and sprinkle with sea salt. Bake in a preheated oven at 400°F/200°C/gas mark 6 for 45 minutes, or until risen and golden brown.

PIZZA ALLA MARINARA
Follow the recipe for Gluten-free White Bread, using olive oil. Divide the dough between two greased and floured (with rice flour or cornmeal) baking sheets. Using the back of a wet spoon, spread the dough out into two circles measuring approximately 10 in./25 cm across. The dough should be just under ½ in./1 cm thick. Neaten the edges of the pizza dough by running a spoon around the edge of each. Drizzle each pizza dough with 1 Tbsp. olive oil and bake in the preheated oven at 400°F/200°C/ gas mark 6 for 20 minutes, or until the pizzas are golden brown on both sides. Spread each pizza with Rich Italian Tomato Sauce (page 80), arrange 8 anchovy fillets over the top, and sprinkle over 1½ tsp. capers, 1 Tbsp. pitted black olives, 1 tsp. mixed dried herbs, a little salt and pepper, and a drizzle of olive oil. Bake for another 15 minutes, then serve immediately.

GLUTEN-FREE BROWN BREAD

This wholesome brown bread has the texture, color and flavor that you would expect in a conventional wheat-based brown bread. It is good enough to use for sandwiches. **Makes one medium loaf**

INGREDIENTS

14 Tbsp./110 g potato flour

14 Tbsp./110 g cornstarch

7 Tbsp./55 g tapioca flour

7 Tbsp./55 g rice flour

2 tsp. salt

2 tsp. dark brown sugar

2 tsp. xanthum gum powder

¼ oz./14 g or 2 packets dried yeast granules

⅓ cup/55 g finely ground whole almonds

● NUTS   7 Tbsp./55 g potato flour and 2 extra tsp. oil

1 Tbsp. rice bran

2 Tbsp. sunflower or olive oil

a large pinch each millet flakes and buckwheat flakes to decorate (optional)

1 Preheat the oven to 400°F/200°C/gas mark 6. Lightly grease and flour a 9 by 5-inch/900-g loaf pan, pouring out any excess flour.

2 Sift together the flours, cornstarch, salt, sugar, and xanthum gum powder into a mixing bowl.

3 Stir in the yeast, ground almonds, and rice bran.

4 Measure out 1½ cups/350 ml lukewarm water. Add the oil to the water.

5 Pour 1⅓ cups/300 ml of water and oil onto the dry ingredients and beat with a wooden spoon until smooth, and firm enough to hold its shape but soft enough to fall slowly from a spoon. If the mixture seems too firm or dry, stir in more water a tablespoon at a time, until the bread mixture reaches the required consistency. The mixture should fall slowly from a spoon in the same way as cake batter. If the dough is too stiff or too wet, it will not rise.

6 Spoon the bread mixture into the prepared loaf pan and level out with the back of a spoon dipped in water. Sprinkle over the millet and buckwheat flakes.

7 Place on the middle rack of the oven and bake for 45 minutes, or until the bread is crisp and golden brown on all sides. The bread is done when all sides are brown and firm and the underside of the bread sounds hollow when tapped gently with your knuckles.

8 Place the baked bread on a wire rack to cool. The texture of the bread improves as it cools and is best eaten cold. Store the bread for up to 2 days in an airtight container or sliced in the freezer in a sealed plastic bag.

Chapter 17

DESSERTS AND SWEET SAUCES

DESSERTS

Homemade desserts are commonly made with butter, cream, eggs, nuts, and flour while store-bought desserts often contain soy products. The reason for this is that these ingredients add creaminess, structure, texture, flavor, and color to foods that are sweet and delicate in consistency. Sometimes their presence is essential—meringues, for example, rely on the unique properties of egg white. However, this chapter demonstrates how recipes for many popular and well-known desserts easily can be adapted for gluten-, egg-, dairy-, nut-, and soy-free diets by substituting or simply omitting certain ingredients—and with delicious results, too.

MOUSSES

Rich-tasting, airy mousses make wonderful desserts, served alone, with a rich custard sauce, or as part of an assembled dessert. Mousses are made by gently folding flavoring ingredients, such as melted chocolate, into whisked eggs or whipped cream.

GENERAL RULES FOR MAKING MOUSSE

- Each time a whipped or whisked mixture is stirred, it loses air and volume so use a large metal spoon that turns over a large portion of the mixture at a time.
- Mixtures with similar consistencies mix together with minimal stirring. To retain as much air as possible in the mousse, make the consistency of mousse ingredients more similar by stirring a large spoonful of whipped cream or whisked egg whites into the thinner flavoring ingredients before folding the two together.
- Whisk egg whites in a grease-free glass, china, or metal bowl. Plastic bowls scratch easily and harbor grease, which prevents egg whites from foaming properly.
- Whisk egg whites until they stand in soft peaks and wobble slightly when shaken.
- Whip cream until it just holds its shape so that the mousse ingredients can be mixed easily together. Stiffly whipped cream forms a lumpy, heavy mousse.

NOTES FOR FOOD ALLERGY SUFFERERS

Mousses are gluten-, nut-, and soy-free. Due to the rich flavor and thickening properties of chocolate, chocolate mousse also can be made dairy-free, by using whisked eggs; or egg-free, by using whipped cream (see pages 189–90).

Beware egg-based mousses

These are made with raw eggs, so ensure the eggs are as fresh as possible, and chill the finished mousse to reduce the risk of salmonella poisoning. Do not serve mousses to pregnant women, young children, and elderly people.

BITTER CHOCOLATE MOUSSE

This wonderfully rich but light dairy-free mousse contains nothing but dark chocolate, eggs, and sugar. It's a real treat. For an egg-free mousse, see page 190. Use the best-quality chocolate you can find because the flavor of the dessert relies on it. **Serves 4**

INGREDIENTS

4 oz./110 g best-quality dark chocolate containing 70% cocoa solids, broken into small pieces

● **NUTS** check label for traces of nuts

● **SOY** check label for soy lecithin

4 egg whites

1 Tbsp. superfine sugar

2 egg yolks, at room temperature

1 Melt the chocolate very gently in an ovenproof bowl placed over a pan of simmering water, stirring occasionally. Once melted, set aside.

2 Place the egg whites in a medium bowl and whisk until they form soft, wobbly peaks. Sprinkle the sugar over and continue to whisk until the egg whites stand upright but bend over at the tip.

3 Stir the egg yolks into the warm, melted chocolate.

4 Mix 2 large spoonfuls of whisked egg whites into the chocolate and egg mixture, then gently fold in the remaining egg whites. Pour into four ramekins, holding the mixing bowl close to the ramekins to limit the loss of air.

5 Cover with plastic wrap and chill for at least 4 hours, preferably overnight before serving.

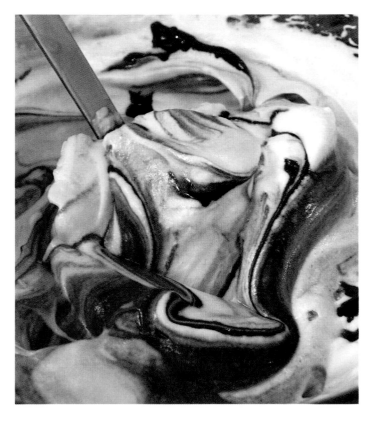

RICH CHOCOLATE MOUSSE

This mousse is enriched and lightened with whipped cream rather than egg whites. It is unsuitable for a those on a dairy-free diet but is great for chocolate lovers and those avoiding eggs. It is delicious dusted with good-quality cocoa powder and served with Coffee Custard Sauce (page 207) or with soft fruit and Fresh Summer Berry Sauce (page 209). To allow the mousse to set properly, make this mousse a day in advance. Serves 4

INGREDIENTS

6 oz./170 g best-quality dark chocolate containing 70% cocoa solids, broken into small pieces

● NUTS check label for traces of nuts

● SOY check label for soy lecithin

1¼ cups/290 ml whipping cream

2 Tbsp. good-quality cocoa powder

● GLUTEN check label for wheat flour

1 Melt the chocolate very gently in an ovenproof bowl placed over a pan of simmering water, stirring occasionally. Set aside.

2 In a large mixing bowl, whip the cream until it just holds its shape. Be careful not to overwhip it.

3 Stir one-quarter of the whipped cream into the cooled melted chocolate, then pour the chocolate mixture into the remaining whipped cream and gently fold together with a large metal spoon until just mixed.

4 Pour into four ramekins, leaving ½ in./1 cm headspace. Cover with plastic wrap and chill overnight to set. Dust with cocoa powder before serving.

VARIATION

RICH CHOCOLATE MOUSSE TORTE

This impressive egg-free dessert is great for dinner parties and special occasions. It can also be made gluten-, nut-, and soy-free by using suitable cookies to make the base.

Preheat the oven to 350°C/180°C/gas mark 4. Finely crush 4 oz./110 g chocolate-covered cookies or digestive biscuits (or gluten-free plain cookies). Stir the crushed cookies into ¼ cup/55 g melted butter and pour into a lightly oiled 8-in./20-cm round tart pan. Press the cookie mixture down firmly until the bottom of the pan is thinly and evenly covered. Bake for 10 minutes. Meanwhile, make a double recipe of the Rich Chocolate Mousse above. Spoon the mousse on top of the hardened cookie base and level off the top by passing a palette knife across the rim of the pan. Loosely cover the dessert with plastic wrap and leave to set in the refrigerator overnight. Run a sharp knife around the edge of the pan, lift off the sides, and dust with cocoa powder before serving.

SPONGE CAKES FOR ROULADES

Sponge cakes are often used as a base for fruit, cream, and mousse desserts. The light consistency of sponge cakes relies on the air bubbles incorporated into whisked egg, which expands and lightens the mixture as it bakes.

GENERAL RULES FOR MAKING WHISKED SPONGE

- Oil the baking pan, line with parchment paper, and brush the paper with a light coating of oil. Sprinkle 1 Tbsp. superfine sugar into the lined pan, shake from side to side until it is coated with sugar, and pour out any excess sugar. Do the same with 1 Tbsp. flour. Do this before beginning the recipe because the whisked sponge mixture quickly loses volume if left to stand.
- Whisk the eggs in a spotlessly clean china, glass, or metal mixing bowl. Plastic bowls harbor grease, which prevents eggs from foaming to their full potential.
- Whisk egg yolks until they become pale, double in volume, and are thick enough to leave a trail on the surface as the whisk is lifted out of the mixture.
- Whisk egg whites until they quadruple in volume and stand in firm peaks but are not stiff.
- Gently fold the mixture together using a large metal spoon.
- Fold the thinner yolks into the thicker egg white foam. The two are easier to fold together if a third of the whites are stirred into the yolks beforehand to make both foams closer in consistency. This way the mixture will require less folding, which means less chance of precious air being lost.
- Fold melted butter and flour into the mixture until just blended. Overfolding will cause the mixture to lose volume.

NOTES FOR FOOD ALLERGY SUFFERERS

DAIRY-FREE DIET: Melted butter is sometimes added to sponges to moisten and enrich the cake. If butter is included in a recipe for whisked sponge, replace it with melted dairy-free margarine.

GLUTEN-FREE DIET: Although flour is not necessary for the success of whisked sponge, it is sometimes added to give the cake a more substantial texture. In place of wheat flour, use an equal quantity of gluten-free flour made with 50 percent rice flour, 25 percent ground almonds, and 25 percent cornstarch.

EGG-FREE DIET: The unique properties of whisked egg are essential in whisked sponges and cannot be replaced with any other ingredient. In place of whisked sponge, use egg-free Victoria Sponge Cake (page 172).

NUT-FREE DIET: Whisked sponge is suitable for nut-free diets, provided recipes using nuts are avoided and any fat used to enrich it does not contain nut oils.

SOY-FREE DIET: Whisked sponge is suitable for soy-free diets, provided any fat used to enrich it does not contain soy-bean oil.

CHOCOLATE ROULADE FILLED WITH BITTER CHOCOLATE MOUSSE AND RASPBERRIES

This dessert is dairy, gluten, nut and soy free, but very rich and wicked. The whisked sponge does not contain flour or added fat and relies solely on eggs to form its airy mousse-like texture. **Serves 6**

FOR THE SPONGE

4 eggs, separated into yolks and whites

1¾ cups/170 g confectioners' sugar

● GLUTEN check label for wheat flour

½ cup/55 g good-quality cocoa powder

● GLUTEN check label for wheat flour

FOR THE FILLING

Double recipe Bitter Chocolate Mousse (page 189), made the day before

8 oz./200 g raspberries

1 Preheat the oven to 400°F/200°C/ gas mark 6. Oil a shallow 9 by 12-inch/ 25 by 30-cm jelly-roll pan and line with lightly oiled waxed paper, to stand an inch or so above the rim.

2 Whisk the egg yolks with half the confectioners' sugar until thick and pale.

3 Clean the whisk and dry thoroughly. Whisk the egg whites until they form soft peaks. Add half the remaining confectioners' sugar and continue to whisk the egg whites until stiff.

4 Stir a large spoonful of whisked egg whites into the whisked egg yolks and mix well. Pour the remaining egg whites into the egg yolks and gently fold together.

5 Mix the cocoa powder and remaining confectioners' sugar and sift onto the whisked egg mixture. Gently fold into the eggs until the mixture is just blended.

6 Holding the bowl just above the pan, pour the mixture into the lined baking pan, spreading it from side to side.

7 Bake for 8–10 minutes, or until the sponge is lightly set and feels springy in the center. Do not open the door for at least 6 minutes or the sponge may collapse. Once done, cover with a damp kitchen towel to prevent it from drying out.

8 Once cold, turn it out onto a large piece of waxed paper dusted with confectioners' sugar. Peel away the paper, spread the mousse over the sponge and evenly scatter the raspberries onto the mousse.

9 To roll the roulade, align one of the long ends of the rectangle with the edge of the work surface. Tightly fold the long end of the roulade farthest from you over the first 1 in./2.5 cm of filling, then pull the waxed paper up and over the center, towards you, supporting the roulade as you roll it.

10 Using the paper to support the roulade, roll the cake onto a serving plate and dust with more confectioners' sugar. Trim away any rough ends of the roulade and serve cut into thick slices.

PANCAKES

Pancakes are traditionally made with a batter consisting of eggs, milk, and flour, but they are just as good made with egg-, dairy-, and gluten-free ingredients. Savory pancakes are delicious in baked dishes with lots of sauce, and sweet pancakes make a great dessert topped with fruit, ice cream, or chocolate sauce.

GENERAL RULES FOR MAKING PANCAKES

- Use a large bowl to mix the batter ingredients.
- Carefully and gradually blend the dry and liquid ingredients, to make a lump-free batter. If lumps appear, pass the batter through a fine-meshed sieve.
- Once the batter is made, stop stirring or gluten, contained in wheat flour, will become too developed, resulting in tough pancakes.
- Leave pancake batter to stand and thicken, covered in the refrigerator, for at least 30 minutes before cooking. The flour grains swell in the liquid and burst open as the batter is cooked to make light, tender pancakes. Pancake batter for thick, risen pancakes should be cooked immediately so that the rising agents in the flour lighten the consistency of the pancakes as they bake.
- For light, tender pancakes, the batter should be no thicker than the consistency of heavy cream. When batter is too thick, add more milk or water, 1 tablespoon at a time, until it reaches the required consistency.
- Cook a small sample pancake to test the consistency of the cooked pancake batter before making the pancakes. The batter may require thinning down with a little more milk or water.
- To avoid thick, soggy pancakes, pour excess batter that does not immediately set on the bottom of the hot pan back into the bowl.
- To prevent pancakes from sticking as they cook, apply a very thin coating of oil to the frying pan, using oiled paper towels.

NOTES FOR FOOD ALLERGY SUFFERERS

DAIRY-FREE DIET: Cows' milk is usually used to make pancake batter because it is bland in flavor and readily available. Soy milk, rice milk, and almond milk all make delicious pancakes with a mild flavor and delicate texture.

GLUTEN-FREE DIET: Light-textured and tender gluten-free pancakes can be made by using finely ground rice flour, which has a suitably bland flavor, tapioca flour, and arrowroot powder, which help bind the pancakes, and egg.

EGG-FREE DIET: Although eggs bind and lightly set the ingredients in cooked batter, pancakes can be made very successfully without egg. Egg-free pancakes rely on the binding properties of gluten in wheat flour and a small quantity of arrowroot powder and tapioca flour, to hold the batter together as it cooks.

NUT- AND SOY-FREE DIETS: Pancake batter is enriched and moistened with a small quantity of neutral-flavored oil, such as sunflower oil, corn oil, or canola oil stirred into the batter, and it is also fried in oil. Check that the oil you use does not contain peanut or soybean oil.

FRENCH CRÊPES

These pancakes are nut and soy free and are easily adapted for gluten- and diary-free diets. They are not egg free – for egg-free pancakes, see page 197. Top or fill these delicious pancakes with Dark Chocolate Sauce (page 208), Fresh Summer Berry Sauce (page 209), or simply with honey, maple syrup, jam, or lemon juice and sugar.
Makes about 12 pancakes

INGREDIENTS

● **GLUTEN**

1 cup/110 g all-purpose flour

½ cup/55 g brown rice flour, ¼ cup/30g tapioca flour, and ¼ cup/30 g arrowroot powder

½ tsp. salt

1 Tbsp. superfine sugar

1 egg and 1 egg yolk, beaten together

1½ cups/350 ml milk

● **DAIRY**

soy, rice, or almond milk

finely grated zest of 1 orange

sunflower or corn oil

1 Sift the flour, salt, and sugar into a bowl and make a wide well in the center. Pour in the beaten eggs and add a little milk. Using a wooden spoon, stir in small circles so that the flour is slowly drawn into the liquid from the sides.

2 As the egg and flour mixture thickens, add the milk, stirring it in little by little, until all the milk is incorporated and the batter is smooth. Stir in the orange zest and 1 Tbsp. oil, cover with plastic wrap, and leave to stand for 30 minutes.

3 Pour some oil into a 8–10-inch/ 20–25-cm frying pan, swirl it around the pan, then pour off the excess into a bowl to re-use. Heat until the oil starts to smoke. French crêpes should be wafer thin, so test your batter by swirling 1 Tbsp. batter in the heated pan. Once the top of the pancake starts to bubble, turn the pancake over and brown the second side. If the pancake seems a little thick, thin the batter with 1–2 Tbsp. milk or water.

4 Stir the batter well and pour a small ladle of batter into the hot pan. Swirl the pancake batter over the bottom of the pan and pour any excess batter back into the bowl. After 30–40 seconds, when the top of the pancake starts to bubble, turn the pancake over using a palette knife and brown the second side for another 30 seconds. Repeat with the remaining batter. Cover the cooked pancakes with waxed paper and keep warm in a very low oven before serving.

BUCKWHEAT PANCAKES WITH CARAMELIZED CINNAMON APPLES

These pancakes can be adapted for gluten-free diets but are not egg free. Buckwheat gives a wholesome flavor that is delicious complemented by caramelized apples and Vanilla Ice Cream (page 204). **Serves 4 (2 pancakes each)**

FOR THE PANCAKES

½ cup/55 g buckwheat flour

½ cup/55 g all-purpose flour

● GLUTEN rice flour

½ tsp. salt

1 Tbsp. superfine sugar

1 egg and 1 egg yolk beaten together

1¼ cups/290 ml milk

● DAIRY sweetened dairy-free milk

sunflower or corn oil

FOR THE APPLES

½ cup/85 g granulated sugar

6 Tbsp./85g unsalted butter

● DAIRY dairy-free margarine

4 Granny Smith apples, peeled, cored, and thickly sliced

1 tsp. ground cinnamon

1 To make the pancake batter, sift the flours, salt, and superfine sugar into the bowl and make a wide well in the center of the flour. Pour in the beaten eggs and a little milk.

2 With a wooden spoon, stir the egg mixture in small circles so that the flour is slowly drawn from the sides of the well into the liquid.

3 As the egg and flour mixture thickens, add the remaining milk, little by little, continuing to stir until all the milk is incorporated and the batter is smooth. If it contains a few lumps, pass it through a sieve into a clean bowl. Stir in 1 Tbsp. oil, cover with plastic wrap, and leave to stand for 30 minutes in the refrigerator.

4 Meanwhile, heat the granulated sugar in a dry frying pan over a medium heat until it melts and turns golden brown. Turn off the heat and stir in the butter to make the caramel sauce.

5 Stir the sliced apples and cinnamon into the caramel, cover with a lid, and gently simmer over a low heat for about 20 minutes, or until the apples are tender and golden brown. Remove from the heat and keep warm.

6 To cook the pancakes, heat some oil in a frying pan, stir the batter, and pour a small ladle of butter into the pan. When the top of the pancake starts to bubble, turn the pancake over and brown the second side. Continue until all the batter is used.

7 To serve, place a pancake flat on a warmed plate and top with a large spoonful of warm apples and caramel sauce and loosely fold or roll the pancake.

EGG-FREE PANCAKES

These pancakes have a fine, lacy texture very similar to French crêpes. Serve them with sugar and lemon, or chocolate sauce and ice cream. Or omit the sugar and make savory pancakes as the basis for an egg-free savory dish. They are not suitable for those who suffer from a gluten allergy. **Makes about 12 pancakes**

INGREDIENTS

½ cup/55 g all-purpose flour

¼ cup/30 g arrowroot powder

¼ cup/30 g tapioca flour

½ tsp. salt

1 Tbsp. superfine sugar

1½ cups/350 ml milk

● DAIRY   sweetened dairy-free milk

1 Tbsp. sunflower or corn oil, plus more as needed

finely grated zest of 1 orange

1 Sift the all-purpose flour, arrowroot powder, tapioca flour, salt, and superfine sugar into a bowl and make a wide well in the center.

2 Pour one-third of the milk into the well. With a wooden spoon, stir the milk in small circles so that the flour is slowly drawn from the sides of the well into the liquid.

3 As the milk and flour mixture thickens, slowly add more milk, stirring it in little by little until all the milk is incorporated and the batter is smooth. If the batter contains a few lumps, pass it through a sieve into a clean bowl.

4 Stir in the oil, add the orange zest, cover with plastic wrap, and leave to stand for 30 minutes.

5 Pour some oil into a 8–10-inch/ 20–25-cm frying pan, swirl it around the pan, then pour off the excess into a bowl to re-use. Heat until the oil starts to smoke. Stir the batter well and pour a small ladle of batter into the hot pan. Swirl the batter over the bottom of the pan and pour any excess back into the bowl. After 30–40 seconds, when the top of the pancake starts to bubble, turn the pancake over and brown the second side for another 30 seconds. Repeat with the remaining batter. Cover the cooked pancakes with waxed paper and keep warm in a very low oven before serving.

MERINGUES

Meringue is made by folding superfine sugar into whisked egg whites. As the egg whites are whisked, they fill with bubbles of air, which give meringues their airy lightness. The sugar dissolves in the egg white foam to form a syrup coating around each bubble. As meringues bake, the moisture around each bubble evaporates leaving a crisp sugary shell.

GENERAL RULES
FOR MAKING
MERINGUES

- Egg whites should be at room temperature, because they foam better than cold eggs.
- Whisk egg whites in a clean china, stainless steel, or glass bowl. Plastic bowls tend to scratch and harbor grease. If the bowl is not spotlessly clean and dry, the egg whites will not foam to their full potential.
- Do not whisk too vigorously—begin slowly and gradually increase the speed as the foam thickens with tiny bubbles.
- Sugar should not be added to whisked egg whites until they are stiff and no longer wobble when shaken.
- Only add half of the sugar, or you risk the egg whites collapsing. Whisk on a fast speed until the egg whites stand in stiff peaks and have a smooth pearly appearance.
- Fold the remaining sugar into the stiff meringue as gently and as briefly as possible to avoid the meringue losing too much air and collapsing. Use a large metal spoon to reduce the number of stirs necessary for mixing in the sugar.

INDIVIDUAL MERINGUES

This recipe makes five to six large meringues to serve with fresh fruit steeped in Summer Berry Sauce and your favorite ice cream. It can also be used to make twenty baby meringues for children's parties. This recipe is not suitable for egg allergy sufferers. **Serves 5–6**

INGREDIENTS

2 egg whites

½ cup/110 g superfine sugar

TO SERVE

12 oz./350 g mixed berries, steeped overnight in Fresh Summer Berry Sauce (page 209)

homemade ice cream (pages 203–5)

1 Preheat the oven to 250°F/120°C/ gas mark ½. Line a baking sheet with parchment paper.

2 Whisk the egg whites in a clean bowl slowly, gradually increasing the speed as the foam thickens, until the egg whites form soft peaks.

3 Sprinkle half of the sugar onto the whisked whites and whisk until the mixture is very stiff and has a pearly sheen. Gently fold the remaining sugar in, using a large metal spoon.

4 Using two tablespoons, spoon five large piles of meringue onto the baking sheet, spacing them well apart. (To make individual baby meringues, use two teaspoons to spoon piles of meringue onto the lined baking sheet.)

5 Place the meringues on the lower rack in the oven, to ensure they remain white. Bake large meringues for 2 hours (baby meringues for 1 hour). The meringues are done when they are crisp and dry on the outside, soft in the center, and no longer stick to the parchment paper.

6 Place on a wire rack and leave to cool before serving with the sauce and ice cream.

VARIATION
MERINGUE BASKETS
To make five meringue baskets, spoon the meringue mixture into a piping bag with a medium nozzle. Draw around a cup, five times, on a sheet of parchment paper, spacing the circles well apart. Place the parchment, pen side down, on a baking sheet and pipe from the center of the circles, round and round, forming a spiral until the circle is filled. To form the sides, pipe two hoops of meringue one on top of the other on the edge of the base. Pipe the four other baskets in the same way. Bake for 1½–2 hours until the baskets are crisp and no longer stick to the paper.

NOTES FOR FOOD ALLERGY SUFFERERS

There is no such thing as an egg-free meringue because no other ingredient has the same set of properties as egg white. However, meringues make an ideal base for dairy-, gluten-, nut-, and soy-free desserts. Confectioners' sugar is sometimes used to make meringues and can contain wheat flour to prevent it from forming lumps. Check the label before using it.

FRUIT CRISPS

Fruit crisp is an ideal dessert to make for large family meals in the autumn, when the weather is beginning to change and robustly flavored fruits such as apples and pears are in plentiful supply. You can assemble a crisp a few hours before it is to be eaten and bake it in a hot oven while everyone enjoys their main course. Crisp toppings can also be made well in advance, stored in an airtight container, and refrigerated for up to 2 days, or frozen. Allow frozen crisp topping to defrost before sprinkling it over freshly prepared fruit. Bake the assembled fruit crisp in a preheated hot oven.

GENERAL RULES
FOR MAKING
FRUIT CRISPS

- Use a dish approximately 2 in./5 cm deep. For a generous filling, the dish should be filled to three-quarters full of prepared fruit, leaving ½ in./1½ cm for the crisp topping.
- Cut fruit into bite-size pieces to retain some texture once it is baked. Fruit cut too small will become mushy.
- Taste the fruit before sweetening it with sugar. It might require more or less than the recipe suggests.
- Use chilled butter or margarine cut into dice. Soft fat is hard to rub into the dry ingredients without the mixture lumping together.
- Use your fingertips only to rub the fat into the dry ingredients to avoid warming up and softening the fat. The cooler the ingredients, the easier it is to rub them together.
- The topping mixture is ready to use when it looks like coarse bread crumbs.
- Bake crisps in a preheated hot oven. The crisp is done when the topping is golden brown and lightly crunchy and the fruit below is soft when tested with a sharp knife.

NOTES
FOR FOOD
ALLERGY
SUFFERERS

DAIRY-FREE DIET: Hard baking margarine is an ideal alternative to butter for producing the golden brown color and crunchy texture of the topping.

GLUTEN-FREE DIET: Crisp topping is traditionally made with flour and oats but can be made just as well with a mixture of rice flour, flaked rice, millet, and buckwheat.

EGG-FREE DIET: Egg is not used in crisps.

NUT-FREE AND SOY-FREE DIETS: Crisps are suitable for nut- and soy-free diets, provided butter or nut- and soy-free margarine is used.

APPLE AND BLACKBERRY CRISP

Blackberry and apple crisp is one of the most rewarding ways to eat blackberries. Serve with Vanilla Ice Cream (page 204), Crème Anglaise (page 207,) or heavy cream. **Serves 4–6**

FOR THE FILLING

1½ lb./675 g tart apples, such as Granny Smiths, peeled, cored, quartered, and thickly sliced

8 oz./225 g blackberries, hulled and rinsed

3 Tbsp. brown sugar

FOR THE TOPPING

1 cup/110 g all-purpose flour

● GLUTEN rice flour

1 cup/110 g rolled oats

● GLUTEN ⅔ cup/55 g millet flakes, 3 Tbsp./30 g rice flakes and 3 Tbsp./30 g buckwheat flakes

6 Tbsp./85 g Demerara sugar

½ tsp. salt

½ cup/110 g butter, chopped into small pieces

● DAIRY dairy-free hard baking margarine

1 Preheat the oven to 400°F/200°C/ gas mark 6.

2 Scatter the apples and blackberries over the bottom of an 7 by 11-inch/ 20 by 28-cm ovenproof dish. Sprinkle the brown sugar over the fruit.

3 To make the topping, mix the flour, oats (or millet flakes, rice flakes and buckwheat flakes), Demerara sugar, and salt together in a mixing bowl.

4 Add the butter to the dry ingredients and lightly rub together with your fingertips until the mixture resembles coarse bread crumbs.

5 Sprinkle the topping over the fruit, spreading it out so the fruit is completely covered.

6 Bake for 30–40 minutes, or until the topping is crisp and golden brown. Serve warm or cold.

VARIATION
RHUBARB CRISP
Use 2 lb./900 g rhubarb, chopped into 2-in./5-cm pieces, in place of the apples and blackberries. Increase the amount of Demerara sugar in the topping to ½ cup/110 g

Sorbets make colorful, refreshing, and delicious desserts, served with meringues, cookies, fresh fruit, or sweet fruity sauces. Sorbet is made by freezing fruit syrup or puree, then beating it to a soft, smooth consistency.

RASPBERRY SORBET

Vivid and fresh in flavor and color, this sorbet is a wonderful egg- and dairy-free alternative to ice cream. It is also gluten-, soy-, and nut-free. It is delicious served simply with fresh fruit, or with Fresh Summer Berry Sauce (page 209). It also makes great frozen popsicles. **Serves 6**

INGREDIENTS

1¾ lb./750 g raspberries

1¾ cups/400 ml cold Sugar Syrup (page 209)

juice of 1 lemon, plus more as needed

superfine sugar

1 Press the raspberries through a sieve into a bowl and mix in the sugar syrup and lemon juice. Taste and if necessary, balance the flavor with a squeeze of lemon juice or a little superfine sugar.

2 Pour the raspberry mixture into a plastic container, cover with a lid, and freeze for 4 hours, or until half frozen.

3 Cut the freezing mixture into chunks and blend in a food processor or beat with a wooden spoon in a mixing bowl until smooth. Return the sorbet to the freezer and freeze for another 2 hours. Beat once again, then return the sorbet to the freezer until firm.

4 Remove the sorbet from the freezer 15 minutes before serving to soften.

NOTES FOR FOOD ALLERGY SUFFERERS

Sorbets consist of sugar, water, and fruit and make ideal desserts for those on a dairy-, egg-, gluten-, nut-, or soy-free diet.

EGG-FREE DIET: Egg white is sometimes added to sorbet to soften its texture because it prevents large ice crystals from forming in the mixture. It is not necessary to add egg white to sorbet, provided sugar is used in the correct concentration and the frozen sorbet mixture is beaten until it is smooth and soft.

ICE CREAM

The richest, smoothest ice cream is made from a basic mixture of milk, cream, sugar, and egg yolks. However, you can make a delicious dairy-free version with soy milk and soy cream (see Rich Chocolate Ice Cream and Vanilla Ice Cream, page 204). For an egg-free ice cream that has a rich flavor and smooth consistency, mashed banana mixed with cream (or soy cream), sugar, and orange and lemon juice is a great alternative (see Banana Ice Cream, page 205).

GENERAL RULES FOR MAKING CUSTARD-BASED ICE CREAMS

- Measure the amount of sugar accurately. Too much sugar will lead to a soft, overly sweet ice cream and too little results in hard, bland-tasting ice cream. Sugar generally makes up about one-third of the weight of the ingredients in ice cream.
- Add milk and cream (or soy milk and soy cream) in equal quantities to ensure the correct consistency.
- Use very fresh eggs (generally, 4 egg yolks per 2½ cups/570 ml of liquid) because they are only partially cooked when the custard is made and could still carry the salmonella bacteria. Never refreeze custard-based ice cream once it has thawed.
- Cook the custard over a gentle heat, stirring continuously so that the egg thickens slowly and doesn't coagulate.
- Remove custard from the heat when it starts to steam and thicken and the bottom of the pan feels slippery as you stir with a wooden spoon.
- Taste buds are less sensitive to frozen foods. The ice cream mixture should therefore taste overflavored and too sweet, before it is frozen.
- If you do not have a food processor to churn the frozen ice cream, allow it to soften slightly before beating it with a wooden spoon until smooth but firm enough to hold its shape. Do not overchurn or the ice cream will melt.

NOTES FOR FOOD ALLERGY SUFFERERS

DAIRY-FREE DIET: Soy milk and soy cream are the most suitable dairy-free alternatives for making ice cream. Use good-quality sweetened soy milk because the cheaper varieties tend to be watery and have a very beany flavor. The beany flavor of soy does come through in subtly flavored ice creams, such as vanilla, but it is masked by the addition of chocolate, fruit purees, or coffee.

GLUTEN-FREE DIET: Homemade ice cream does not contain gluten unless ingredients containing gluten are included in a recipe for added texture and flavor.

EGG-FREE DIET: Custard-based ice cream is not suitable for egg-free diets. Instead, try making Banana Ice Cream (page 205).

NUT-FREE DIET: Basic homemade ice cream does not contain nuts unless they are included in a recipe to add texture and extra flavor. Read the labels of chocolate and other products used to flavor ice cream because they could contain nuts.

SOY-FREE DIET: Traditional homemade ice cream does not contain soy products. Soy cream and soy milk are, however, extremely useful for making dairy-free ice cream. If you are allergic to soy and dairy products, Banana Ice Cream (page 205) can be made using rice milk or almond milk. The resulting frozen dessert is much lighter and tastes more like a sorbet.

RICH CHOCOLATE ICE CREAM

This ice cream is very rich, intensely chocolatey, and just as delicious made with dairy-free soy milk and soy cream. Use a good-quality dark chocolate for a really intense chocolatey flavor. Serve this ice cream with Meringues (page 199), pancakes, or as a trio with Banana Ice Cream (page 205) and Raspberry Sorbet (page 202). This recipe contains egg—for an egg-free ice cream see opposite. **Serves 4**

INGREDIENTS

4 egg yolks

½ cup/110 g superfine sugar

4 oz./110 g good-quality dark chocolate with 70% cocoa solids, broken into pieces

● NUTS — check label for traces of nuts

● SOY — check label for soy lecithin

1¼ cups/290 ml whole milk

● DAIRY — good-quality sweetened soy milk

1¼ cups/290 ml whipping cream

● DAIRY — soy cream

1 Stir the egg yolks and superfine sugar together in a medium-sized bowl until smooth.

2 Place the chocolate pieces in a saucepan and pour in the milk. Warm the milk over low heat, stirring continuously, until the chocolate is completely melted. Remove from the heat.

3 Slowly pour the hot chocolate milk in a thin, continuous stream onto the egg and sugar mixture, stirring continuously, until thoroughly blended.

4 Pour the mixture back into the pan and stir over low to medium heat until the custard starts to steam heavily and thickens to the consistency of heavy cream.

5 Remove the pan from the heat and immediately pour in the cream to stop the cooking, or lumps of coagulated egg may form.

6 Pour the custard through a sieve (to catch any lumps of coagulated egg) into a shallow container. Allow to cool, then place in the freezer for at least 3 hours, or until half frozen. Cut the freezing ice cream into pieces and beat until smooth in a food processor or in a bowl with a wooden spoon.

7 Return the ice cream to the freezer for another hour or so or until firm. Remove the ice cream from the freezer for 15 minutes before serving to soften.

VARIATIONS

STRAWBERRY OR RASPBERRY ICE CREAM
Push 8 oz./225 g hulled berries through a fine sieve and stir into the cooled custard after the cream is added. Balance the flavor with lemon juice or a little more sugar before freezing.

VANILLA ICE CREAM
Replace the chocolate with 2 split vanilla pods. Add the pods to the milk and bring to a simmer. Remove from the heat, scrape the black seeds into the milk, and pour the vanilla milk onto the egg yolk and sugar mixture. Follow the recipe from step 4 onwards.

BANANA ICE CREAM

This smooth and fruity ice cream is egg free and by replacing the dairy cream with soy cream, it can be dairy free, too. It's very easy to make and delicious served with fresh fruit, fruit pies, and chocolate desserts or brownies. **Serves 4**

INGREDIENTS

4 firm but ripe bananas, peeled

juice of 1 lemon

juice of 1 orange

2 Tbsp. superfine sugar

⅔ cup/150 ml whipping cream

● **DAIRY** soy cream

1 Break the bananas into pieces and place in a food processor with the lemon juice, orange juice, superfine sugar, and cream.

2 Puree the ingredients until completely smooth, pour into a plastic container, cover with a lid, and place in the freezer for 3 hours, or until half frozen.

3 Break the half-frozen ice cream into chunks and churn in the food processor, or beat in a large bowl with a wooden spoon until smooth.

4 Return the ice cream to the plastic container, cover, and freeze until firm.

5 Remove the ice cream from the freezer for 15 minutes before serving to soften.

SWEET SAUCES

Sweet sauces add color, flavor, and texture to a wide variety of desserts and can make a simple dessert look and taste special. This section covers sweet sauces that complement the desserts included in this book.

CUSTARD

Custard is a smooth, creamy, pale yellow sauce made with milk, sugar, and egg yolks or cornstarch. Fresh custard thickened with egg yolks is also known as crème Anglaise and is served as a more interesting alternative to cream. It is also used to make custard-based ice cream. Cornstarch is often used in crème Anglaise to help thicken it and to stabilize egg yolk as it is heated, or in the case of custard powder, used alone to form an egg-free, smooth, slightly gelatinous milky yellow sauce best served with warm puddings.

GENERAL RULES FOR MAKING CRÈME ANGLAISE

- Use very fresh eggs, because they are only partially cooked. To reduce the risk of salmonella poisoning, store the custard, covered, in the refrigerator, for no more than 24 hours and do not serve to very young children, pregnant women, and the elderly.
- Cook custard over a gentle heat, stirring continuously so that the egg thickens slowly and doesn't coagulate.
- Remove custard from the heat when it starts to steam and thicken and the bottom of the pan feels slippery as you stir with a wooden spoon.
- To stop hot custard from cooking further, pour it into a bowl standing in cold water. As the custard cools, it thickens to the consistency of heavy cream.

NOTES FOR FOOD ALLERGY SUFFERERS

DAIRY-FREE DIET: Although both custard made with custard powder and crème Anglaise are traditionally made with cows' milk, they are just as good made with dairy-free milk. Sweetened soy milk is best because it most closely resembles dairy milk in appearance and consistency. Rice milk and almond milk also can be used for making custard; however, their thin consistency tends to make thin, watery custard. To enrich and thicken custard made with rice milk or almond milk, use 4 egg yolks per 1¼ cups/290 ml milk.

GLUTEN-FREE DIET: Crème Anglaise is ideal for gluten-free diets because it is thickened with egg yolks not flour. Where flour is needed to thicken a custard, cornstarch is generally used.

EGG-FREE DIET: Although egg yolks enrich, color, and thicken crème Anglaise, a very similar egg-free sauce can be made using cornstarch to thicken, a small quantity of custard powder for color, and milk or cream to enrich its flavor (see Vanilla Cream Sauce, page 208).

NUT- AND SOY-FREE DIETS: Crème Anglaise is entirely suitable for nut- and soy-free diets. Check custard powder for traces of nuts or soy flour before using to make cornstarch-thickened custards.

CRÈME ANGLAISE

Fresh custard is a luxurious, creamy sauce to serve warm with hot fruit tarts, pies, crisps, and steamed puddings or chilled with mousses, ice creams, and cold tarts and cakes. For an egg-free alternative, see page 208. **Serves 4**

INGREDIENTS

● **DAIRY**

1¼ cups/290 ml milk

soy milk, rice milk, or almond milk

1 vanilla pod, split along its length

2 egg yolks

3 Tbsp./40 g superfine sugar

1 Slowly bring the milk to a boil with the vanilla pod.

2 In a bowl, stir the egg yolks and superfine sugar together until smooth.

3 Slowly pour the boiling milk onto the egg mixture, stirring continuously. Pour the mixture back into the pan and stir over low heat until the custard starts to steam and thicken.

4 When the custard reaches the consistency of heavy cream, remove the pan from the heat. Strain the custard through a sieve to remove the vanilla pods and any lumps of coagulated egg. Pour the custard into a cold bowl—this prevents it from cooking further. Serve hot or chilled.

VARIATIONS

CHOCOLATE CUSTARD SAUCE
Allow the hot custard to cool a little before gradually mixing in 2 oz./40 g chopped dark chocolate. Serve warm or cold with chocolate, coffee, banana, vanilla, and almond-flavored desserts.

ORANGE CUSTARD SAUCE
Add the finely grated zest of 1 orange to the milk with the vanilla pod. Add 1 Tbsp. Cointreau or Grand Marnier to the hot custard sauce. Serve hot or cold with rich chocolate, vanilla, or almond desserts.

COFFEE CUSTARD SAUCE
Dissolve 1 heaped tsp. instant coffee in 1 Tbsp. boiling water and stir into the hot custard. Serve hot or cold with vanilla, coffee, or chocolate desserts.

RUM CUSTARD SAUCE
Replace the superfine sugar with ¼ cup/55 g light brown sugar and mix 2 Tbsp. rum into the hot custard. This sauce is delicious served with fruitcake.

VANILLA CREAM SAUCE

This recipe is a wonderfully smooth, rich, egg-free alternative to crème Anglaise. Vanilla cream sauce can be served as it is, hot or cold, or flavored with chocolate, coffee, or orange (see the variations for Crème Anglaise, page 207, which also apply to this recipe). For a lighter sauce, use soy milk only. **Makes 1¼ cups/290 ml**

INGREDIENTS

2 tsp. egg-free custard powder (Birds is egg-free)

⅓ cup/70 ml whole milk
soy milk

● DAIRY

1 cup/220 ml heavy cream
½ cup/100 ml soy milk mixed with
½ cup/100 ml soy cream

● DAIRY

2 Tbsp. superfine sugar

2 vanilla pods, split along their length

1 Place the custard powder in a heavy saucepan and slowly incorporate the milk to make a smooth mixture.

2 Add the cream, superfine sugar, and vanilla pods and bring to a boil, stirring continuously. Simmer gently for 30 seconds and remove from the heat. Remove the pods.

3 Serve hot or chilled. This sauce can be made in advance and reheated.

DARK CHOCOLATE SAUCE

This smooth, glossy sauce is wonderful served with dairy or soy vanilla ice cream. The chocolate sauce sets as it cools and can be used as a chocolate fudge frosting on cakes and cold brownies. **Makes 1¼ cups/290 ml**

INGREDIENTS

4 oz./110 g good-quality dark chocolate (70% cocoa solids), broken into pieces
check for traces of nuts
check for soy lecithin

● NUTS
● SOY

6 Tbsp./85 g butter
dairy-free margarine

● DAIRY

½ cup/100 ml corn syrup

1 Combine the chocolate in a heavy saucepan with the butter and corn syrup. Melt the ingredients together over low heat, stirring continuously until the sauce is glossy and smooth. Alternatively, cook in a microwave for 15–20 seconds, then stir thoroughly and repeat until the sauce is smooth and glossy. Don't allow the chocolate sauce to boil or it will curdle.

2 Remove from the heat and serve immediately or gently reheat when required.

SUGAR SYRUP

Sugar syrup is simply sugar dissolved in water—the greater proportion of sugar, the thicker the syrup. It is useful for adding extra sweetness to fruit salads or softening the texture of sorbet. **Makes 1¼ cups/290 ml**

INGREDIENTS

¾ cup/200 ml water

1 cup/225 g granulated sugar

1 strip lemon zest

1 Combine the water in a pan with the sugar and lemon zest and bring slowly to a simmer, stirring frequently until the sugar is dissolved.

2 Boil the syrup until it is thick enough to coat the back of a spoon. Immediately pour the thickened syrup into a cold bowl to prevent it from cooking and thickening further. Allow to cool, remove the lemon zest, and use as required.

FRESH SUMMER BERRY SAUCE

A versatile, vibrantly colored and flavored sauce made from fresh raspberries, strawberries or blueberries or a mixture of all three. Serve with fruit and chocolate desserts, ice cream, meringues, and cakes. Pour into popsicle molds and freeze for the most wonderful homemade popsicles you have ever tasted. **Serves 4**

INGREDIENTS

4 oz./110 g raspberries

4 oz./110 g strawberries, hulled

2 oz./55 g blueberries

1 Tbsp. lemon juice

2 Tbsp. superfine sugar

1 Blend all the ingredients in food processor or with a hand-held blender until smooth.

2 Pass the sauce through a fine-meshed sieve into a bowl to catch the seeds and any fibrous parts of the fruit. Use a wooden spoon to help press the pureed fruit through. The sauce should evenly coat the back of a spoon. If the sauce is too thick, add water tablespoon by tablespoon until the sauce is the correct consistency.

3 Taste the sauce and add more lemon juice or sugar if necessary. Serve as required or store covered in the refrigerator for up to two days.

Chapter 18 | BABY FOODS

Introducing your baby to solids is exciting because it marks an enormous leap in your baby's development and the start of your baby joining the family at meal times. However, with the increased numbers of children suffering allergies, it can also be a daunting time because you may be unsure which foods are best to give to your baby. This chapter is about preventing food allergies, as well as cooking for those with allergies, because it is at this stage that parents can do much to reduce the likelihood of their child developing food allergies or intolerances.

Whether or not there are food allergies in the family, feeding your baby exclusively on breast milk or infant formula milk is recommended for the first 6 months. This allows your baby's immune and digestive systems to develop and prepare for processing solids. Before 6 months, a baby's intestine is porous and may allow molecules of partially digested food to enter the bloodstream. The immune system may see these molecules as foreign and dangerous, stimulating an immune (or allergic) response. If this occurs, the baby's immune system may react more and more strongly each time you feed your child that particular food, resulting in increasingly severe allergic symptoms. At 6 months, the majority of your baby's diet still should be breast milk or infant formula because it contains the perfect combination of nutrients your baby needs at this stage. The nutritional content of the purees you feed your baby becomes increasingly important as he starts to eat more and consume less milk.

INTRODUCING YOUR BABY TO SOLIDS

In addition to delaying the introduction of solids until your child is at least 6 months old, it is advisable to avoid the common allergens—gluten, eggs, dairy, nuts, fish, and shellfish—at least for the first month of weaning. An ideal starter food is flaked baby rice, mixed to the consistency of runny yogurt with a little breast milk or infant formula. Although the consistency of milk and baby rice is slightly thicker than plain milk, the taste is the same and your baby is unlikely to reject or react in any way to such a simple food. To begin with, your baby may only eat one or two teaspoons but as he becomes more efficient at swallowing, his intake will increase. Once your baby is keenly eating a few tablespoons of baby rice and milk a day, make the mixture slightly thicker, and start to introduce your baby to other simple, mild-flavored purees. The question at this stage is do you buy ready-prepared baby food or make your own?

THE MERITS OF HOMEMADE BABY FOOD

Jars of prepared baby food are invaluable for providing your baby with an instant meal when you are away from home or when you are too tired or too short of time to cook. However, they are not as fresh, pure, varied, or as inexpensive as the purees you can make at home. When you make your own purees, you are in control of the quality and proportions of ingredients used, allowing you to tailor the consistency and flavor to your child's taste and to ensure your child is receiving the best possible nutrition.

By preparing a number of servings of puree at one time, cooking for your baby need not take up much time. Instant purees can be made with ripe avocados and peeled bananas, mashed separately or together with a fork. Freshly made purees made from cooked ingredients can be covered and stored for up to 2 days in the refrigerator or divided into portions and frozen. All you have to do is defrost and gently heat a portion of puree in a small pan or in the microwave.

MAKING HOMEMADE PUREES

Start by making small quantities of very smooth purees from raw or cooked fruits and vegetables: mashed avocado or banana, or pureed apple, pear, root vegetables, sweet potato, or butternut squash are ideal foods to start with because they have appealing flavors, are easy to puree to a fine consistency, and are easy for your baby to digest. To get your baby used to a new flavor, mix a spoonful of puree into your child's baby rice and milk so that the consistency remains familiar and mild in flavor. You can also start to introduce iron-rich foods, such as well-cooked, pureed beans and lentils, green vegetables, dried fruit (such as apricots), and iron-enriched cereal.

Introduce your baby to one ingredient at a time over a period of 2 to 3 days, so that your baby has a chance to get used to the new taste and texture. By introducing one food at a time, it also allows you to associate any signs of allergic reaction, such as tummy aches, diarrhea, or rashes, directly with it. Your baby's reaction to a food will also help you decide which foods suit him and which do not. If he holds his mouth open for more and looks excited, you're onto a winner! If there are no adverse reactions to that food, then you can give it to him again, either on its own or combined with another new or tried-and-tested food.

Recognizing an allergic reaction

When a particular food does not suit your baby, it may cause an allergic reaction immediately or later on in the day in the form of diarrhea, tummy aches, and gassiness. Immediate allergic reactions can range from mild to severe. Mild allergic reactions include itchy redness and slight swelling around the mouth, nettle rash or hives, and the onset of eczema. More dramatic reactions include swelling around the eyes, nose, and mouth, shortness of breath or, far more serious, anaphylactic shock.

If your baby suffers a mild allergic reaction to a new food, avoid giving it to him again for a few months. Giving your baby the food a second time, on its own or mixed with other foods, may well result in a more serious allergic reaction. When the initial allergic reaction is serious and threatens the health of your child, you may be advised by your doctor to avoid that food entirely until the child is much older. In such cases, it is important to see an allergy specialist and dietician to ensure your child is receiving a balanced diet and is developing normally. Sometimes it is unclear what is causing the onset of eczema, hives, asthma, or other allergic reactions, because other factors, such as allergies to pollen, house dust mites, pets, and cleansing products also may be contributing factors.

When he is not sure of the flavor or the food is irritating him in some way, he'll soon make it clear by turning away. Respect this response as much as a positive one but do try again another time—as your baby grows and his digestive system continues to mature, his preferences and requirements will change.

INTRODUCING
MORE COMPLEX
FOODS

At around 7 to 9 months, your baby will be used to eating simple purees made with fruit and vegetables, and you will have a clear idea which foods suit your baby. He will now be relying on solids more, to satiate his growing appetite, and the nutritional content of his purees must now increase to compensate for his decreasing milk consumption. Start to mix a small quantity of gently poached and pureed chicken and fish or tender, slow-cooked lamb, beef, and pork, into the savory purees your baby enjoys. You can also slowly introduce each of the allergenic ingredients you have been careful not to use until now, such as bread and pasta, egg, and dairy products, including mild-flavored hard cheese, baby yogurts, and cows' milk. Nuts should be avoided until your baby is at least 1 year old. If there are nut allergies in the family, you may be advised to avoid giving nuts to your child until he is 4 or 5 years old.

As your baby becomes more proficient at chewing and swallowing, you can gradually increase the thickness of his purees and blend them more coarsely so they contain small, soft lumps. Your baby may be ready to try simple finger food, cut into bite-sized pieces, such as bread, melon, ripe bananas, and cooked carrots and sweet potato.

If your child appears to enjoy and thrive on these foods, you can have fun introducing a whole variety of foods to your child, but do it slowly and watch out for any adverse reactions.

SUBSTITUTING
INGREDIENTS
IN BABY FOODS

When your baby is allergic to particular foods, cooking fresh food for your baby becomes essential. Jarred baby food is very clearly labeled and may well be suitable for an allergic baby but it will never provide the variety and freshness of food that you can with freshly cooked food. There are many allergy-free substitutes available to use in the place of the most common allergens.

Dairy products: To thin purees and as a base for milky sauces, use breast milk or soy-based infant formula in place of cows' milk and dairy-based infant formula. After your child's first birthday, cook with calcium- and vitamin-enriched soy milk or rice milk. You can also introduce your baby to soy yogurt in place of dairy yogurt. See Substituting for Dairy Products, page 50.

Gluten: Use gluten-free cereals and flours to make breakfast cereals, baked goods, and to thicken sauces. See Substituting for Wheat, page 40.

Eggs: Avoiding eggs is straightforward when your child is eating purees, but as he starts to eat more grown-up foods, you'll need to be more vigilant. See Substituting for Eggs, page 34.

Nuts: Because nuts commonly cause the severest allergic reactions, cooking fresh food from scratch for your baby becomes a necessity. As your baby grows, you will want to introduce him to more complex foods. For ways of adapting recipes that contain nuts, see Substituting for Nuts, page 55.

Soy: In particular, watch out for soy in jarred baby food and use cows' milk or rice milk in cooking. See Substituting for Soy, page 58.

These recipes are gluten-, dairy-, egg-, soy-, and nut-free and were great favorites with my boys when they were babies.

PARSNIP AND APPLE PUREE

This puree has a delicate fruity flavor and light, creamy consistency. It can be stored in the refrigerator for up to 2 days or divided into servings and frozen. **Makes 6–8 servings**

INGREDIENTS

4 small parsnips, peeled and cut into small dice

2 apples, peeled, cored, and sliced

1 Place the parsnips in a steamer over water or in a saucepan and cover with water. Steam or simmer for 15 minutes.

2 Add the apple and continue to cook for another 5 minutes, or until tender. Drain the parsnip and apple and reserve the cooking liquid.

3 Blend the parsnip and apple until smooth with ¼ cup cooking water. Add more liquid to the puree, a tablespoon at a time, until it is just thick enough to hold its shape.

POTATO, LEEK, AND PEA PUREE

This is an ideal puree for introducing your baby to the aromatic flavor of leeks or onion. It can be stored in the refrigerator for up to 2 days or divided into servings and frozen. **Makes 6–8 servings**

INGREDIENTS

1 baking potato, peeled and diced

1 leek, trimmed and thinly sliced

2 Tbsp. frozen peas

water, or White Chicken or Vegetable Stock (pages 64, 66)

1 Place the potato in a pan, cover with water and a lid, and bring to a boil. Simmer for 10 minutes, then add the leek and peas. Simmer for another 10 minutes, or until the potato is tender.

2 Drain the vegetables, reserving the cooking liquid.

3 Using a hand-held blender or food processor, blend the vegetables to a smooth puree with 2 Tbsp. cooking water or stock. If the puree is too thick, add more hot stock or water, a tablespoon at a time, until the puree is just thick enough to hold its shape.

AVOCADO AND BANANA PUREE

Instant and highly nutritious, this delicately flavored puree is ideal to serve to your baby when you are out and about. It is rich in vitamin E and B complex vitamins, for growth, a healthy nervous system, and for the maintenance of healthy body tissue. **Makes 1 serving**

INGREDIENTS

1 small or ½ large banana, peeled

½ small ripe avocado, cut into slices

Combine the banana and avocado in a bowl and mash to a smooth puree with a fork. Avocado discolors quickly so serve immediately or within a few hours.

APPLE AND PEAR PUREE

Unsweetened apple puree, even when made with the sweetest apples, can sometimes taste a little sharp for babies. Pear softens and sweetens the flavor of apple to make a puree your baby will love. Store in the refrigerator for up to 2 days or freeze in servings. **Makes 6–8 servings**

INGREDIENTS

2 apples, peeled, cored, and diced

2 ripe pears, peeled, cored, and diced

1 Place the apple in a pan and just cover with water. Cover with a lid, bring to a boil, and simmer for 5 minutes.

2 Add the pear, cover, and continue to cook for another 5 minutes, or until both

the apple and pear are tender, but not mushy.

3 Drain the fruit and reserve the cooking water. Blend with 2 Tbsp. cooking water and if necessary, add more, a tablespoon at a time, until the puree is smooth and just holds its shape.

CARROT AND BUTTERNUT SQUASH PUREE

This sweet puree is rich in vitamin A, which is important for growth, the immune system, good vision, and strong bones. It is particularly good made with stock and can be stored in the refrigerator for up to 2 days or divided into servings and frozen. **Makes 6–8 servings**

INGREDIENTS

1 butternut squash, peeled, seeded, and cut into large dice

2 large carrots, peeled and cut into small dice

Vegetable Stock (page 66) or water

1 Place the vegetables in a medium pan and cover with stock and a lid. Bring to a boil, then reduce the heat and simmer

the vegetables for 20 minutes, or until tender. Drain the vegetables, reserving the cooking water.

2 Using a hand-held blender or food processor, puree the vegetables with 2–3 Tbsp. cooking water, until the puree is smooth and just holds its shape.

First finger foods for babies of 7 months plus

Between 7 and 9 months, your baby will start developing an interest in feeding himself. Choose soft-textured, unseasoned foods that are large enough for him to hold easily in his hand while he chews and sucks them. Avoid hard foods that may crumble into small, sharp pieces and very small foods, such as raisins, because both may cause your baby to choke. Simple finger foods that are unlikely to cause allergic reactions include:
• Peeled cucumber sticks
• Carrot and sweet potato sticks and broccoli florets, steamed until soft
• Chunks of soft ripe, peeled, pitted or cored fruit, such as pear, peach, nectarine, mango, banana, and avocado
• Plain rice cakes
• Large pieces of soft dried fruit including apple rings and ready-to-eat pitted apricots and prunes
• Gluten-free toast strips and breadsticks
• Gluten-free pasta shapes

Once you have established which of the more complex, allergenic foods, containing dairy, egg, gluten, and soy are suitable for your baby, you can introduce him to:
• Strips of wheat-based toast
• Cooked wheat pasta shapes
• Breadsticks
• Lumps of mild-flavored hard cheese

PUREES FOR BABIES 8 TO 10 MONTHS OLD

CHICKEN, POTATO AND CORN PUREE

This nutritious meal also can be made using skinned fillets of mild-flavored white fish, such as cod, haddock, and sole. This puree will keep in the refrigerator for up to 2 days or divide it into servings and freeze. **Makes 6–8 servings**

INGREDIENTS

¼ onion, finely sliced

1½ tsp. vegetable oil

2 baking potatoes, peeled and diced

White Chicken or Vegetable Stock (page 64, 66) or water

1 boneless, skinless chicken breast, cut into 1-in./2.5-cm dice

¼ cup frozen corn

1 Gently fry the onion in the oil, covered with a lid, until very soft. Add the potatoes and cover with stock. Simmer for 10 minutes, then add the chicken and corn, and gently simmer for 10 minutes, or until the chicken is cooked through and the potatoes are tender. Do not overcook the chicken, or it will become tough.

2 Strain half the cooking liquid into a bowl and coarsely blend or finely chop the remaining contents of the pan. If the mixture is too dry, mix in a little more of the strained cooking liquid.

CHICKEN AND APRICOT RICE

The soft texture of cooked risotto rice makes it an ideal base for smooth, coarsely blended, or chopped meals for your baby. Once your baby is eating food with lumps, try making this meal with more fibrous, nutritionally superior brown rice. This dish will keep in the refrigerator for up to 2 days or divide it into servings and freeze.
Makes 4–6 servings

INGREDIENTS

¼ onion, diced

1 Tbsp. sunflower or corn oil

½ cup/55 g Arborio or other white rice

1¼ cups/290 ml White Chicken or Vegetable Stock (page 64, 66) or water, plus more as needed

1 boneless, skinless chicken breast, cut into large cubes

1 cup/55 g dried apricots

1 Gently fry the onion in the oil, covered with a lid, until soft. Stir the rice into the onion, add the stock, and simmer for 10 minutes.

2 Add the chicken and apricots to the pan and simmer for 10 minutes, or until the chicken is cooked through and the rice is swollen and tender.

3 Coarsely blend or finely chop the contents of the pan. If the mixture is too stiff, mix in some water or hot stock, a tablespoon at a time.

RICE PUDDING

Made with flaked rice, this is a satisfying pudding to serve warm or cold. It is delicious flavored with a tablespoon or two of your baby's favorite fruit puree. This dish can be stored for up to 2 days but should not be frozen. **Makes 4 servings**

INGREDIENTS

1¼ cups/290 ml cows' milk, infant formula, or dairy-free milk fortified with calcium

¼ cup/45 g flaked rice

1–2 tsp. brown sugar

1 Slowly bring the milk to a boil to prevent it from scorching on the bottom of the pan. Add the rice, cover, and simmer gently for 20–30 minutes, until the rice is very soft.

2 Stir in the sugar and serve warm or cold.

FOOD FOR CHILDREN BETWEEN 9 AND 12 MONTHS OLD

Once your baby reaches 9 months old, you will have a clear idea of the foods that suit him. At this stage, cooking for your family becomes easier because you can start to give your baby some of the food that you serve to the rest of the family. If your baby is allergic to certain foods, you may be able to adapt recipes to suit his requirements so you can all eat the same things (see Part 2: Knowing How to Substitute). Choose dishes that are soft in texture and require minimal chewing, such as soup or spaghetti Bolognaise. Avoid using salt, pepper, and spices in dishes your baby will be eating, until you have separated his portion.

The following recipes from this book are suitable for babies above 9 months old:
- Chunky Winter Vegetable Soup, pureed (page 69)
- Bolognaise, with spaghetti (page 122)
- Lasagna (page 122)
- Homemade Pork and Apple Sausages (page 94)
- Chicken and Mushroom Pie (page 128)
- Mediterranean Roast Chicken with Vegetables (page 114)
- Salmon Fish Cakes (page 89)
- Mashed Potato (page 136)
- Oven Fries—avoid seasoning the potatoes until you have separated some for your baby (page 136)
- Crushed New Potatoes—peel the potatoes because the skins could cause your baby to choke (page 137)

There are also lots of baked foods and desserts your baby can try (although always remember that sweet foods should be an occasional treat, not a regular part of their diet):
- Gluten-free Bread—substitute ground almonds in the recipe with more potato flour (pages 185–87)
- Victoria Sponge Cake (page 172)
- Plain Scones (page 174)
- French Crêpes (page 195)
- Buckwheat Pancakes with Caramelized Apple (page 196)
- Apple and Blackberry Crisp (page 201)
- Vanilla Cream Sauce—always make an egg-free custard for babies because the egg in crème Anglaise is partially cooked and could cause salmonella poisoning (page 208)
- Banana Ice Cream (page 205)

CHILDREN'S PARTY FOODS

Cooking for children's parties can be an unbearably daunting experience if you have a young child who cannot eat dairy, eggs, wheat, soy, or nuts, because all these ingredients are commonly used in manufactured foods and in home-cooked party food. However, you'll find many of the recipes in this book are suitable for children—and for parties, often all that is required is for them to be made in smaller pieces or sliced or cut into smaller servings. This chart offers an at-a-glance guide to which child-friendly recipes can be adapted for particular allergies (Y means yes, the recipe can be adapted for that allergy and N means no, it can't).

Party Food Ideas	page	Dairy	Egg	Gluten	Soy	Nuts
SAVORY FOOD						
Mini Beef Burgers	92	Y	Y	Y	Y	Y
Mini Salmon Fish Cakes	89	Y	Y	Y	Y	Y
Crispy Fish Ribbons	104	Y	Y	Y	Y	Y
Mini Homemade Sausages	94	Y	Y	Y	Y	Y
Honey-Baked Sausages	119	Y	Y	Y	Y	Y
Oven Fries	136	Y	Y	Y	Y	Y
Slices of Pizza Marinara	186	Y	Y	Y	Y	Y
Sticky Finger Chicken Drumsticks	123	Y	Y	Y	Y	Y
Sandwiches—ham, cucumber (use gluten-free bread)	185	Y	Y	Y	Y	Y
SWEET FOOD						
Chocolate Chip Cookies	180	Y	Y	Y	Y	Y
Shortbread Rounds	179	Y	Y	Y	Y	Y
Chewy Rice Krispies Squares	178	Y	Y	Y	Y	Y
Mini Scones	174	Y	Y	Y	Y	Y
Fudgy Chocolate Brownies	176	Y	N	Y	Y	Y
Egg-Free Rich Chocolate Brownies	177	Y	Y	N	Y	Y
Victoria Sponge Cake	172	Y	Y	Y	Y	Y
Date and Orange Muffins	175	Y	Y	Y	Y	Y
Banana Cinnamon Honey Cake	167	Y	Y	Y	Y	Y
Jam Tarts	163	Y	Y	Y	Y	Y
Individual Meringues	199	Y	N	Y	Y	Y
Rich Chocolate Ice Cream	204	Y	N	Y	Y	Y
Raspberry Sorbet Ice Popsicles	202	Y	Y	Y	Y	Y
Banana Ice Cream with	205	Y	Y	Y	Y	Y
Dark Chocolate Sauce	208	Y	Y	Y	Y	Y

INDEX

A

air travel, 24–25
allergic reactions, 210
almond milk, 51
almonds
  Apricot and Orange Tart, 160
  Moist Almond Cake with Lemon
    Syrup, 173
  Rice and Almond Shortcrust
    Pastry, 155
Anchovy Mayonnaise, 84
apples
  Apple and Blackberry Crisp, 201
  Apple and Chorizo Stuffing, 117
  Apple and Pear Puree, 215
  Buckwheat Pancakes with
    Caramelized Cinnamon Apples,
    196–97
  French Apple Tart, 164
  Homemade Pork and Apple
    Sausages with Rich Onion Gravy,
    94
  Parsnip and Apple Puree, 213
  Unsweetened Applesauce, 166
apricots
  Apricot and Orange Tart, 160
  Apricot Puree, 166
  Baked Moroccan Chicken with
    Fennel, Olives, and Apricots,
    121
  Chicken and Apricot Rice, 217
avocados
  Avocado and Banana Puree,
    214
  Avocado and Watercress Dip,
    84

B

baby foods, 210–18
Baked Fillet of Salmon with Shallots,
  Tarragon, and Lemon, 120
baking, 118–23
  bread, 182–87
  cakes, 165–77
  cookies, 178–81
  pastry, 149–64
bananas
  Avocado and Banana Puree,
    214
  Banana Honey Cake, 167
  Banana Ice Cream, 205
barley, 138

Basic Shortcut Pastry, 152
Basic Vinaigrette, 81
Battered Cod, 102–03
Béchamel Sauce, 74
beef
  Beef Burgers with Tomato and
    Corn Salsa, 92
  Corned Beef and Cabbage, 129
  Brown Beef Stock, 65
  Fillet Steak with Red Wine Sauce,
    93
  Lasagna al Forno, 122–23
  steaks, 93
  Traditional Roast Rib of Beef, 113
binding agents
  egg-free, 37
  gluten-free, 45–46, 47–48
Bitter Chocolate Mousse, 189
Blackberry Crisp, Apple and, 201
bran, rice, 143
bread, 43, 48, 182–87
  crumbs, 43, 100
  Gluten-Free Brown Bread, 187
  Gluten-Free White Bread, 185
  Italian Focaccia with Rosemary,
    186
  Onion Focaccia, 186
  White Bread Rolls, 186
breakfast cereals, 141
broiling, 105–8
brownies
  Egg-Free Rich Chocolate
    Brownies, 177
  Fudgy Chocolate Brownies, 176
Brown Beef Stock, 65
Brown Chicken Stock, 64
Brown Rice, Mushroom, Oregano,
  and Orange Stuffing, 116
Brown Rice, Mushroom, Parsley,
  and Lemon Stuffing, 116
Brown Rice Tabbouleh, 140
Brown Vegetable Stock, 66
buckwheat, 138, 139
  Buckwheat Pancakes with
    Caramelized Cinnamon
    Apples, 196–97
bulgur, 138
  Tabbouleh, 140
butter, dairy-free substitutes for, 53–54
buttercream frostings for cakes, 171
Butternut Squash Puree, Carrot and,
  215

C

Cabbage, Corned Beef and, 129
cakes, 165–77
  Banana Honey Cake, 167
  buttercream frostings for, 171
  Chocolate Roulade Filled with
    Bitter Chocolate Mousse and
    Raspberries, 192–93
  egg-free, 37, 165, 166
  gluten-free, 47–48, 165
  Lemon and Orange Marmalade
    Cake, 169
  Moist Almond Cake with Lemon
    Syrup, 173
  Rich Chocolate Mousse Torte, 190
  Rich Fruit Cake, 170–71
  Victoria Sponge Cake, 172
carbohydrates, 27, 29
Carrot and Butternut Squash Puree,
  215
cereals, breakfast, 141
Champ, 136
cheese
  Cheese Sauce, 74
  dairy-free substitutes for, 52
  Parmesan and Potato Pastry, 157
Chewy Rice Krispies Squares, 178
chicken. *See also* poultry
  Baked Moroccan Chicken with
    Fennel, Olives, and Apricots,
    121
  Brown Chicken Stock, 64
  Chicken and Apricot Rice, 217
  Chicken and Mushroom Pie,
    128–29
  Chicken, Potato, and Corn Puree,
    216
  Crispy Chicken Ribbons, 104
  Lebanese Chicken Kebabs,
    106–07
  Mediterranean Roast Chicken
    with Vegetables, 114–15
  Moroccan Chicken Tagine,
    132–33
  Singapore Stir-Fried Noodles, 96
  Sticky Finger Chicken Drumsticks,
    123
  Thai Green Chicken Curry, 130
  White Chicken Stock, 64
children, 14–18
  parties for, 16, 219
chocolate, 59
  Bitter Chocolate Mousse, 189
  Chocolate Buttercream Icing, 171

Chocolate Chip Cookies, 180
Chocolate Custard Sauce, 207
Chocolate Roulade Filled with
    Bitter Chocolate Mousse and
    Raspberries, 192
Chocolate Sponge Cake, 172
Dark Chocolate Fudge Frosting,
    171
Dark Chocolate Sauce, 208
Egg-Free Rich Chocolate
    Brownies, 177
Fudgy Chocolate Brownies, 176
Rich Chocolate Ice Cream, 204
Rich Chocolate Mousse, 190
Rich Chocolate Mousse Torte, 190
Chorizo Stuffing, Apple and, 117
Cod, Battered, 102–03
Coffee Custard Sauce, 207
cookies, 178–81
    Chewy Rice Krispies Squares, 178
    Chocolate Chip Cookies, 180
    Shortbread Rounds, 179
corn
    Beef Burgers with Tomato and
        Corn Salsa, 92
    Chicken, Potato, and Corn Puree,
        92
Corned Beef and Cabbage, 129
cornstarch, 74, 139
cornmeal, 139
    Cornmeal and Potato Pastry, 157
    Rice and Cornmeal Shortcrust
        Pastry, 156
    Sweet Rice and Cornmeal Pastry,
        156
cream
    dairy-free substitutes for, 52
    sauces and, 77
Creamy Oatmeal, 141
Creamy Rice Pudding, 141
Crème Anglaise, 207
crêpes, 195
crisps, 200–201
Crispy Chicken Ribbons, 104
Crispy Fish Ribbons, 104
Crushed New Potatoes, 137
curry
    Curry Mayonnaise, 84
    Lamb Rogan Josh, 134
    Thai Green Chicken Curry, 130
custard, 36, 38, 166, 206–07

D

dairy-free diets, 21, 26
    baby food, 212
    baked goods, 149, 165, 191,

200
    dairy substitutes, 50–54
    frying, 87, 95, 101
    ice cream, 203
    pancakes, 194
    poaching, 125
    roasting, 109
    salad dressings, 82
    sauces, 77, 81, 206
    soups, 68
    stews, 131
    stuffings, 111
Dark Chocolate Fudge Frosting,
    171
Dark Chocolate Sauce, 208
Date and Orange Muffins, Spiced,
    177
deep-frying, 100–104
Dip, Avocado and Watercress, 84
drizzle frostings, 171
Duck Breasts with Braised Lentils,
    90–91

E

eating out, 14–15, 19–23
egg-free diets, 22, 26
    baby food, 212
    baked goods, 37, 149, 160,
        165, 166, 177, 191, 201
    egg substitutes, 34–39, 166
    frying, 95, 101
    ice cream, 203
    pancakes, 194, 197
    poaching, 125
    salad dressings, 82
    sauces, 77, 81, 206
    sorbets, 202
    soups, 68
    stuffings, 111
Egg-Free Pancakes, 197
Egg-Free Rich Chocolate Brownies,
    177
Egg-Free Tart, 160
eggs
    in meringues, 198–99
    in mousses, 188
emulsion sauces, 81–85

F

fats, 27, 29, 86, 109. See also
    oils
fennel
    Baked Moroccan Chicken with
        Fennel, Olives, and Apricots,
        121

Provençal Fish Stew with Fennel
    and Potatoes, 126–27
fiber, 27, 29
Fillet Steak with Red Wine Sauce,
    93
finger foods, for babies, 216
fish. See also specific kinds
    baking, 118–19
    broiling, 105–06
    Crispy Fish Ribbons, 104
    doneness defined, 119
    Fish Stock, 64
    poaching, 124–25
    Seafood Kebabs, 107
flour. See also wheat
    gluten-free, 45, 47
    rice, 143
    –thickened sauces, 72–75
focaccia, 186
food labels. See labels
French Apple Tart, 164
French Crêpes, 195
Fresh Summer Berry Sauce, 209
Fritto Misto di Mare, 103
frostings for cakes, 171
fruit. See also specific kinds
    Fruit Cake, 170–71
    fruit crisps, 200–201
    Fruit Scones, 174
    Fruit Shortbread, 179
frying, 86–104
    batters for, 100
    gluten-free coatings for, 43–44

G

Garlic Mayonnaise, 84
glazing baked foods, 39
Gluten-Free Brown Bread, 187
gluten-free diets, 21–22, 26
    baby food, 212
    baked goods, 47–48, 149,
        153–54, 165, 182–87, 191
    cereal, 141
    frying, 87, 95, 101
    gluten substitutes, 40–49
    grains, 138–39
    ice cream, 203
    pancakes, 194
    pasta, 147
    poaching, 125
    roasting, 109
    salad dressings, 82
    sauces, 77, 81, 206
    soups, 68
    stews, 131
    stuffings, 111

Gluten-Free Muesli, 141
Gluten-Free White Bread, 185
grains, 138–41
Greens, Leafy, Stir-Fried, 99
ground rice, 143

H

herbs
    Herb Velouté Sauce, 75
    Tomato and Herb Sauce, 80
honey
    Banana Honey Cake, 167
    Honey Baked Sausages, 119
Horseradish Cream, 85
hotels, 25–26
hygiene, 13

I

ice cream, 203–05
    dairy-free substitutes for, 54
Individual Meringues, 199
Italian Focaccia with Rosemary,
    186

J

Jam Tarts, 163
jellied stock, reconstituting, 63

K

kebabs, 106–07

L

labels for food, 13
    with dairy products, 54
    with eggs, 39
    with gluten, 48–49
    with nuts, 55
    with soy products, 59
lamb
    Lamb Kebabs, 107
    Lamb Rogan Josh, 134
    Lamb Tagine, 133
    Marinated Broiled Lamb Steaks,
        108
Lasagna al Forno, 122–23
Lebanese Chicken Kebabs, 106–7
leeks
    Leek and Mustard Sauce, 79
    Potato, Leek, and Pea Puree,
213
lemon
    Lemon Buttercream Frosting, 171
    Lemon and Orange Marmalade
        Cake, 169

Lemon Sauce, 79
Lemon Shortbread, 179
Lemon Sponge Cake, 172
Lemon Tart, 162
Lemon Velouté Sauce, 75
    Moist Almond Cake with Lemon
        Syrup, 173
Lentils, Braised, Duck Breasts with,
    90–91

M

margarine, 53, 59
marinades, 105
Marinated Broiled Lamb Steaks,
    108
Marmalade Cake, Lemon and
    Orange, 169
mayonnaise, 82–84
    egg-free, 39
meat. *See also specific kinds*
    baking, 118
    broiling, 105–06
    doneness defined, 112, 118
    poaching, 124, 125
    roasting, 109–10
    stewing, 131
Mediterranean Roast Chicken with
Vegetables, 114–15
meringues, 198–99
milk, substitutes for, 50–51
millet, 138, 139
    Millet and Rice Flake Porridge,
        141
    Millet Tabbouleh, 140
minerals, 28, 31
Mint Sauce, Red Currant and, 78
Moroccan Chicken Tagine,
    132–33
mousses, 188–90
Muesli, Gluten-Free, 141
Muffins, Spiced Date and Orange,
    175
mushrooms
    Chicken and Mushroom Pie,
        128–29
    Brown Rice, Mushroom,
        Oregano, and Orange
        Stuffing, 116
    Brown Rice, Mushroom, Parsley,
        and Lemon Stuffing, 116
    Mushroom Velouté Sauce, 75
    Red Wine Sauce with Shallots
        and Mushrooms, 78
mustard
    Leek and Mustard Sauce, 79
    Mustard Cream Dressing, 85

Mustard Dressing, 81

N

noodles, 143. *See also* pasta
    Singapore Stir-Fried Noodles, 96
nut-free diets, 22–23, 24
    baby food, 212
    baked foods, 149, 165, 201,
        191
    frying, 87, 95, 101
    ice cream, 203
    pancakes, 194
    poaching, 125
    roasting, 109
    salad dressings, 82
    sauces, 77, 81, 206
    soups, 68
    stuffings, 111
    substitutes for, 55–57
nutrition, 27–31

O

oat milk, 51
oats, 43, 138
    Chewy Rice Krispies Squares,
        178
    Creamy Oatmeal, 141
oils, 27
    for bread-making, 183
    as dairy substitute, 53
    for frying, 86, 100
    for roasting, 109
olive oil, 53
onions
    Homemade Pork and Apple
        Sausage with Rich Onion
        Gravy, 94
    Onion Focaccia, 186
    Sage and Onion Sauce, 74
    Tomato, Red Onion, and Basil
        Tart, 159
oranges
    Apricot and Orange Tart, 160
    Lemon and Orange Marmalade
        Cake, 169
    Orange Buttercream Frosting,
        171
    Orange Custard Sauce, 207
    Orange Sponge Cake, 172
    Orange Shortbread, 179
    Spiced Date and Orange
        Muffins, 175
Oven-Baked Fries, 136
oven-baking, 118–23

P

pan-frying, 86–94
pancakes, 194–97
    Buckwheat Pancakes with
        Caramelized Cinnamon
        Apples, 196–97
    Egg-Free Pancakes, 197
    French Crêpes, 195
    gluten-free, 44
Parmesan and Potato Pastry, 157
Parsley Sauce, 74
Parsnip Puree, Apple and, 213
parties, children's, 16, 219
pasta, 147–48
    gluten-free, 42
    Lasagna al Forno, 122–3
    rice, 143
    Tomato and Garlicky Pasta with
        Shrimp and Lemon, 148
pastry, 149–64
    gluten-free, 46, 153–54
Pear Puree, Apple and, 214
Peppercorn Sauce, 78
pies. See also pastry
    Chicken and Mushroom Pie,
        128–29
    pastry quantities, 153
    single-crust pies, 151
Pizza alla Marinara, 186
Plain Scones, 174
poaching, 124–30
pork
    Homemade Pork and Apple
        Sausages with Rich Onion
        Gravy, 94
    Singapore Stir-Fried Noodles, 96
potatoes, 135–37
    Champ, 136
    Chicken, Potato, and Corn Puree,
        216
    Cornmeal and Potato Pastry, 157
    Crushed New Potatoes, 137
    Mashed Potato, 136
    Mediterranean Roast Chicken
        with Vegetables, 114–15
    Oven-Baked Fries, 136
    Parmesan and Potato Pastry, 157
    Potato, Leek, and Pea Puree, 213
    Provençal Fish Stew with Fennel
        and Potatoes, 126–27
    Roast Potatoes, 135
poultry. See also specific kinds
    baking, 118
    doneness defined, 112, 118
    poaching, 124, 125
    roasting, 110–11

stewing, 131
protein, 27, 29
Provençal Fish Stew with Fennel and
    Potatoes, 126–27
Puddings. See also custard; mousses
    Creamy Rice Pudding, 141
    Rice Pudding, 217
purees
    baby food, 211–16
    as egg substitutes in cakes, 166

Q

quinoa, 139
    Quinoa Tabbouleh, 140

R

raspberries
    Chocolate Roulade Filled with
        Bitter Chocolate Mousse and
        Raspberries, 192–93
    Fresh Summer Berry Sauce, 209
    Raspberry Ice Cream, 204
    Raspberry Sorbet, 202
Red Currant and Mint Sauce, 78
restaurants, 19–23
Rhubarb Crisp, 201
rice, 142–46
    Brown Rice, Mushroom, Oregano,
        and Orange Stuffing, 116
    Brown Rice, Mushroom, Parsley,
        and Lemon Stuffing, 116
    Brown Rice Tabbouleh, 140
    Chewy Rice Krispies Squares,
        178
    Chicken and Apricot Rice, 217
    Creamy Rice Pudding, 141
    Millet and Rice Flake Porridge,
        141
    Rice Pudding, 217
    Rice Salad with Pistachio Nuts
        and Pomegranate Seeds,
        144–45
    Seafood Risotto, 146
rice bran, 143
rice flour, 143
    Rice and Almond Shortcrust
        Pastry, 155
    Rice and Cornmeal Shortcrust
        Pastry, 156
    Whole-Grain Rice and Almond
        Pastry, 155
rice milk, 51
rice noodles, 143
rice pasta, 143
Rich Chocolate Ice Cream, 204

Rich Chocolate Mousse, 190
Rich Chocolate Mousse Torte, 190
Rich Fruit Cake, 170–71
Rich White Sauce, 74
Risotto, Seafood, 146
roasting, 109–17
Roast Potatoes, 135
Rolls, White Bread, 186
roulades, 191–93
Rum Custard Sauce, 207
rye, 138

S

safety, 13, 100, 188
Sage and Onion Sauce, 74
salad dressings, 82
    Basic Vinaigrette, 81. See also
        mayonnaise
salads
    Rice Salad with Pistachios and
        Pomegranate Seeds, 144–45
    Tabbouleh, 140
salmon
    Baked Fillet of Salmon with
        Shallots, Tarragon, and Lemon,
        120
    Salmon Fish Cakes with Tartar
        Sauce and Lemon, 89
sauces, 72–81
    custard, 38, 166, 206–07
    emulsion, 81–85
    flour-thickened, 72–75
    Fresh Summer Berry Sauce, 209
    reduction, 76–79
    Rich Italian Tomato Sauce, 80
    sweet, 206–09
    thickening, 38, 43, 72, 74
sausages
    Apple and Chorizo Stuffing, 117
    Homemade Pork and Apple
        Sausages with Rich Onion
        Gravy, 94
    Honey Baked Sausages, 119
school meals, 17–18
scones, 174
sea bass
    Crispy Fillet of Sea Bass, 88
    Provençal Fish Stew with Fennel
        and Potatoes, 126–27
seafood. See also specific kinds
    Fritto Misto di Mare, 103
    Provençal Fish Stew with Fennel
        and Potatoes, 126–27
    Seafood Kebabs, 107
    Seafood Risotto, 146
Shortbread Rounds, 179

shortcrust pastry, 150–56
shrimp. *See also* seafood
    Seafood Kebabs, 107
    Singapore Stir-Fried Noodles, 96
    Stir-Fried King Shrimp with Garlic,
        Black Pepper, and Lime, 98
    Tomato and Garlicky Pasta with
        Shrimp, 148
Singapore Stir-Fried Noodles, 96
solid food, introducing to babies,
    211–12
sorbets, 202
    egg-free, 39
    Raspberry Sorbet, 202
soups, 67–71
    Chunky Winter Vegetable Soup,
        69
    Peppery Watercress and Spinach
        Soup, 70
    thickening, 43, 67
soybean oil, 58–59
soy cheeses, 52
soy cream, 52
soy-free diet, 23, 26
    baby food, 212
    baked goods, 149, 165, 191,
        201
    frying, 87, 95, 101
    ice cream, 203
    pancakes, 194
    poaching, 125
    roasting, 109
    salad dressings, 82
    sauces, 77, 81, 206
    soups, 68
    soy substitutes, 58–60
    stuffings, 111
soy margarine, 59
soy milk, 51
soy sauce, 58
soy sour cream, 52
soy yogurt, 52
Spiced Date and Orange Muffins,
    175
Spinach Soup, Peppery Watercress
    and, 70
sponge cakes
    for roulades, 191–93
    Victoria Sponge Cake, 172
steaks, cooking times, 93
stews, 131–34
    thickening, 43
Sticky Finger Chicken Drumsticks,
    123
Stir-Fried Leafy Greens, 99
stir-frying, 95–99
stock, 62–66

for thickening sauces, 74
strawberries
    Fresh Summer Berry Sauce, 209
    Strawberry Ice Cream, 204
stuffings, 111
    Apple and Chorizo Stuffing, 117
    Brown Rice, Mushroom, Oregano,
        and Orange Stuffing, 116
    Brown Rice, Mushroom, Parsley,
        and Lemon Stuffing, 116
substituting ingredients
    for dairy, 50–54
    for eggs, 34–39
    for gluten, 40–49
    for nuts, 55–57
    for soy, 58–60
Sugar Syrup, 209
Sweet Rice and Cornmeal Pastry,
    156
Sweet Rich Shortcrust Pastry, 152
Sweet Shortcrust Pastry, 152

T
Tabbouleh, 140
tagines, 132–33
Tarragon and White Wine Sauce,
    79
Tartar Sauce, 84
tarts. *See also* pastry
    Apricot and Orange Tart, 160
    Egg-Free Tart, 160
    egg substitutes for, 38
    French Apple Tart, 164
    Jam Tarts, 163
    Lemon Tart, 162
    pastry quantities for, 153
    Tarte Niçoise, 158
    Tomato, Red Onion, and Basil
        Tart, 159
Thai Green Chicken Curry, 130
tomatoes
    Rich Italian Tomato Sauce, 80
    Beef Burgers with Tomato and
        Corn Salsa, 92
    Tomato and Garlicky Pasta with
        Shrimp and Lemon, 148
    Tomato, Red Onion, and Basil
        Tart, 159
Torte, Rich Chocolate Mousse, 190
Traditional Roast Rib of Beef, 113
travel, 24–26
tuna
    Tarte Niçoise, 158

U
Unsweetened Applesauce, 166

V
vacations, 24–26
Vanilla Cream Sauce, 208
Vanilla Ice Cream, 204
Velouté Sauce, 75
vegetables. *See also specific kinds*
    baking, 119
    canned and frozen, 59
    Chunky Winter Vegetable Soup,
        69
    Mediterranean Roast Chicken
        with Vegetables, 114–15
    pureed sauces, 80
    Stir-Fried Leafy Greens, 99
    Stir-Fried Vegetables, 99
    Vegetable Fritto Misto, 103
    Vegetable Stock, 66
Victoria Sponge Cake, 172
Vinaigrette, Basic, 81
vitamins, 27–28, 30

W
watercress
    Avocado and Watercress Dip, 84
    Peppery Watercress and Spinach
        Soup, 70
wheat, 138, 182
    substitutes for, 40–49
White Bread Rolls, 186
White Sauce, 73–74
White Wine Velouté Sauce, 75
Whole-Grain Rice and Almond
    Pastry, 155
Whole-Wheat Pastry, 152
Whole-Wheat Scones, 174
wine
    Fillet Steak with Red Wine Sauce,
        93
    Red Wine Sauce with Shallots
        and Mushrooms, 78
    White Wine Sauce, 79
    White Wine and Tarragon
        Sauce, 79
    White Wine Velouté Sauce, 75

X
xanthum gum, 183

Y
yeast, 183
yogurt, dairy-free substitutes for, 52